SKEPTICAL
PHILOSOPHY
for
EVERYONE

Skeptical Philosophy for Everyone

EVERYONE

RICHARD H. POPKIN
& AVRUM STROLL

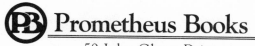 Prometheus Books

59 John Glenn Drive
Amherst, New York 14228-2197

Published 2002 by Prometheus Books

Inquiries should be addressed to
Prometheus Books
59 John Glenn Drive
Amherst, New York 14228-2197
VOICE: 716-691-0133, ext. 207
FAX: 716-564-2711
WWW.PROMETHEUSBOOKS.COM

06 05 04 03 02   5 4 3 2 1

Library of Congress Cataloging-in-Publication Data

Popkin, Richard Henry, 1923–
    Skeptical philosophy for everyone / Richard Popkin & Avrum Stroll.
        p. cm.
    Includes bibliographical references and index.
    ISBN 1-57392-936-0 (alk. paper)
    1. Skepticism. I. Stroll, Avrum, 1921– II. Title.

B837 .P67 2001
149'.73—dc21   2001049237

Printed in the United States of America on acid-free paper

To **Julie Popkin** *and* **Mary Stroll,**
who have aided and abetted us throughout this venture,
with the most heartfelt thanks.

CONTENTS

ACKNOWLEDGMENTS

We would like to thank three assistants who helped very much in getting this volume together—Sarah Burges, Stephanie Chasin, and Gabriella Goldstein. We hope that the work is worthy of their efforts.

1 WHY DO PEOPLE PHILOSOPHIZE?

INTRODUCTION

Why do people marry? Why do people play tennis? Why do they philosophize? There are, of course, many answers to these questions. People marry for all sorts of reasons: for love, for companionship, for money. They play tennis for love of the game, for exercise, for money. They philosophize for various reasons—even for money. Let us ignore most of these. We propose in this chapter to concentrate on one that is important. It is this: In the course of every human life certain pressing problems arise that cut deep, often to the bone. They typically demand a decision, or some kind of sensible response or action. Yet the issues they raise are complex and difficult to resolve. To deal with them requires deep reflection and careful deliberation. It is this kind of thought process that is traditionally called "philosophizing." People philosophize because they need to grapple with certain kinds of urgent problems.

What sorts of problems are these? It is difficult to give an exact definition. But here are some examples: Does life have any meaning or purpose? Does God exist? Is there life after death? Can one really be sure of what is right or wrong? Is suicide ever justifiable? Is lying always wrong? Is abortion a case of murder? Should I, a pacifist and democrat, join the army if my country is attacked by a totalitarian state? The list of such problems is virtually endless. It is important to emphasize that reflection about such matters is common and that nearly every human being at some time or other has engaged in it. How rigorously one probes any of these issues is what distinguishes the "professional" philosopher from the ordinary person. The difference is a matter of degree, of how deeply one is prepared and able to explore such dilemmas. In the remainder of this chapter we shall attempt to describe what the professionals do. But it should be kept in mind that ordinary persons are doing much the same thing, only, perhaps, less systematically.

This point is important and worth expanding upon before we enter the technical domain of professional philosophy. A glance at the world today reveals that human beings are beset by problems that require profound thought and judicious action. These issues are not restricted to academics; they affect nearly everyone. Though the Cold War between the Soviet Union and the major Western powers has now vanished, the threat of nuclear annihilation has not. Nuclear weapons have been dispersed to various nations and perhaps even to terrorist organizations. The possibility of their use cannot be discounted; if they were ever used the consequences would be horrendous. The world population is increasing astronomically, causing major pollution, the exhaustion of natural resources, starvation, and disease. There are extremely tense political confrontations in large sectors of the globe: in the Balkans, the Middle East, Korea, Africa, and India. Any of these could erupt into major wars affecting everyone. In all of these situations the picture is one of nations, groups, individuals, and even whole races taking adversary positions toward one another. What accounts for these attitudes—the bitterness, hatred, and lack of tolerance that seem to be the order of the day?

No doubt each case requires a specific explanation, and none is likely to be simple. Yet each derives from a specific philosophical position. Such positions may and typically do arise from different sources, but they may also have the same source. For instance, fundamentalist groups in both the Middle East and the United States find common ground in a tradition that derives from the Bible. Yet this common source may also serve to divide them. Religious warfare often stems from differing construals of how a given text is to be understood and in the assessment of a group's fidelity to the principles contained in that document. Such antagonisms turn on differing interpretations about the importance and value of the individual person, the purpose and function of the state, and the degree to which it is justified in controlling individual conduct. Such matters as whether women should wear veils in public, or whether abortion is justifiable, create profound divisions that are not easily reconcilable. In nearly all of the cases mentioned above—racism, conservation of resources, the population explosion, the range of control that the state should exercise—conflicting sets of principles or disagreements about the interpretations of commonly accepted principles seem to be at the core of these disputes, and nearly all of them represent different philosophical attitudes and convictions.

It is sometimes claimed that philosophy as a subject is no longer of any importance to the contemporary, technologically oriented person, yet the situations we have mentioned belie such an affirmation. It is obvious that to the degree that differences in fundamental lifestyle and conviction divide people there is no more important subject for study in the world today than philosophy. Accordingly, if one is to acquire some understanding of the forces that motivate human beings, one must acquire some understanding of the nature of philosophy and its influence on human action.

Our effort in this work is to make such comprehension possible. But this, as we shall see, is not a simple job. Setting Oriental philosophy aside, one can trace Western philosophy back nearly three thousand years. It is difficult to compress into a neat general account the full range of activities that in the West have been called "philosophy." In some respects philosophy has changed dramatically from its earliest beginnings among the Greeks, and yet in other respects it has not changed at all. As an intellectual activity, it seems to deal with new problems and with the same old problems. How can one capture the nature of the subject if these activities seem so contrary?

Historically, philosophers have offered many accounts, definitions, characterizations, and descriptions of what they are doing—and some of these are incompatible with one another. Some authors have asserted, for example, that philosophy is dedicated to explaining the ultimate nature of reality, while others have rejected this description and have stated that philosophy is not a fact-finding activity and therefore cannot tell us anything about reality. It has been affirmed that philosophy is a rational activity in which good reasons are adduced in support of a particular conclusion. On this view philosophy is identical with argumentation. Yet others have denied that the use of reason and argument in philosophy is either important or even relevant, and some of these persons, mainly skeptics, have claimed that no arguments in philosophy are any good. From the skeptical perspective, argumentation is thus pointless and a waste of time. It was widely held for centuries that philosophy is the Queen of the Sciences, that is, the most synoptic and universal science, as distinct from such particular sciences as biology, chemistry, and physics. But this thesis has also been challenged and indeed today is hardly accepted at all. The attempt to provide a coherent, consistent, and precise account of the subject thus seems to be an attempt to embrace within a simple model a gamut of apparently incompatible theories, practices, outlooks, and traditions. How can one possibly impose some sort of order on such a wide array of diverse conceptions?

In order to respond to the question, What is philosophy? we shall pose and then answer six questions in this book. These are: (1) Why do people philosophize? (2) Do humans possess knowledge of the external world, including knowledge of the minds of others? (3) What is the relationship between mind and body? (4) Is there a supreme being? (5) What is the good for man? and (6) Is an ideal society possible? In answering these queries we shall be covering most of the main branches of philosophy—epistemology (or the theory of knowledge), the philosophy of mind, philosophy of religion, ethics, and political philosophy. Our approach to these topics is both historical and analytic. We shall be referring to the main views developed by major philosophers of the past and present, and at the same time considering these views critically, that is, asking whether and to what degree they can be defended or rejected as correct.

These two approaches, the historical and analytic, will be given a further, special twist in what follows. Unlike any other text with which we are familiar, ours will emphasize the skeptical challenges that have been developed in each of these areas. The justification of this unusual emphasis will be given below and in the individual chapters that follow.

A SPECIFIC EXAMPLE: EUTHANASIA

As we have indicated above, philosophical problems are typically complex and composed of various strands: factual, scientific, technological, and moral. They involve elements of judgment, decision, the comparison of cases with one another, the drawing of precise distinctions, and so forth. We will illustrate some of the complexities such problems generate by considering the case of euthanasia, which will involve most of the elements just mentioned. It is the kind of problem that raises fundamental concerns for parents, senior citizens, many married persons, close friends and associates of the ill, legislators, sociologists, social workers, psychologists, physicians, and, of course, philosophers. Let us begin by drawing a distinction—this is the first move that a philosopher must make in order to acquire a perspicuous understanding of the problem.

Euthanasia must be distinguished from cases of suicide on the one hand, and physician-assisted death on the other. Suicide, for example, is an activity in which a person takes his or her own life. It is primarily an individual action, that is, taken by the person in question. If another person helps that individual to die—say, by injecting drugs or by throwing the individual off a cliff—those actions would not be considered suicide. The person who ultimately does commit suicide may, of course, discuss the prospective action with others before engaging in the act, but the resulting action is basically individual in character.

Euthanasia, in contrast, necessarily involves at least one other person. Yet, euthanasia, as a multiparty action, must be distinguished from other multiparty interactions, in particular from physician-assisted death, even though in both cases one of the parties will be responsible for the other's death. The difference between euthanasia and physician-assisted death, in part though not wholly, consists in the relationship that doctors in Western countries have to their patients. Generally speaking, physicians are bound by the Hippocratic Oath, a moral/professional code which forbids physicians to knowingly and intentionally harm persons whose health and well-being are in their care. Thus, an immediate moral issue arises when a physician (such as Dr. Jack Kevorkian) provides medication or other means to assist persons who are terminally ill to end their lives. Many doctors believe that such actions are prohibited by the Hippocratic Oath, and accordingly there is considerable controversy about the propriety of physican-assisted death. What counts as "physican-assisted death" is itself complex. Is a physician who refuses to put an elderly, comatose patient on a life-support respirator assisting that patient to die? That case seems to be different from one in which the physician removes a life-support system from a terminally ill patient. In such an instance there is a direct intervention by the doctor. Providing drugs that ease pain but which may end the patient's life is still a different sort of case. Let us distinguish all of these, and in speaking of physician-assisted death refer only to those cases where there is active intervention by the doctor to terminate a patient's life, such as turning off a respirator. It is this issue that has caused such a furor within and outside the medical community.

Physician-assisted death is also illegal in many states. Dr. Kevorkian has been tried several times in Michigan, for example, and juries had exonerated him on all such occasions until, in 1999, he was found guilty of giving a fatal dose of a drug to a patient dying of a terminal disease. In some states suicide is regarded as illegal and, in principle, a person who tries but fails to commit suicide can be subject to legal sanctions; but in practice such cases are hardly ever brought to court by prosecutors.

Both legal and moral issues also arise in standard cases of euthanasia, but the latter are not usually tied to a specific code such as the Hippocratic Oath. Thus, a wife who assists her terminally ill husband to die is not bound by any particular provision that makes her action immoral. If the act is judged to be immoral or reprehensible, it will be for different reasons. It is therefore essential to distinguish such cases from those that involve physicians or others with specific institutional obligations, such as priests, ministers, or rabbis, that may forbid euthanasia. We should thus draw a distinction between physician-assisted death and euthanasia, since the evaluation of those actions will be importantly different.

Let us now look at euthanasia itself. This will also be found to be complex, but let us start with a prototypical case. A husband and wife who have been married for a long time have been discussing what would happen if one of them developed a lingering, extremely painful, and ultimately fatal illness, such as Lou Gehrig's disease (amyotrophic lateral sclerosis, or ALS), for which there is no known cure. Suppose they agree now, while they are still in good health, that if something like this should happen, the suffering party will ask for his or her life to be terminated, perhaps by the administration of sleeping pills or a fatal injection. The important points to notice in this arrangement are three: (1) there is now a contract or agreement between the parties, which will be implemented if and when one of them becomes disabled; (2) the contract has been entered into voluntarily by both parties, each of whom is in good health and of sound mind; and (3) one of the parties has agreed actively to intervene in order to terminate the life of the other. This last point is especially important. If the healthy party does nothing and simply allows his or her spouse to die naturally, this would not be a case of euthanasia. Some specific action must be taken for the act to qualify as such.

Let us now suppose that one of the parties, the husband, falls ill. At this point we enter the realm of scientific fact. There may be all sorts of different diagnoses of the case made by physicians, and there may be disagreements, even between experts, about what is wrong with him and what his prospects are. However, the assessment that the patient is in pain is not determined in the same way as the assessment or diagnosis that he is suffering from a specific disease. The latter is an objective matter that does not wholly depend on the patient's feelings. But whether the patient is in pain or not, and how bad the pain is, are pieces of information that can be conveyed to physicians only by the patient himself. Thus, not only are there degrees of pain and diverse thresholds for bearing pain, but the exact status of the patient's feelings and suffering is primarily a subjective matter. Because that is so, the patient's wife may be faced with a difficult decision. Is the pain really unbearable? How much suffering can and should husband bear before she should take the drastic action of terminating his life? How long should she wait? Are there any alternatives to euthanasia? What she elects to do is thus a personal decision, and, of course, it is possible for her to be mistaken. Indeed, one of the complaints voiced about Dr. Kevorkian is that he acted too quickly in some cases. But a parallel issue might arise (say, if the couple has children) in a case of euthanasia. The children might feel that their father should not have been put to death, and that the action of their mother was precipitous. A spouse who must make the decision to proceed thus bears an enormous responsibility, and the mere existence of the contract does not necessarily justify one's intervening at a particular time.

Let us complicate the case slightly. In the contractual agreement both parties may have also agreed that even if the prospective patient decides to change his or her mind, that fact should not override the original decision to terminate his or her life. That is, the patient might agree at the time of his or her original decision that it should not be set aside if he or she suddenly decides otherwise. In such an instance, the original contract would recognize that at the moment of termination the patient may not be wholly rational or in a position to make a proper decision; the healthy party is thus authorized from the outset to carry out the original agreement no matter what.

Once again, a profound judgmental question is raised at this juncture. Suppose the husband changes his mind and decides he does not want to undergo euthanasia. His wife now has a serious problem: whether or not to end her husband's life against his current wishes. One can imagine heartrending scenes at this moment: an ill person pleading not to be put to death and his spouse torn by anxiety about what she should do. If despite all this, the wife decides to proceed as they had originally planned, is her action justified? Can she be absolutely sure that her husband is not rational now? Would it not be better to wait? If she waits, then she has not carried out the original agreement, and is acting irresponsibly. So what should she do?

At this point, philosophical issues begin to arise. Can one *ever* be sure what another is thinking or really wants? And if one cannot, what should one do in this kind of circumstance? When such doubts are generalized the outcome may be a kind of paralysis with respect to any action. Is one ever in possession of the kind of certainty that would justify any action, drastic or otherwise? Still, let us not push the skeptical challenge too far in this particular situation. We shall look at skepticism in detail later on. Apart from any theoretical form of skepticism, the healthy spouse finds him- or herself in a difficult situation if the invalid has suddenly changed his or her mind. How can one *rationally* determine what the best course of action should be in such a case?

There are numerous possible variations on the standard case besides that just mentioned. Suppose, for instance, that a healthy person cannot bring him- or herself to put his ailing spouse to death? At that moment, it is just too difficult to do—to see a human being with whom one has lived for years die at one's own hands. But if this is the ultimate decision, then the contract has been violated. Should the unwilling or unable spouse be held responsible for failing to act, *and by whom*? Can anyone ever be held responsible for refusing to put another to death?

But let us ignore these complications and return to the standard case. Who is right with respect to euthanasia? On this point there are a spectrum of differing answers. At one end of the spectrum, it is argued that euthanasia is *always* wrong, since it requires someone knowingly and intentionally to kill another person who has not committed any offense against society, has not done any harm to anyone else, and thus is not guilty of any legal or moral offense. In effect, the contention is that this amounts to killing the innocent. The position thus rests upon a philosophical principle, that no one is ever justified in killing the innocent. That principle, in turn, rests upon another: Justice requires that equal crimes should be treated equally, and that it is unjust to punish people differently for the same crime. Where no crime has been committed, then no penalty should be exacted. But this is precisely the situation in standard cases of euthanasia; the person being put to death is innocent of any crime. It follows from this perspective that the action is always wrong. The argument thus seems to be a variant of the right-to-life position on abortion, where it is argued that abortion is never justified since it amounts to killing the innocent.

This position is controversial. A completely opposite point of view holds that there are overriding reasons that justify taking the life of another. A proponent of this view might argue that in real life the principle that equal offenses deserve equal punishment has many exceptions. Suppose two people are convicted of robbing a bank. One of them is a hardened criminal, arrested and convicted many times for various offenses. His stealing is part of a pattern of behavior. The second person has recently lost his job, his family is starving, and it is his first brush with the law. Many juries would hold it unreasonable—indeed, *unjust*—to give the two individuals identical sentences. There are other grounds for holding that the killing of the innocent is sometimes justified. In cases of war, for instance, it is not generally held to be immoral to kill an enemy soldier in order to protect one's country. From this philosophical perspective the fundamental question is, What grounds can one advance in support of taking the life of another? A typical response would assert that if the patient is terminally ill, if no drugs will relieve unbearable pain, and if no cure or prospect of a cure is in sight, then one is acting compassionately in ending that individual's life. It is the optimal course of action in that particular circumstance. Those in favor of abortion access might advance similar reasons: When the life of the mother is at stake, or if the pregnancy is the result of rape or incest, then terminating the pregancy is justified. The argument is thus that there are considerations that are more important than the maintenance of life. These essentially have to do with the quality of life. On that view, although life is *an* important value, it is not necessarily *the* most important value. There are thus overarching factors that justify euthanasia. In between these two radically different positions one can find a host of intermediate views, all of them defended on rational grounds.

Which of these positions is correct is not an issue we shall attempt to debate here. Our point is rather to show that the issues raised are not only legal, sociological, medical, and practical, but to a great extent are concerns of a different type or order, namely, philosophical. This can be shown by asking the question, How much pain should a person suffer before his spouse is justified in terminating his existence? The answer to this question clearly involves conceptual issues, requiring for their resolution such matters as whether one is ever entitled knowingly and deliberately to terminate the life of the innocent, whether a society that legalizes euthanasia is just, and so forth. Such matters fall squarely into the domain of philosophy. In the next section, we shall try to bring out, in terms of this example, what is meant by describing a problem as "philosophical" and, in so doing, will try to explain how such problems involve and yet transcend scientific, legal, medical, or practical solutions.

Generally speaking, the sorts of issues we have mentioned—abortion, racism, control of the environment, contraception—involve considerations of principle that have been discussed by philosophers of the past and present. From these kinds of problems important and influential theories have developed, such as those of Plato, Aristotle, Thomas Hobbes, John Stuart Mill, and others. In the course of this book we hope to show how seemingly simple and ordinary features of our human experience can give rise to conceptual difficulties that have led to the development of theories for solving these problems. Such reflection is what it means to philosophize.

SIX INGREDIENTS OF A PHILOSOPHICAL PROBLEM

**Philosophical problems are typically complex,
and exhibit strands that are factual and nonfactual**

It is sometimes not sufficiently stressed that factual, technological, and scientific factors often play roles in philosophical problems. This is true in the case of euthanasia. As we have indicated, there may be a debate among physicians about the nature of the patient's illness: What is it exactly? Is it progressive? Is it generally unbearably painful? Is it terminal? Whether a spouse should intervene to end her husband's life may well depend on the answers to some or all of these questions. But suppose it is agreed by the experts that the disease is progressive, it will be increasingly painful, and it is terminal. At that point, the question of potential intervention arises. But the decision to intervene or not to intervene is not factual. As we have pointed out, all sorts of other factors may now come to the fore: Can I really bring myself to kill my spouse? Even if I can, should I? Is this the right time or should I wait? It is clear that these are not scientific or factual issues. One characteristic of a philosophical problem is that it crucially involves considerations that go beyond the merely factual or scientific.

A philosophical problem is not solvable solely by an appeal to the facts

This statement is true if the statement that philosophical problems are not wholly factual is true. We believe that both statements are true. Normally, a philosophical problem does not arise through a lack of factual information. Consider the previous case of the two persons arrested for stealing money. The facts are all there for the jury to decide. They are given accurate information about the backgrounds and the characters of the accused. There is no question but that both persons stole some money. The jury's problem is now of a different order: How shall these two persons be treated? Is it just to punish them equally, or not? The answer or answers the jury members arrive at are not wholly determined by the facts in the two cases, but by considerations of a different kind. Note that we are not claiming that factual information does not play a role in the solution or resolution of philosophical problems. Clearly it does, as described in the above situation. Our claim is that such problems cannot be resolved *merely* by an appeal to the facts. In the cases of the two thieves, we can imagine a debate among the jurors, some of whom might argue that, independent of the histories of the accused persons, equal crimes should be treated equally, and some of whom argue that background factors should be taken into consideration in dispensing justice. Each side will argue its case, that is, advance philosophical grounds for its position.

A philosophical problem is fundamentally a conceptual problem

If such problems are *not* merely factual or scientific problems, then what additional considerations must be brought to bear in their resolution? The question gives rise to a third feature of philosophy, namely, that it is primarily a *conceptual* activity. This is a somewhat complicated notion which can be explained by contrasting conceptual and factual problems. Because of its importance, we shall spend a little time explaining the point.

Suppose the question is, "How far is it from Vancouver, British Columbia, to New York City?" Before answering the question, certain clarifications are in order. We obviously have to know what the words in the question mean. But let us assume that the context will make that query clear, for example, that we are speaking of distance by road, rather than distance by air. Given this understanding, the answer to the question will be straightforwardly factual. It will consist of remarks such as, "It is 2,850 miles," or "I drove it last year and according to my odometer it was 2,933 miles," and so on. The information contained in such answers might be arrived in various ways: by driving the distance personally and seeing what one's mileage reads, by checking the distance on a road map, and so forth. The key point is that the facts resolve the issue: No special conceptual residue remains when such answers are given.

But the issue of euthanasia—and, indeed, all philosophical problems—is not simply decided by an appeal to matters of fact. The problem of abortion provides a good example of what is meant by a conceptual problem. Let us consider the issue in some detail for a moment. The extreme right-to-life position advances the following considerations in support of its position: First, it argues that from the moment of conception, a human fetus is a human being, and that all human beings are persons. Second, as mentioned above, it states that such persons are innocent of any crime. Third, it contends that it is necessary to find a consistent set of principles—that is, a reasonable philosophy—that would justify killing them. Fourth, it affirms that since similar cases must be treated in similar ways, such principles would justify the abortion of a prenatal child only if they would also justify the killing of an innocent postnatal infant. Fifth, it holds that no considerations can be found that would justify the latter course of action, and, accordingly, it concludes that no principles can be found that justify the former. Therefore, abortion is never justified.

The pro-choice position attacks each of these premises and disagrees with the conclusion. But to bring out the special nature of a conceptual problem, let us simply concentrate on the first premise of the extreme right-to-life argument. It holds, as indicated, that the fetus from the moment of conception is a both a human being and a person. Some advocates of the pro-choice position hold that the so-called conceptus or zygote is not a human being, let alone a person, although it has the potentiality of becoming both. This contention is supported by an analogy. Suppose everyone agrees that cutting down an oak tree is, in a specific case, a bad thing to do. Yet those same persons would agree that an acorn is not an oak tree, so destroying an acorn that eventually might become a tree is not identical with destroying a tree. According to this comparison, the conceptus or zygote is like an acorn. It is not yet a human being, and is certainly not a person. The zygote is simply a mass of living tissue, analogous to a benign growth, and is not yet human since it lacks all human features or characteristics. It can thus be excised and abortion can be thought of as analogous to a surgical procedure that eliminates an unwanted cyst or tumor.

Let us set aside this position and concentrate on a more common variant of it, namely the notion that the conceptus is not a *person*. On this pro-choice position, which is less extreme than the previous, it is conceded that the conceptus or zygote is a human being, but it is denied that it is as yet a person: something with a mind, feelings, desires, thoughts, and so forth. Curiously enough, this point of view is sometimes advanced by persons with religious commitments. A common formulation of their position would state that the conceptus or zygote does *not* yet have a "soul," and therefore is not yet a person. A well-known philosopher who denies that the conceptus or zygote is a person puts her position in this way: "At this place, however, it should be remembered that we have only been pretending throughout that the fetus is a human being from the moment of conception. A very early abortion is surely not the killing of a person."[1]

In the famous *Roe* v. *Wade* decision of 1973, the United States Supreme Court agreed that fetuses "are not fully legal persons," and that a woman has the right to an abortion. The decision also mentioned that the right to an abortion is not absolute, and is limited by the state's right to regulate medical practice to protect maternal health. Justice Harry A. Blackmun wrote that "a state may properly assert important interests in safeguarding health, in maintaining medical standards, and in protecting potential life."

What we wish to emphasize in describing the difference between the extreme right-to-life and the pro-choice positions is that the issue of whether a conceptus or fetus is a person is not a factual issue. Everyone would agree on the key facts involved in conception. The facts include such pieces of information as the following: The female germ cell, or "ovum," is fertilized by the male germ cell, the "spermatozoan." When this occurs, the cell possesses a full complement of twenty-three pairs of chromosomes, one in each pair from each parent. At that stage, the ovum is called a "single-cell zygote." Within twenty-four hours, the single cell begins to divide. It acquires sixteen cells by the third day, and continues to grow as it moves through the Fallopian tube into the uterus. During the first week, it implants itself in the uterine wall, and then is called a "conceptus." By the end of the second week, it is firmly embedded in the uterine wall, and from this point until the eighth week it is called an "embryo." Some human features appear by the fourth week—the embryo acquires a face and incipient limbs—and by the eighth week brain waves can be detected. From this point until birth at nine months, it is called a "fetus."

The facts, as just described, are not disputed by either side. The question is, rather, When does the fertilized egg become a person? But as one examines the facts they do not speak to that issue. Is a "single-cell zygote" a person? Or is the "conceptus" a person? Is neither a person? The facts are silent. So how is the judgment to be made? That clearly depends on the point of view one takes, and, no doubt, such positions are complex. They may arise from religious or nonreligious perspectives. But whatever their origins, they are not determined solely by rehearsing the scientific facts. The issue of whether an unborn child is a person or not must thus be resolved in some different way. This is the typical situation in dealing with philosophical issues. Such issues typically turn on crucial premises that are conceptual in character. Our third point, then, is that philosophical problems are conceptual and not straightforwardly factual.

Philosophical problems arise from perplexity

In the case of the problem of abortion, for instance, there is a perplexity about the relationship between bits of tissue and persons. When do pieces of flesh become persons? If a person is not merely flesh, what it is? Is it some kind of nonmaterial entity, and if so, how can we identify it? If one is speaking of the soul, for instance, what is that? Where does it exist and how do we know what it is like? Where does it come from? This particular question gives rise to one of the deepest and most intractable philosophical issues, the so-called Mind/Body Problem. We shall explore the problem later in this chapter, but one can already sense the nature of the difficulty. Philosophers from the time of the Greeks to the present, theologians of all stripes, and ordinary persons have been puzzled about the relationship between personhood and the material constitutents that constitute living objects. When the Gospel According to Saint John states that "the word was made flesh" (1:14), we have a theological version of this problem.

Philosophy begins in wonder, as Aristotle once said. In words different from his, we might say that philosophers are concerned to make sense of the world—a world that for all sorts of reasons they find puzzling or baffling: a "booming, buzzing confusion," as William James called it. Thus, there is need for clarification, explication, and the overcoming of difficulties. If the guiding principles of the world were obvious philosophizing would not be necessary, and indeed would not arise at all. But given that the world is a puzzle, reflection about its characteristics is unavoidable and is an essential ingredient in the human psyche.

A philosophical problem requires a rational explanation

The next feature of philosophy is connected with the need for a rational explanation of things. Not any old explanation will do; it must be an account in which good reasons are given in support of a particular conclusion. We have seen in the case of abortion that both the extreme right-to-life and pro-choice positions satisfy this requirement. Each is a reasoned viewpoint that leads to a well-supported conclusion. More generally, one might say that a rational explanation makes an appeal to a system of principles. In the case of abortion, such principles might include a theory about the nature of personhood, about the rights that the unborn have, about the conditions under which some rights are said to override others when rights conflict, and so forth. This is a complex array of notions, and unless one is careful, it might be inconsistent. It is easier to measure consistency when a theory is made explicit, and this requires a critical assessment of it. The explanation ultimately presented by the philosopher—say, whether abortion is justifiable or not—thus quickly escalates to a higher level of theoretic generality. Accordingly, the fifth feature of philosophy consists in the requirement that an explanation be rational, that it appeal to a set of principles that are cogent and consistent, and that such principles amount to a theory applying to the issue at hand.

Philosophical problems lead to deep explanations

What is the advantage of philosophical theorizing? The answer is that it provides a deeper understanding than any commonsense or habitual interaction with the world. The aim of the philosopher is to penetrate superficial phenomena and to reach and articulate their underlying principles. A scientist does much the same sort of thing. It was a remarkable discovery, made only in the nineteenth century, that ice, steam, and water, whose observable properties radically differ, are all composed of H_2O. It is this kind of penetration of the familiar to arrive at a fundamental level of comprehension that is also characteristic of philosophy. The philosopher who notes that all phenomena obey the laws of mechanics may arrive at the conception that human beings, trees, and sewing machines are all, in some profound sense, mechanical objects, subject to the laws of physics in terms of their behavior. From such an insight some philosophers have inferred that human beings are simply machines. On their view, the commonsense notion that there is a soul or a mind that differs in kind from the body is wrong. There is simply chemical and electrical activity in the human brain that initiates action. As the seventeenth-century philosopher Thomas Hobbes said, "What is the heart but a pump, and the nerves so many strings?"

Whether such a view is right or wrong is open to debate, but that it is a deep insight cannot be denied. It is characteristic of the great philosophers of the past and present to have plumbed the depths to create new understandings of relationships never previously recognized.

From Plato to the present, philosophers have searched for *essences*, or common qualities or the fundamental principles, that connect particular cases, and thus provide for understandings that transcend the familiar and commonplace.

Summary

The preceding list of six features is not, of course, exhaustive. They are simply among the more important characteristics of philosophical activity. We can summarize what a person does when he or she philosophizes.

Philosophy is a complex, intellectual activity that (a) involves reflection about the world and its inhabitants; (b) is a conceptual, rather than a straightforwardly scientific, empirical, or factual discipline; (c) is a rational activity, demanding the use of argument in an attempt to support a particular conclusion; (d) arises in part because the world is complex and not well understood, and is therefore directed toward clarifying or resolving problematic issues or doctrines; (e) involves the quest for deeper explanations to get at what is fundamental and not superficial; and (f) does so by developing a theory or theories to account for the matters under consideration. The problems of euthanasia and abortion illustrate many of these features. They raise questions about what is true, or right, and what kinds of actions are ultimately justifiable.

PHILOSOPHY AND THE PRACTICAL

Having produced, above, a certain picture of philosophy, we must now, in the interests of accuracy, modify it somewhat. In dealing with euthanasia and abortion, we were discussing problems having significant social, political, and legal implications. We might thus have inadvertently created the impression that *all* philosophical problems are essentially practical problems. But this is not true and, unless qualified, would be highly misleading.

In confronting problems that have little or no practical implication, philosophy is similar to science. Science in its purest forms must be distinguished from technology, for example. It is concerned with understanding the world, and arises from human curiosity. Technology, in contrast, arises from the need to solve practical problems, and is thus primarily concerned with changing the world. Many of the most important scientific (as distinct from technological) discoveries have no practical implications. The Newtonian revolution changed the scientific picture from a geocentric to a heliocentric conception. This change was unquestionably of monumental historical importance. It revolutionized man's apprehension of the nature of the earth and its status in a broader range of astral phenomena. It also applied to such matters as the religious story told in the Bible, and for many thinkers had antireligious implications. Yet in a certain sense, Isaac Newton's discoveries had no practical implications for ordinary daily life. With the possible exception of religious practice, the practical, everyday activities of most human beings continued in more or less the same fashion after Newton's work had become disseminated.

But the same cannot be said of technology. It has drastically changed the way we live. The invention of the automobile, the telephone, computers, and even such earlier technologies as the printing press, gunpowder, and the saddle for horses greatly altered the practical activities of human beings. It is possible for a civilization to develop a high degree of technology without ever developing science: This was true of China for most of its lengthy history. Indeed, even today its science is imitative of developments in the West.

Philosophy is like pure science in some ways, and is like technology in others. It has both an abstract, nonpractical side and an important, applied side. Let us, for a moment, turn to its nonpractical side. Some of the deepest and most stubborn problems are of this sort, and some of the most ingenious theories have been developed in an effort to solve them.

Here is a classical example. It is generally agreed that there is something called "the world," or "the universe." For the moment, we shall bypass the issue of what it is. The question we wish to pose is, Where did it come from? This question goes beyond anything that science can currently answer. According to present physical theory, the universe evolved from a dense, comparatively tiny object, an "original atom," which exploded, sending pieces outward. These pieces have become galaxies, stars, planets, and other sorts of celestial objects. But the question that the philosopher poses is, Where did the original object come from? Let us assume that the big bang theory of what happened is correct. This conjecture does not tell us where the primal atom originated. Was it caused by something else: say, a supreme being, God? But if so, where did God come from? It seems plausible to hold that if anything exists, it must have been caused by something else. But then there could be no absolute first cause. But if there was no first cause, then there is no second, third, and so on cause. Hence, if no first cause, then no last cause, and therefore no present universe. Since there *is* a present universe, however, there must have been a first cause that was uncaused. We thus have a difficult puzzle. It seems true to say that universe must have a first cause, which is uncaused, but it also seems true to say that there could not be any uncaused cause, since everything must have a cause. So where did the universe come from?

This is a dilemma that many of the greatest philosophers, such as Saint Thomas Aquinas and Benedict de Spinoza, have addressed and to which they have offered answers. We shall explore their views later in this book. The point we are emphasizing now is that many philosophical problems, such as this about the existence of a first cause, raise mind boggling perplexities. Yet neither they, nor the theories designed to solve them, have any obvious practical implications. It is thus important to realize that purely intellectual dilemmas constitute much of the subject matter of philosophy.

TWO LEVELS OF SKEPTICISM

We indicated earlier that the previous picture of philosophy, as concerned with providing a cogent account of the world, has been challenged by various forms of philosophical skepticism. In the chapters that follow we shall bring out the nature of these challenges. But it is important to notice that they are *philosophical* in character. They express the doubts of sophisticated reflection, and should be distinguished from everyday, practical doubts, which are more local. The latter allow for the existence of knowledge and certainty in some some cases, while denying it in others. All doubts, whether practical or philosophical, begin from concerns about the propriety of claims made about daily events and experiences. A politician might promise to provide funds for schools and the environment, but experience teaches persons to accept his avowals with a grain of salt; a lover utters remarks that an experienced companion soon learns to question; a theologian provides an argument about the exact date of the creation of the universe, and so forth. Many events and interactions in everday life give rise to queries about the veracity of things people say.

But for most persons such doubts tend to be specific and temporary. They do not give rise to a general skepticism about all assertions, promises, and verbal commitments, and they surely do not end in outlooks that challenge the very existence of knowledge and certainty. It is the philosophical forms of skepticism that go this extra distance. They also typically arise from reflection on everyday experience. But as the philosopher ponders these matters, he or she may come to feel that human beings live in a world in which the commonly accepted veracities are more vulnerable than are ordinarily supposed. As such reflections deepen and as their scope widens, the result may be profound doubts about the very existence of other persons, of a world external to the mind of the doubter, and so forth. In such cases, we have arrived at classical forms of philosophical skepticism.

To the ordinary person, such doubts may seem fantastic and bizarre. Yet the train of reflection leading to them may seem, upon careful scrutiny, to be without flaw. We shall have to examine such lines of reasoning carefully in what follows. One thing we can say categorically: In the history of Western philosophy, philosophical skepticism has been taken very seriously. It is unquestionably one of the fundamental traditions in Western thought, running from its beginnings among the ancient Greeks to the present time.

Here is how a recent commentator describes the importance of philosophical skepticism. In *The Skeptic Way*, Benson Mates writes:

> If philosophical authors were to be ranked in order on the basis of their relative influence on the subsequent history of Western philosophy, Plato and Aristotle would be at the top of the list, no doubt. But a good case can be made that the third place should be assigned to a rather obscure Greek physician of the second century A.D., Sextus Empiricus. . . . His writings were immensely influential. Due largely to the work of Richard Popkin and his students and associates, it is now clear that the rediscovery and publication of these works in the sixteenth and seventeenth centuries led directly to the skepticism of Montaigne, Gassendi, Descartes, Bayle, and other major figures, and eventually to the preoccupation of modern philosophy, right down to the present, with attempts to refute or otherwise combat philosophical skepticism.[2]

As these remarks make plain, one cannot write an introductory book about philosophy without a detailed examination of the history and contemporary importance of skepticism. Therefore, beginning in the next chapter, this topic will play a fundamental role in the discussions that follow.

GETTING INTO THE SUBJECT

No brief introduction, such as we have tried to provide above, can function as a substitute for the reader's getting involved in the subject. To understand the nature of this activity one must steep oneself in particular texts, in the political, social, and historical contexts that give rise to real problems for real people. We will thus emphasize in this book that the particular historical setting in which a problem arises is critical for a full appreciation of the issues that were under debate. Textbooks can make living issues seem abstract and unreal. We shall try to avoid such an approach.

Here, again, let us refer to the Mind/Body Problem. It takes many forms historically. In early Christian theology, it dealt with the question of how a spiritual being, such as Christ, could also be material, that is, a human being composed of flesh and blood. As we enter a new millennium, the problem has dropped its theological gloss. Now the issue is whether the brain—a complex material object—is the same thing as the mind, something which does not seem material at all. The current debate thus involves such questions as: What are thoughts? What are beliefs? What are intentions? Are they simply various forms of neural activity, that is, neurons firing at 40 Herz, and so forth? Or are they sui generis kinds of things, not describable in physical, material, or mechanical terms? The current debate is in some respects the same as it was in the year 300 C.E., and in some respects, because of scientific developments, it is quite different.

Because the historical circumstances are so important, we feel that that there is no better procedure for coming to understand the nature of this discipline than a study of the history of philosophy. Such an approach will recreate the intellectual and social climates in which the great problems of human life arose, and will indicate how they were viewed, both by their contemporaries and by later thinkers, and how they were addressed in various temporal periods. In the chapters that follow, we attempt to recreate some of these ambiences, thus adding flesh to the bare bones we have uncovered in this introduction. By this method, the reader will add a deeper dimension to his or her exposure to the subject and its impact on human lives. We shall begin with the theory of knowledge, or epistemology, as it is also labeled. We shall then proceed to discuss the other major domains of the discipline: metaphysics, ethics, political philosophy, and the philosophy of religion. In all of these discussions, we shall keep a close eye on the role played by various forms of skepticism.

NOTES

1. Judith Jarvis Thomson, "Symposium on Abortion," *Philosophy and Public Affairs* 1, no. 1 (1971): 47–56.

2. Benson Mates, *The Skeptic Way: Sextus Empiricus's Outlines of Pyrrhonism* (Oxford: Oxford University Press, 1996), p. 4.

2 DOES ANYONE EVER KNOW ANYTHING?

IS RADICAL SKEPTICISM BELIEVABLE?

Epistemology is the field of philosophy in which skepticism finds its natural turf. As the name indicates, epistemology provides theories about the nature, origin, and limits of human knowledge. The persistence and long history of this discipline presuppose that many philosophers have believed and still believe that knowledge exists and that through a careful and intensive intellectual effort they can describe its essential characteristics. But skeptics challenge this point of view. They cast doubt on such theories, often in the form of arguments, but sometimes using nonargumentative techniques. We shall focus on these challenges in what follows. But let us begin with some intuitive remarks that support the notion that knowledge exists.

Suppose two nonphilosophers are having a discussion about the history of baseball, and that they are mostly in agreement about which players were on which teams. They concur that in the 1930s Lou Gehrig and Babe Ruth were members of the New York Yankees, that in the 1960s Sandy Koufax and Don Drysdale were Los Angeles Dodgers, and so forth. A philosopher listening to their conversation might say that such assertions as "Sandy Koufax pitched for the Los Angeles Dodgers" and "Babe Ruth played right field for the Yankees" were things that both speakers knew. These remarks could be taken as examples of pieces of knowledge. It thus seems obvious that many persons know all sorts of things: their own names, the names of their spouses and children, their home addresses, and where they work.

Now it also might be that in their discussion there was some discord. They might have disagreed, for example, about whether Babe Ruth ever played for the Boston Braves. Either he did or he didn't. If one asserts that he did, and the other demurs, it is a logical truth that one of them must be wrong and the other right. A person who is wrong about this matter cannot be said to know what he is claiming. Suppose both also agree that Hank Aaron played for the Dodgers. In this case, the facts show that both are wrong.

A philosopher, listening to their conversation, might infer that there are some things about baseball history that both know, some things that one of them knows but that not both know, and some things that neither knows. The philosopher might generalize from their conversation and conclude that there are many things humans know and many things they do not know. This would be the commonsense position. It seems obviously true. Yet it is this position that the radical skeptic challenges. According to such a skeptic, nobody really knows anything.

The skeptic's position seems prima facie peculiar. Given the previous discussion, how can one plausibly suggest that nothing is known? After all, didn't both discussants know that Sandy Koufax was a Dodger? What possible considerations could justify such a counter-intuitive posture? Isn't it too extreme to be credible? Oddly enough, the answer is no. The fact that skepticism has had such a long and lively career suggests that it must have real substance, and that the commonsense view described above, when scrutinized, is less compelling than it seems. The skeptic is urging such scrutiny, asking that we look deep into and beyond the obvious. Let us describe some of the considerations that make this request persuasive.

SOME PRELIMINARY CONSIDERATIONS IN FAVOR OF SKEPTICISM

Much of what we think we know comes from seeing, touching, hearing, tasting, and smelling things. I know there is a tree in my front yard because I see it there. I know that motorcycles exist because I can hear them going by, and if I glance out the window, I can see them. Philosophers thus say that some of our knowledge derives from sense experience. It is the sense of touch, the sense of smell, and so forth, that provide us with information about many things. The ordinary person tends to trust the senses, and to assume that the information they generate is reliable. But the skeptic finds such acceptance too facile. Consider some simple counter-cases.

We use mirrors for all sorts of purposes: to shave, to examine our skin, and to observe the positions of cars behind us on the highway. When one shaves, for example, one assumes that the image of one's face that appears in the mirror is accurate, and that, because this is so, the process of shaving will be successful. Yet if one thinks about mirrors a little more carefully, one realizes that every mirror image distorts the world's features. If one holds up an English language book to a mirror, one cannot read it, because the print runs backward. Yet the print on the book does not. One looking in a mirror never sees one's own face directly, that is, in the way other persons do. What one sees is reversed and subtly altered. We can shave because we adjust our habits to this situation, but it is a mistake to think that one is seeing one's own face, just as it is.

There are many ordinary, daily-life situations like this. A straight stick dipped in water looks bent, yet we do not believe it is really bent. Railroad tracks seem to converge in the distance, and yet when we walk to the spot where they apparently merge we find them to be parallel. The wheels of automobiles seen on television seem to be going backyard when the automobile is seen to be moving forward. Yet this is impossible. Such examples of distorted perception could be multiplied endlessly. Each of these sense phenomena is thus misleading in some way. If human beings were to accept the world as being exactly how it looks they would be deluded as to how things really are. They would think the stick in water was really bent, the writing on pages was really reversed, and the wheels were really going backward.

These are visual anomalies, and they represent the sorts of ordinary occurrences that provide ammunition for the skeptic. Starting from these cases, the skeptic can show that, as we scrutinize them, our commonsense beliefs become increasingly vulnerable to doubt.

Consider the case of the stick that looks bent when immersed in water. How can one be sure that it does not become bent when put in water? How can one be sure that it is straight when it is out of the water? Of course it looks straight, but it also looks bent. What justifies giving priority to some sense impressions over others?

A commonsense philosopher might respond by saying that *seeing* is not a sufficient condition for knowledge. One needs to correct vision by some of the other senses. Thus one might claim that the stick in water is not really bent because one can feel it with his hands to be straight when it is in the water. One corrects aberrant visual sensations by tactile impressions. But the skeptic can easily meet this move. What, he might say, justifies accepting one mode of perception as more accurate than another? After all, there are common occurrences that cast doubt upon the reliability of touch. Suppose one were to cool one hand and warm the other, and then insert both into a bucket of water having a uniform thermometric reading. The water will feel warm to the cold hand, and cold to the warm hand. But, by stipulation, the water has the same uniform temperature, and therefore cannot be both hot and cold at the same time. Does this imply that one is not sensing the water at all? It is an interesting possibility, and some skeptics have argued that such an inference is correct. But whether it is or not, the experiment surely suggests that the tactile sense cannot be fully trusted, either, and in particular that there is no justification for giving it priority over vision.

Later, we shall see that these preliminary remarks merely scratch the surface. In his famous Dream and Demon Hypotheses, René Descartes propounded even deeper skeptical objections to the commonsense view. He pointed out, for instance, that it is possible for us to have all the sense impressions we normally have when awake, but might be asleep and dreaming. In such a case, we would not be aware of external reality at all. This is radical skepticism in a full-blown form. But let us defer consideration of his arguments until the next chapter and instead return to our theme, which we shall now deepen a bit.

Suppose in the light of the previous difficulties, it is proposed that no mode of sense perception is sufficient to guarantee that one has knowledge, and hence that one needs to correct the senses by some other mode of awareness, say, by reason. Reason tells us that, despite appearances, it is illogical to believe that parallel steel tracks, without any apparent reason, suddenly converge or that water bends rigid objects such as sticks. So independent of what our senses say, we can count on reason as a corrective that will give us an accurate picture of the world's features.

Yet reason has its own difficulties. It suffers from various liabilities: forgetting, jumping to unwarranted conclusions, miscalculations, misunderstandings, and misinterpretations. Almost everybody has forgotten or misremembered something important. One remembers having met Smith at the airport in Boston; yet Smith has never been in Boston. One has added a column of figures incorrectly, getting the wrong sum. So why should one trust reason if its conclusions sometimes run counter to sense perception?

As these various examples show, the skeptical attitude cannot merely be dismissed. If it is ultimately mistaken, one will have to show how and why. That will require some hard thinking in order to arrive at a clear and defensible explanation of the apparently simple claim that the stick is really straight. A person who attempts to meet this challenge will need to develop a theory for justifying the commonsense belief that our senses are reliable. Such a theory will, in effect, be an attempt to solve the famous problem "Our Knowledge of the External World." That problem, in its deepest forms, raises two issues. The first is the so-called egocentric predicament, that is, whether there is a reality that exists outside the circle of our own ideas and sense impressions. What reason do we have to believe that anything exists except our own sensations? They are the only things we are directly aware of, and there is no conceivable way of getting outside them to access some supposititious external reality. The second aspect of the problem is, in effect, one that we have touched on in the preceding discussion. How can anyone know what anything is really like if the perceptual evidence is conflicting? Is the water really hot or really cold? This problem, in these dual forms, has bedeviled philosophy since its inception, and in the following pages we shall examine the views of various thinkers who have tried to solve it—as well as the views of radical skeptics who deny that it can be solved.

SCIENCE, COMMON SENSE, AND SKEPTICISM

Another highly surprising source of skepticism is to be found in science. It is complicated to show why this is so. Let us begin with some comments about the nature of knowledge. As we have seen from the previous examples, if someone asserts a statement p, but is wrong, that person cannot be said to know that p is true. Thus, one of the main features that characterizes the concept of knowledge is that one cannot know that which is false. If I assert that the moon is only one hundred miles from the earth, that assertion, being mistaken, cannot be a piece of knowledge. In analyzing the concept of knowledge, then, all scholars concur that one cannot know that p if p is false.

A second criterion that the concept of knowledge must satisfy is that of certainty. This condition is connected with the former. If it is possible to be mistaken about p, then one cannot know that p. Thus, if it is possible that it will rain tomorrow, or possible that it will not rain tomorrow, I cannot know today that it will rain tomorrow or that it will not rain tomorrow. The existence of possibility thus implies a kind of uncertainty in one's awareness of a given situation. Hence, many writers have argued that if one knows that p, then it is not possible to be mistaken about p. And if this is so, then it is true that if one knows that p one knows that p with certainty. Thus, a second criterion of knowledge (which we shall accept here for purposes of our general exposition) is that if one knows that p, then one knows that p with certainty. It is this particular provision that science rejects and which allows it, therefore, to be described as a form of skepticism.

According to most scientists and philosophers of science, scientific theories are based upon observation. Some observations are, of course, about presently occurring events, such as the appearance of a supernova. Such observations might be mistaken for various reasons: the technical equipment may be faulty, or the observer may be tired, hallucinating, or dreaming. For the present, however, let us ignore these kinds of objections. The more immediate point is that all scientific laws are based on past observation. The physical principle that water at sea level boils at 100°C is arrived at through many past observations, conducted over a vast period of time. In the past, and under the appropriate conditions, scientists have always found water to behave in just that particular way. Would any scientist, therefore, be committed to the thesis that it is *absolutely certain* that water will always boil at 100°C at sea level? The answer is no. It is no because past experience is not an infallible guide to the future. Here is where the notion of possibility excludes certainty. It is possible, for instance, that water has boiled at that temperature for the past 3 million years, but that next week it will start to boil at a different temperature. It could be that the real physical law is cyclical: according to it, water boils at one temperature for 3 million years, at another temperature for the next 3 million years, at the original temperature for the next 3 million, and so on. Since this scenario is possible, then no scientist can know with certainty that water in the future will continue to boil at 100°C. Realizing this possibility, scientists tell us that it is *highly probable* given past experience that water will continue to boil at 100°C, but that it is not certain.

Some philosophers of science agreeing with this analysis have attempted to redefine "knowledge" in such a way as to eliminate its connection with certainty. According to their proposal, "knowledge" simply means whatever the scientific community at a given point in time agrees is true. Thus a case of high probability, such as a well-established physical law, is a case of knowledge on that construal. But if one were to accept such a revision, a particular scientific law might have the characteristic that it could be true in the year 2000 C.E. and false in the year 2001 C.E. This consequence, however, would be inconsistent with the condition that one cannot know that which is false. Therefore, this interpretation would have to be rejected as a satisfactory analysis of the concept of knowledge. Since skeptics claim that human beings can never arrive at knowledge and/or certainty, and scientists agree that certitude about the world is not attainable, then science is a form of skepticism. It is not radical skepticism, as we shall see later, but it is skeptical in character nonetheless.

Apart from this particular feature, science possesses another that calls into account our ordinary, commonsense picture of the world. The commonsense picture is based on everyday experience. Our experience is of a macroscopic world, one whose components we can see, touch, hear, taste, and feel. The macroscopic world is composed of inanimate objects, such as rocks and mountains, and of animate objects, such as insects, animals, and persons. We can all see the sun and the moon, and feel ourselves standing on the earth. Observation makes it plain that the earth is flat, and that the sun moves around it from east to west. Since time immemorial this has been the accepted picture of the cosmos. Yet science tells us that it is all wrong. The earth is not flat; it does not stand still, the sun does not revolve around it, and so forth. It follows that if science is right the information generated by the senses is wrong.

Consider a second example. The ordinary person tends to think of water as a kind of liquid that is useful for various purposes: for drinking, washing, mixing with other substances. What science tells us about water differs from this conception. It claims that water is H_2O. On this view, water is a collection of hydrogen and oxygen molecules. But molecules are things we cannot see. Water is thus not identical with its observable, overt properties, such as its liquidity and transparency, but with some features not accessible to the naked eye. In liquidity and transparency, we see the manifestations of these invisible ingredients, but the essential nature of water is hidden from the ordinary perceiver. Once again, our senses have misled us.

Let us turn to a third example. Common sense believes that many objects are perfectly solid. The table I am writing on is a good example. But according to scientific theory, the table is mostly empty space and is not really solid. Its perceptible solidity is thus misleading as to its real nature. The truth of the matter is that the table is a cluster of invisible electrical particles occupying mostly empty space. The conclusion to be drawn from these examples (and one could add an extensive list of others) is that common sense is mistaken as to the nature of reality. We have no reason to believe that our ordinary sense experience gives us an accurate picture of the world. In undermining common sense in favor of a highly complex, very counterintuitive picture of the real nature of things, science supports skeptical doubts about the apparent knowledge the senses give us. It demonstrates that they do not provide an accurate account of how things are.

Let us summarize the discussion in this chapter so far. It began with the commonsense idea that human beings do possess knowledge, indeed plenty of it. But it was agreed that such knowledge mostly derives from sense experience. And as one carefully scrutinizes the information that sense experience generates, it begins to look less solid and reliable than initially assumed. Science lends further support to such doubts. It thus seems patent that we cannot dismiss the skeptic's concerns. Yet it is an interesting fact that a majority of the greatest philosophers of past and present have rejected skepticism. We shall therefore have to scrutinize their reasons for doing so. Let us call philosophers of this stripe "dogmatists." By this locution, we do not mean that these philosophers are stubborn or unreasonable. The term is historically used in a technical sense to refer to views that assert that knowledge and certainty are attainable by human beings. That is how we shall employ it in what now follows. We shall begin with the Greeks and, in particular, with Plato, the most famous of all dogmatists.

PLATO'S THEORY OF KNOWLEDGE

Plato's theory of knowledge is extraordinary, the creation of a philosophical genius. It has three main features. (1) It holds that knowledge and certainty exist, and, indeed, that one who knows something knows that thing with certainty. (2) Although affirming that knowledge and certainty exist, it denies that everyone is capable of acquiring knowledge and attaining certainty. It limits this capacity to an elite given special physical and intellectual training. (3) It makes a considerable concession to skeptical reservations about the senses. On Plato's view, sense experience will never produce knowledge/certainty. In this respect, he concurs with the skeptics. But unlike them, he believes that the acquisition of knowledge and certainty is possible. He argues, therefore, that in order to achieve knowledge and certainty, one must transcend sense experience and employ reason instead. Plato's theory of knowledge is thus ultimately a form of rationalism.

In order to explain this complicated and subtle view, we need to describe the social and political conditions, as well as the philosophical theories, that were prevalent in Athens in the fifth century B.C.E. Plato's theory of knowledge arises, at least in part, as a reaction to the increasing democratization of Athens on the one hand, and to burgeoning relativistic and skeptical philosophies on the other. As he saw the situation, these developments were intimately connected, and both had to be resisted. Let us begin with the sociopolitical background.

The sociopolitical background

As distinct from modern Greece, which is one nation with a central government, ancient Greece was a composite of separate city-states, each with its own political system. These ranged from military oligarchies, such as Sparta, to the first known democracy, Athens. Because of commercial and ideological rivalries, these autonomous states engaged in frequent warfare with one another. But in the fifth century B.C.E. they united against a common threat. Persia invaded from the East with an army that later historians have estimated to contain more than a million men. For more than a decade—starting in 490 B.C.E. where, on the plains of Marathon, the Athenians defeated a force of thirty thousand Persians, down to 480 B.C.E., when the Athenian navy destroyed the Persian fleet at Salamis—the Greeks managed to beat back the Persians. By 466 B.C.E., under the Athenian general Cimon, the Greeks had taken the offensive and were freeing Greek cities in Asia minor. From this period on, the Persians abandoned Europe and never again represented a threat to Greece.

The psychological impact on the Persian court of the naval disaster at Salamis is depicted, interestingly enough, by an Athenian, the famous playwright Aeschylus. His drama *The Persians*, first presented in 472 B.C.E., is a sympathetic portrayal of the Persian shock and reaction to their defeat. He invents conversations between the

Persian king and his advisors, who cannot understand how a major power such as theirs could be beaten by so few men. The point of the play is to bring out that those committed to democracy, and fighting for its survival, are different from troops hired to do battle but not motivated by the defense of a free society.

As a result of these victories, Athens and Sparta emerged as the two most powerful states in Greece. Given their differing political and social orientations, it was inevitable that they would eventually collide. When they did, the result was the destructive Peloponnesian War (431–404 B.C.E.) brilliantly described by the Athenian historian Thucydides. His narrative, for unknown reasons, breaks off in 411 B.C.E., six and one-half years before the end of the war. The outcome of this lengthy struggle was the defeat of Athens and the disappearance of political democracy from Greece for more than two thousand years.

From its earliest days, and even after it had lost its power, Athens was the cultural center of the Western world. It produced such great playwrights as Aeschylus, Sophocles, Euripides, and Aristophanes; such great historians as Herodotus and Thucydides; and a host of distinguished philosophers, among them Socrates, Plato, and Aristotle.

Because Athens was a democracy, and because a democracy is a system of self-government, the question arose about the best way of educating the citizenry to rule themselves, that is, to develop the skills needed to formulate and implement wise public policies. A group of philosophers called "Sophists," assumed this task. Some of these teachers were major thinkers in their own right. Much of what we know about their views comes from the writings of Plato, who vigorously opposed them and the democratic state for reasons to be described in more detail below. In such dialogues as *Protagoras, Gorgias*, and *The Republic*, he describes their positions and the arguments developed against them by his teacher, Socrates.

The Sophists and skepticism

The Sophists were clever, adept at argument, and prepared to teach people what they needed to know in order to get along in the world and to persuade others to adopt their views. The content of their teaching was thus practical, the art of winning arguments. They scorned theoretical and abstract subjects, such as pure mathematics, which did not apply to ordinary, everyday human interactions. The Sophists were not necessary dishonest, but because of their lack of commitment to any point of view, they gave this impression to their opponents, especially to Socrates and Plato, who felt that winning was less important than striving for truth. In the Platonic dialogues they are inevitably depicted as developing arguments for the sake of argument, doing anything to emerge victorious in a dispute. As a result, Plato's characterizations have colored the historical assessment of the Sophists. This construal has even become a linguistic staple of modern English. Words like "sophist," "sophistry," "sophism," and "sophistical" now have negative connotations that they did not bear in the ancient world. Thus, Webster's Dictionary defines a "sophism" as clever but fallacious reasoning; a "sophist" as one who uses fallacious or specious arguments; and "sophistical" as to deceive by using sophisms.

In order to justify their emphasis upon the practical and their rejection of abstruse and theoretical speculation, the Sophists developed a negative, highly skeptical theory of knowledge. It was this theory that Socrates and Plato both strongly opposed. Its most famous expression is attributed to Protagoras, who held that "man is the measure of all things." Another sophist, Gorgias, went even further, stating that "nothing exists, and even if it did, nobody could know it, and even if someone did, that person could not communicate this knowledge." From Plato's perspective, the Sophists were contending that human beings cannot ever know what is really going on in the world; that the only information anyone has is derived from appearances. Since appearances differ from individual to individual, each man is an equally good measure of truth. Thus, on their view, there is no such thing as objective truth or an objective reality, by which they meant some absolutely correct description of the way things are independently of any percipient. Each description must be relativized to a particular perceiver, so there are many equally valid and equally competitive truths; none of them completely objective. In contemporary philosophy, such writers as Stephen Stich and Hilary Putnam are sympathetic to this outlook. For them, truth must always be relativized to a particular standpoint or perspective. Putnam calls his view "internal realism." It is similar to what the sophists meant by the apothegm that "man is the measure of all things."

For Socrates and Plato, the implications of this doctrine were pernicious. It entailed that there could be no absolutely true morality, no objective standards in politics, and no descriptions of reality that were categorically true. Thus, for them the views of the democrats, the Sophists, and the skeptics were not merely wrong, but were palpably dangerous to the social fabric.

The Socratic reaction to the Sophists

Socrates (469–399 B.C.E.) was the epitome of what it is to be a philosopher. He was a charismatic figure who walked around ancient Athens, questioning people as to what they meant by "piety," or "justice," or "friendship," and so forth. His intensive probing inevitably led to the conclusion that the average person did not know what these notions meant. Such experiences were but a short step to Plato's later view that the average person could not attain knowledge. And it was but another short step from that notion to Plato's position that only an intellectual elite could do so. Given the additional premise that good governance requires knowledge, Plato arrived at the antidemocratic conclusion that an intellectual elite should be given absolute power to rule society. Socrates never went that far; yet the seeds of Plato's doctrine are embedded in the methods that Socrates used and the findings that his methods revealed.

Socrates' "charisma" produced a host of admirers, especially among the young, aristocratic intellectuals of fifth-century Athens. Many of these are mentioned, sometimes prominently, in Plato's dialogues, and some of the dialogues are named after them. Because he was a kind of gadfly, challenging opinions about the most sacred things, presumably even the existence of the gods, Socrates was tried by Athenian democrats for impiety, and was eventually condemned to death. Plato's description of the democratic case against Socrates clearly suggests that the charges are trumped up or at least exaggerated. This crime against philosophy, as Aristotle was to characterize it, is one of the things for which Plato never forgave the democrats.

His reaction to these events is depicted in detail in three beautiful dialogues: the *Apology*, which describes the trial and conviction of Socrates; the *Crito*, which follows chronologically and portrays him in his prison cell, engaged in conversation with his disciples; and the *Phaedo*, in which the most famous death scene in philosophy is graphically depicted. Here, the conversation is about the possibility of immortality, and, at the end of it, Socrates swallows a potion of hemlock and dies.

As far as is known, Socrates wrote nothing, so information about him derives from the writings of others. There are three main sources. By far, the most extensive consists of the hundreds of pages in the Platonic dialogues, whose central figure is Socrates. There is also a brief portrait of him in Xenophon's *Memorabilia*, which differs from Plato's characterization. A third source is to be found in the comic playwright Aristophones; in his *Clouds*, the philosopher is satirized and shown to be unworldly.

Since the Platonic dialogues are the main sources of information about the life and views of Socrates, a question of persistent scholarly interest has been how accurate the Platonic depiction is of those views. The range of interpretations is wide. Some scholars believe Plato was simply a reporter who followed Socrates around and accurately described his views, though perhaps giving a special literary gloss to them. Others see Plato as a consummate literary artist who is expressing his own ideas, using Socrates as the spokesman for them. Neither of these extreme opinions is widely accepted. The prevailing view is that in what are called the "early dialogues," such as the *Charmides*, *Lysis*, and *Euthyphro*, Plato (still a young man) is accurately reporting Socrates' views; that beginning with the middle dialogues, such as *The Republic*, a more mature Plato is mixing his own thoughts with those of Socrates; and that in the late dialogues, such as the *Laws*, it is primarily Plato's views that are being expressed. This analysis is based in part on textual evidence, but also on the fact that the early dialogues show Socrates to be very cautious in advancing any positive theory. Instead, he is probing the claims to knowledge made by others. There is thus a skeptical, negative aspect in his approach to philosophical matters that has diminished emphasis in the middle and late dialogues. In those, he is shown as increasingly more dogmatic, asserting that there is such a thing as knowledge and giving an elaborate description of what it is. For this reason, many commentators believe that in the late dialogues it is the voice of Plato that is really speaking, even though the mouth is that of Socrates.

Plato's response to the Sophists and skeptics

Insofar as one can demarcate Socrates' own views, separating them from Plato's, he seems to have adhered to two basic principles: (1) that he knew that he knew nothing, and (2) that the unexamined life is not worth living. His main objections to the sophists were that they did not know or even care that their methods of instruction could not give rise to knowledge—that winning an argument was not the same as knowing what the truth is—and, secondly, that they did not really examine anything. On the contrary, they simply pandered to the superficial desires of most people, teaching them those things that they wanted to hear. The outcome of such "instruction" was disastrous. It did not lead to understanding oneself, one's society, the nature of the world, or the nature of the good life for man. Behind such pandering lay the pernicious principle that "man is the measure of all things." This was what Socrates' persistent questioning was designed to undermine. Even though Socrates' statement that he knew that he knew nothing suggests a form of skepticism, his overall approach to philosophical issues suggests the opposite: The truth is there, but it is difficult to find. And it is this aspect of his teaching that Plato pursued and ultimately developed.

With this background, we are now in a position to describe Plato's theory of knowledge. Like the earlier views of Socrates, it is designed to refute Protagoras, the skeptics, and the democratic thesis that the people are competent to govern themselves. As we said earlier, it exhibits three features: (1) that knowledge and certainty exist, something the sophists and the skeptics either denied or were in doubt about; (2) that one who has knowledge of p knows that p with certainty; and (3) that only a few in society can attain knowledge and certainty. This last provision, with some additional premises, such as that proper ruling requires knowledge, led Plato to the antidemocratic position that only an intellectual elite could and should rule society. We shall defer the political, ethical, and social implications of this last point to later chapters. Let us now turn to the first two principles: that knowledge/certainty exist, and that to know p is to know that p with certainty.

To understand Plato's position, we again require some historical background. As mentioned, the ancient Greeks were obsessively speculative thinkers. Perhaps the single most challenging problem they addressed was, What is the world really like? Or in an alternative formulation, they sometimes put the question this way: Is the world made of some fundamental stuff, and if so, what is it?

Two radically different, wholly incompatible answers were given to these questions. One of them, advanced by Heraclitus (540?–475 B.C.E.) was that there was no fundamental stuff, that is, nothing that was wholly immune to change. For him the only reality was the process of change itself. Everything is in flux, so that, according to his celebrated remark, "you cannot step into the same river twice." Every feature of the world comes into being and passes away. The only thing that does not change is a cosmic balance maintained by the continuous alteration of everything. There is no underlying "stuff," like water, as Thales believed, that remains invariant through all temporal processes. Though he himself apparently did not draw explicit skeptical implications from this view, some of his disciples and followers did. One of them, Cratylus (after whom Plato named a dialogue), held that reality is unintelligible. Since it does not stand still long enough to be described, our words and their meanings are constantly changing, as is each speaker. Thus, human discourse is simply gibberish, having no fixed meanings. Cratylus expands on Heraclitus's river metaphor, arguing that one cannot even step once into the same river, since it is not the same by the time one's foot enters into it, nor is it the same individual who is doing the stepping, nor is it the same foot that enters the water. It follows that there is nothing stable to be described and that communication about the world is impossible. It is reported that Cratylus eventually refused to speak, being willing only to wiggle his little finger when asked a question. This extreme form of skepticism thus arises by pushing the notion of changing sense experience to or even beyond its intelligible limits.

An exactly opposite point of view was developed by Parmenides. His view starts from the commonsense observation that if something, say a leaf, changes, then to speak of it as a "leaf" is to imply that some essential feature of it remains constant. Change is thus different from a sequence of different appearances. If change were total, there would be no thing that changed, such as a leaf. In that case, a so-called leaf would consist of number of unconnected states that appear successively in one's visual field. Thus, a leaf that common sense thinks changes from green to brown must, as a matter of logic, have an essence, that is, some "stuff" that remains constant, and this, as distinct from its color and shape, cannot be anything accessible to the senses.

Let us now examine in some detail what Plato says about sense experience. In the Doctrine of the Divided Line in book 7 of *The Republic*, we find an extensive treatment of this topic. In that passage, Plato distinguishes between the World of Appearance and the World of Reality. The World of Appearance is the world revealed to the senses. It consists of different sorts of objects. Each type of object is apprehended by a different mode of sensing. There are images, for instance, captured by the imagination; there are visible objects, such as tables and rocks, which are apprehended by sight and touch; and so forth. Plato suggests that these objects can be arrayed in a spectrum of increasing stability. Images are more fleeting than rocks, for example. So the information we acquire about rocks is better than that about transient images. But such information never reaches certitude. For that we must access unchanging objects in the World of Reality. These he calls "forms" or "ideas," and we shall speak about them in a moment.

Plato says two things about sense experience that explains why it cannot produce knowledge. First, he states that the various objects one apprehends through the senses bear incompatible predicates. Thus, the same rock can be said to be light or heavy. Second, he points out that all such objects are subject to ceaseless change, though, of course, some alter more rapidly than others. Therefore, because these objects change and have incompatible features, they *cannot be known*. Though he does not expand on these arguments, he seems to be suggesting that knowing is a kind of intellectual grasping. If an object changes, then one cannot really grasp it; it is like trying to pick up quicksilver. Moreover, if it has incompatible features, it has no consistent and therefore no real nature. It is merely a collection of appearances. Therefore, to acquire knowledge, one must leave the world of appearance and access those eternal and self-consistent objects that belong to the world of reality.

The metaphysical, epistemological, moral, and political implications of this doctrine have been and still are enormous: It seems to apply to every domain of human life. Its scope is best illustrated in the Allegory of the Cave. This segment immediately follows the Doctrine of the Divided Line in book 7 of *The Republic* and provides a graphic, literary version of the theory of knowledge that the former gives in an adumbrated form. The Allegory of the Cave is probably the most famous passage in all of philosophy. Virtually every philosophy student has read it. Even today it is constantly referred to by novelists, sociologists, political scientists, linguists, and, of course, philosophers.

The scene is set in a dark cave—the World of Appearance. Persons are chained, with heads fixed forward, facing a wall. Behind them there is a fire, and in front of the fire other persons walk on a parapet. Their shadows are cast on the wall, and it is only these shadows that the chained can see. Their perception of reality is thus confined to the world of appearance, and within that world they apprehend only shadows—images of real persons. Each element in the allegory corresponds to an element in the Divided Line. The lowest level of apprehension consists in the awareness of images, fleeting entities. These are the shadows cast on the wall. The real persons walking are equivalent to visible objects. They are particulars who live in the world of appearance; but, being made of flesh and blood, they are more stable and less evanescent than the shadows.

The allegory goes on to describe how human beings can acquire knowledge. First, they must leave their chains; for this they require help, the sort of help that a philosophical gadfly like Socrates can give. In effect, they free themselves by the exercise of reason. When they cast off their chains, they can begin an ascent that will lead them out of the cave. This upward movement is equivalent to that described in the Divided Line, where thinking provides a bridge to the World of Reality. When they emerge from the cave, they are blinded by light. Gradually, they are able to discern and discriminate various kinds of entities, and eventually the sun. These diverse items correspond to numbers, the forms, and to the Good, respectively. In leaving the cave, they have departed from a world of flux and have arrived at unchanging Reality. They are now in a position to acquire knowledge, that is, to grasp unalterable entities. The moral, social, and political implications of their altered status are immediate. Unless they have knowledge, they cannot know what is good. If they cannot know what is good, they cannot be certain that their actions are moral. If they cannot be certain of that, they cannot rule properly. So release from the cave we all inhabit is the necessary condition for leading a good life. This is why the unexamined life is not worth living: It amounts to perpetual existence in a cave. With this brilliant and moving allegory Plato completes his theory of knowledge.

ANCIENT SKEPTICISM: A BRIEF HISTORY

The history of skepticism can be traced back to Ancient Greece via coeval and later documents, but the skeptical attitude has probably always existed. The documents that comprise the historical record reveal an unbroken tradition from the time of Socrates through the Hellenic period, or through, roughly, the fourth century C.E. There is then a thousand-year hiatus when skepticism either disappears or is submerged. Now the dominant intellectual force is Catholic theology. But with the breakup of the medieval synthesis and the rise of humanism, it emerges again in the Renaissance. The scientific discoveries of Copernicus, Galileo, and Newton in the sixteenth and seventeenth centuries give it additional momentum. It has been part and parcel of philosophy ever since.

For the historian it is difficult to describe. Historically, skepticism has taken many different forms, some of which are not easily characterizable. Still, in order to make some sort of headway here, we can begin with two major classifications. The first distinguishes *assertive* from *nonassertive*, and the second *radical* from *mitigated* forms of skepticism. We shall begin with the former.

Assertive skepticism

One form of assertive skepticism has its origin in Plato's Academy, and in particular exhibits the influence of Socrates on the Academy. It is therefore generally called "Academic skepticism," although the name "dogmatic skepticism" is sometimes applied to it. Skeptics of this kind advanced a thesis based on Socrates' remark that the only thing he knew was that he knew nothing. Following the Socratic maxim, the Greek philosopher Arcesilaus (c. 315–c. 240 B.C.E.) claimed that nothing is known. Since none of his writings is extant, the evidence for his view derives from later sources, from Cicero (who was himself an Academic skeptic), Sextus Empiricus, and Diogenes Laertius.

An objection to this form of skepticism was widely voiced in the ancient world. One version of the objection is attributed to the Stoic Antipater (fl. c. 135 B.C.E.), who pointed out that the view is self-contradictory. To know that knowledge is unattainable is to know something; therefore, Academic skepticism asserts both p and not-p, and is therefore self-refuting. But there were defenders of Arcesilaus as well. Carneades (c. 213–129 B.C.E.), who was a member of the Academy, stated in response that Arcesilaus's remark was misunderstood. It should be interpreted as a kind of presupposition rather than as an explicit affirmation. The presupposition is that knowledge is impossible. The skeptic does not try to prove this assumption but rather defends it against dogmatic arguments to the contrary by showing that such arguments invariably fail. Whether Carneades' response is compelling is a matter we shall not discuss further.

There are also forms of assertive skepticism that offer explicit arguments whose conclusion is that nothing can be known, such as various versions of the Problem of the Criterion and the famous Dream and Demon Hypotheses of Descartes, which we shall discuss critically in chapter 8.

What we wish to emphasize at this stage in our discussion is simply that skepticism can take an assertive, explicitly argumentative form.

Nonassertive skepticism

Let us now turn to nonassertive forms of skepticism. The first of these originated in the fourth century B.C.E. It is called "Pyrrhonism," and is named after Pyrrho of Elis (c. 365–275). None of his works survives and virtually all that is known about him comes from the extensive writings of Sextus Empiricus (second century C.E.). Since Sextus declares himself to be a Pyrrhonist, we shall concentrate upon his version of the view.

Nearly all commentators agree that Pyrrhonism is not a theory, and that it makes no claims or positive assertions. As A. P. Martinich writes, "Ancient Pyrrhonism is not strictly an epistemology since it has no theory of knowledge and is content to undermine the dogmatic epistemologies of others, especially of the Stoics and Epicureans.[1] Other experts concur with this assessment. Benson Mates states that "[t]he single most important point to understand about Pyrrhonism—and a point that unfortunately has been overlooked by many otherwise astute commentators ever since antiquity—is that Pyrrhonism is *not* a doctrine or system of beliefs."[2]

These historians thus tend to interpret Pyrrhonism as a kind of attitude in which judgment is simply suspended. As Richard Popkin describes it,

> Pyrrhonism is first distinguished from the negative dogmatism of Academic skepticism: the Pyrrhonists doubt and suspend judgments on all propositions, even that all is doubt. They oppose any assertion whatsoever, and their opposition, if successful, shows the opponent's ignorance; if unsuccessful, their own ignorance.[3]

The Pyrrhonists call this attitude "epoche." It is the total suspension of judgment. Epoche is consistent with a kind of passive acceptance of the world; one lives in the world, acts in it, takes it as it is without reflection. Epoche is important because it is the first step toward *ataraxia*—a special kind of mental tranquillity. Because no judgments are entertained or made, and because the world is accepted as it is, ataraxia is possible. Pyrrhonism is thus ultimately a philosophy of life, a formula for living well. It reverses the Socratic point of view that the unexamined life is not worth living. For the Pyrrhonist ataraxia is the unexamined life. In this mode of living no assessments or evaluations are made yet mental peace is attainable. Ataraxia is close to the kind of mystic state that is sometimes called "nirvana" or "the peace that passeth understanding." But it is also different since it has no religious resonances.

Yet curiously enough, while nonassertive, Pyrrhonism has historically represented a powerful challenge to dogmatism. But how, if nothing is being affirmed or claimed, can it have any argumentative force? The answer is that it consists of an implicit or covert rhetorical strategy that puts the dogmatist on the defensive.

As we all know, information can be conveyed from one person to another nonverbally. A wink, a raised eyebrow, or a salute can constitute a message even though its initiator remains silent. Even verbal communication can take other than statement-making forms. "There's a bull in the pasture" could be used to tell a joke, to make an offer, to express fear, or to warn or advise someone. In all of these cases the words express nonassertions. The technique of the Pyrrhonist falls into the category of the linguistic nonassertive while expressing a challenge that the dogmatist must make. Here, roughly, is how it works.

Suppose a dogmatist asserts a knowledge claim, for instance, that it is raining now. The Pyrrhonist does not have to deny that it is raining. Instead, he may remark, "How do you know that it is raining?" This question is entirely appropriate. If someone makes an assertion it is proper to ask him why he thinks it is true. The dogmatist might respond by saying, "Because I can see it is raining." At this point, the Pyrrhonist may comment, "But isn't it possible that you could be mistaken? Isn't it possible that you could have all your present sense experience and yet be wrong?" The dogmatist, reflecting on these promptings, might agree that having certain sense experiences, such as experiencing what seems to be rain, could occur, and yet there might be no rain at all. The dogmatist may be hallucinating, or his eyesight might be poor, or water might be leaking from the roof, and so forth. It is thus possible to have sense experiences that are misleading.

This process of systematic questioning by the Pyrrhonist thus reveals a logical gap between the evidence that the dogmatist states he has and the claim that the evidence presumably supports. As long as it is possible that the criterion the dogmatist uses—that is, that he sees something to be the case—is satisfied and yet that he might be wrong, he cannot know what he claims to know. The Pyrrhonist strategy thus reinforces the point made earlier in this chapter, namely, that if one *might* be mistaken one can't know. Without ever asserting anything, the Pyrrhonist has cleverly made his dogmatic opponent acknowledge that the evidence he cites is not conclusive. It is a brilliant strategy because it does not leave the Pyrrhonist open to the counterclaim that he knows that knowledge is unattainable.

Radical and mitigated forms of skepticism

Pyrrhonism and Academic skepticism are both radical forms of skepticism. They are thus to be distinguished from moderate types of skepticism. What all forms of skepticism have in common are reservations about the attainment of knowledge. But the radical skeptic doubts that any piece of information is any better than any other. If the basis for any belief is fallible, then no belief is better founded than any other. The mitigated skeptic disagrees. While concurring that certitude is unachievable, his outlook is that some information is more reliable than other information. Generally speaking, the mitigated skeptic is committed to the thesis that information is to be described in probabilistic terms. The more probable, the more reliable. But in saying this, he is also saying that no degree of probability, no matter how high, is equivalent to knowledge.

It is possible for a philosopher to espouse both forms of skepticism. David Hume is a good example. At times (say, with respect to the problems of the external world and the principle of induction) he is a radical skeptic. Yet in his *Treatise* there is a chapter devoted to probability, and this concept plays an important role in his empiricist outlook. But before turning to Hume, we shall now jump a thousand years from Sextus Empiricus to the seventeenth century, where we shall meet the founder of modern philosophy, René Descartes.

NOTES

1. A. P. Martinich, "Epistemology," in *Encyclopedia Britannica*, vol. 18 (1990), p. 476.

2. Benson Mates, *The Skeptic Way* (New York/Oxford: Oxford University Press, 1996), p. 6.

3. Richard H. Popkin, *The History of Skepticism from Erasmus to Spinoza* (Berkeley: University of California Press, 1979), p. 47.

3 MODERN SKEPTICISM

RENÉ DESCARTES AND THE DREAM AND DEMON HYPOTHESES

The Method of Doubt

Like Plato, Descartes (1596–1650) lived in a world in which traditional verities were being challenged. In France, his birthplace, and in the Netherlands, where he spent most of his adulthood, there were profound religious struggles between Catholics and Protestants about the truth of certain Christian doctrines. Whether the Bible should be read literally or, if not, who should decide what its sentences mean, were issues being debated in churches, public fora, and universities. The Judeo-Christian picture of the origin of the universe, and man's role in it, was confronted by the astronomical theories of Nicolaus Copernicus (1473–1543), Johannes Kepler (1571–1630), and Galileo (1564–1642). The new geographical discoveries in the Americas, Africa, and the Orient, resulting from the voyages of Vasco da Gama, Christopher Columbus, Sir Francis Drake, and others, also opened new frontiers of information. Almost every traditional principle was now susceptible to revision or abandonment.

Descartes, who had studied at the Jesuit school in La Flèche, France, was affected by these developments. He gradually came to mistrust the scholastic doctrines based on Aristotle that were taught at La Flèche, and decided to leave school to discover for himself what was true. After a brief career in the Dutch army as an officer (most of which was spent studying mathematics and physics) he came to the decision that most of the accepted views of the time were suspect. When he returned to Paris in 1628 he met a coterie of intelligent young men who had developed similar caveats. Many of them were complete skeptics and urged Descartes to adopt similar views.

Instead, Descartes reacted negatively and returned to Holland, opting to think the matter through for himself. After several years of intensive reflection, he published his findings in his famous *Discourse on Method* (1637) and, four years later, in his equally celebrated *Meditations on First Philosophy.* In these two works he undertook the task of developing a synoptic metaphysical system to provide the foundation and justification for the materialistic-mechanical picture of nature that the new science was developing. But his vision of philosophy was even larger. He also wished to show how the material world was related to two other aspects of reality—Mind and God. The result was the first major metaphysical system of modern times. It has been the source, both widely copied and widely attacked, of most metaphysical systems since. It also contains one of the most sophisticated defenses of certitude in the face of radical doubt.

One of its most influential theories was that mind and matter are independent substances, that is, that neither could be reduced to the other. Even today, forms of Cartesianism provide the central background against which reductionist theories in cognitive science, psychology, and philosophy spin out their views. Even though his original two-substance doctrine is no longer widely accepted, the thesis of the nonreducibility of mind to matter is still the default position that materialist views, such as the identity theory, functionalism, and eliminativism, seek to overthrow.

Since his mathematical and scientific research had persuaded him that certain propositions were true, and were known by him to be true, he decided to find out by tough-minded self-criticism to see whether these apparent truths were illusory or not. This obsessive questioning was based on the principle that any belief should be rejected if any reason could be advanced for holding it to be dubious. Descartes did not require that anyone, including himself, actually be in doubt. His standard was much more demanding. If, he argued, it is *possible* that a belief could be false, then it should be rejected. In effect, he was requiring that a belief be *certain* before it could be accepted.

This entire process is what has become famous as the Cartesian Method of Doubt.

The method begins with a review of certain individual beliefs that Descartes questions. An object seen from a distance is a different color from that seen close up; when one has a cold food tastes different than it normally does; and so forth. But Descartes realized that if he tried to question each of his beliefs in turn, the task would never end. So the Method of Doubt begins with a generalization. Descartes states that there are two main sources of beliefs, the senses and reason. He argues that if the sources are tainted, one can never be sure that any belief arising from such sources is not also tainted.

His initial application of the Method of Doubt to the senses reveals that they are sometimes misleading. He cites various perceptual illusions, and persons suffering from delusions, as examples of such cases. But even if we are *sometimes* mistaken or deluded it does not follow that we *always* are. We need a still stronger challenge to bring all sense experience into question. This is what the Dream Hypothesis does.

According to that hypothesis, we cannot know at any particular moment that we are not dreaming. If we cannot know at T1 or T2 . . . Tn that we are not dreaming, we can never know for sure that we are awake. The Dream Hypothesis spells out this challenge in detail. It suggests that all experience may well be illusory. The peculiar feature of dreams is that the experiences one has while dreaming are *indistinguishable* from waking experiences. We dream we are seated before a fire, we hear it crackling, we feel its heat—and yet when we wake up, we find ourselves in bed, with no fire present.

Even the experience of awakening might occur in a dream episode and, if so, could not be distinguished from a waking experience. Presumably, when we wake up from a deep sleep, we can perform various tests to see if we are really awake. We can ask another, we can pinch ourselves, we can make a telephone call, and so forth. Yet all these tests may themselves be dreamed. Our experience of waking up may occur in a dream. Any evidence we have, including the sensation of waking up, might be dream evidence. Descartes concluded that we do not have any conclusive reason for believing that any of our sense experiences, past or present, are not part of a continuous dream. It follows that we cannot ever be sure that sense experience puts us into veridical contact with the external world. The Dream Hypothesis thus puts all sense experience at risk.

Does it then follow that we cannot have any knowledge at all?

Not necessarily, Descartes says, for even within dreams, there seem to be verities that we cannot doubt. If we dream that a triangle has 180 degrees, or that $2 + 2 = 4$, we cannot be mistaken about those truths. Or can we? The Demon Hypothesis says that we can. It thus supplements the Dream Hypothesis, so that, taken together, they seem to show that knowledge of any kind is impossible.

The Demon Hypothesis has played a major role in skeptical views ever since Descartes invented it. In contemporary forms it is very powerful. Let us begin with the original version. Suppose, Descartes suggests, that a malicious deity exists who misleads everyone about everything without their knowing it. This demon devises propositions that look obviously true, and yet are not. In reality, $2 + 2$ actually equals 7, but the demon makes everyone believe that the correct answer is 4. According to the hypothesis, there is no way we could find out what is true. Any calculation we might make will be programmed by the demon to seem correct, yet it will not be. There is constant, incessant deception. The point about Descartes's scenario is not that such a demon actually exists, but rather that one might. Thus, given that knowledge entails certainty, the mere possibility that there could be such a diety means that we can never know any of the conceptual products of reason to be true.

There is a famous novelette, *Donovan's Brain* by K. Siodimak, first published in 1943, that presents the Demon Hypothesis in an unforgettable literary form. In contemporary philosophy, Siodimak's science-fiction fantasy has been taken very seriously, and is called the "Brain in the Vat Hypothesis." According to *Donovan's Brain*, a brain (detached from its human body) is kept alive in a jar in the laboratory of a scientist. By means of various electrical and chemical stimuli it thinks that different real events are taking place, for example, that the person it takes itself to be is walking, thinking, and undergoing certain pleasant experiences. Yet none of these things is really happening.

But if such deception is possible, how can we ever know that it is not occurring now. In such distopias as Eugene Zamiatin's *We*, Aldous Huxley's *Brave New World*, and George Orwell's *1984*, humans live in societies that are totally controlled by amoral political forces. They have become brainwashed by conditioning or by the use of drugs into believing that "war is peace," "freedom is slavery," and "2 + 2 = 5." These novels depict the possibility of total intellectual, sexual, and moral control of the populace by totalitarian rulers. In the experience that the Western world has undergone in the twentieth century, with powerful propaganda techniques used by governments to "atrophy the mental organs of" their citizens, as Herbert Marcuse puts it in *One Dimensional Man*,[1] can any of us be sure that we ourselves are not the products of such conditioning? The fact that we might be, that the hypothesis is conceivable, shows that we can never be sure about anything.

The Cartesian quest for certainty: The cogito

Descartes's *Meditations on First Philosophy* consists of six meditations. After the "First Meditation," where the method of doubt is advanced, Descartes seems to leave the reader in despair. He writes, "At the end I feel constrained to confess that there is nothing at at all that I formerly believed to be true, of which I cannot in some measure doubt."[2] All the beliefs deriving from sense experience and reason might be false, and if they might be, then one cannot have knowledge.

Yet, the Method of Doubt for Descartes was not designed to support skepticism. Rather, he insisted that if a challenge of such strength could be met, it would be tantamount to proving that certainty exists. Descartes's so-called skepticism is methodological rather than doctrinal. It is designed as a kind of fulcrum for arriving at certainty. The starting point of the quest for such certitude is found in the "Second Meditation." Deepening his reflections, Descartes describes a startling discovery: one thing that is certainly true.

He says that even if there really is no physical world, even if I live entirely in a dream world, and even there exists a malicious demon, one thing is certain: namely, that no matter what I doubt, or why I doubt it, I must exist to do the doubting.

His point can be put this way: Suppose I think I exist, but am mistaken about this. Still, in order to be mistaken, I must think that *p*. But I cannot think that *p*, even if *p* is false, unless I exist. Thus, the statement, "I think, therefore I exist" has the peculiar property that whenever it is entertained by anyone it is *necessarily* true of that person. No matter how hard I attempt to conceive of some way in which it could be *possibly* false or doubtful, I find I only succeed in confirming its truth. For every occasion on which I engage in thinking, I must exist to do the thinking. Therefore, every consideration against its truth merely confirms its truth. This proposition is not a contingent truth that *might* be false, and thus allow for a logical gap between belief and fact. It is necessarily true, so there is no *possible* gap between "I think" and "I exist." This is thus another way of saying that it is certain. Its Latin version, *cogito, ergo sum*, has given this proposition the name "the cogito." The cogito is Descartes's answer to the Method of Doubt. It demonstrates that he knows one thing for certain, namely, that he exists.

This is a brilliant, original piece of reasoning. It seems obviously correct. Yet in the "Third Meditation," Descartes asks a question that eventually opens his argument to skeptical riposte. We shall see how this develops. He asks, "How do I know that I am a thing that thinks?" His answer is that I can see clearly and distinctly that this is true. This idea is applied to the cogito. He knows it is true because can see this *clearly and distinctly*.

But unfortunately, it is not really clear what he means by these terms. In "The Principles of Philosophy" he writes, "I call that clear which is present and apparent to an attentive mind, just as we say that we see objects clearly when, being present to the perceiving eye, they operate on it with sufficient strength. But the distinct is that which is so precise and different from everything else that it contains nothing within itself but what is clear."[3]

This definition is vague in speaking about "operating with sufficient strength on the eye," and it also seems to assimilate clarity and distinctness to one another. Later in that same work, aware of these difficulties, he makes another try, stating that an idea can be clear without being distinct, but it cannot be distinct without being clear. An experience, he says, is clear but not distinct when we are aware of it, but at the same time are not sure of its precise nature. He offers a toothache as an example. Everyone who has a toothache is aware of it and thus it is "clear" that he has it. But we cannot always be sure where it is located. So that we cannot distinguish it from other things or places, and hence it is not "distinct." In contrast, any distinct idea would also be clear. The idea of a circle is an example. It is distinct since the definition of a circle distinguishes it from any thing else, say, a triangle or tetrahedron, but it is also clear, since we can give a precise mathematical definition of it.

A skeptical objection that arises from his definition is the Problem of the Criterion (also see chap. 8). Clarity and distinctness are now taken to be a criterion of certainty. But if one needs a criterion to establish that a proposition is certain one can ask, "How do you know that this is a good criterion?" The answer will require that one produce another criterion in its support, and so forth endlessly. In the end, no answer will be possible.

Descartes was not aware of this objection while writing the *Meditations*. But it, and other criticisms, were voiced by later scholars. We shall ignore these for the moment. Let us follow the remainder of his argument. In the "Third Meditation" Descartes asserts that the ideas we receive from the senses or the imagination are not both clear and distinct. Some are neither, some are one, some the other. But there is a kind of idea different from these that is both clear and distinct. This he calls "innate." It does not come from either the senses or the imagination, but has its origin in reason. In putting this emphasis upon reason, Descartes joins the long rationalist tradition in epistemology that includes Parmenides and Plato. In fact, some of his arguments for the existence of innate ideas are to be found in such Platonic dialogues as *The Meno* and the *Phaedo*.

Plato, for example, argued that the idea of equality cannot come from experience, since any objects belonging to the world of appearance will never be found to be absolutely equal. Descartes agrees. He states that the ideas of circles, of numbers, and of other mathematical entities, and the idea of God can come neither from the senses nor from imagination since both are based on experience. The idea of a circle as "the locus of all points equidistant from a given point" is not exemplified in the sensible world. "God," in the Judeo-Christian tradition, can be defined as "a substance that is infinite, eternal, immutable, independent, all-knowing, all-powerful, and by which I myself, and everything else, if anything else does exist, have been created." But no object revealed to the senses satisfies this description. Thus, the ideas of God and those of mathematical objects have come to us by other means. We have access to them *prior to* experience, and hence they are inherent or "innate."

Descartes goes on to claim that since I have a clear and distinct idea of God (since the above definition is both clear and distinct), God must exist. Therefore, another truth beyond the cogito has been found, namely, that there must be a God who exists and who is the source of the clear and distinct ideas I have. Having established this thesis, Descartes proceeds to demonstrate that there are many other certitudes I have about the world. These all rest on the notion that God is perfect, and hence benevolent. To be a deceiver is to have an imperfection; but God is perfect, therefore, he cannot be a deceiver. So whatever we discern as clear and distinct are ideas deriving from God and they must be true.

From the fact that God is not a deceiver, we can be certain that God cannot be the evil demon described in the "First Meditation." The "Fourth Meditation" thus eliminates the possibility that we might be the unconscious victims of perpetual deception. Freed from this possibility, we can now proceed to discover what God wishes and forces us to believe. First among these are ideas that are clear and distinct. Whenever we entertain a clear and distinct idea we are compelled to assent to it as true. Since God is omnipotent, and is forcing us to believe this, and given that he is not a deceiver, we can be sure that we are not being misled when we assent to something that is clear and distinct. We also find that we are not constrained to accept anything that is not clear and distinct, and that we can suspend judgment in such situations. If we do make a decision about such matters, we must accept responsibility for it and cannot blame God. Hence, even granting that God exists and is not a deceiver, we have no guarantee that any idea that is not clear and distinct is true. But with respect to ideas belonging to the restricted domain of the clear and distinct we can be sure that they are true.

According to Descartes, falsity and error are human defects. We insist upon deciding questions even when we lack clear and distinct ideas. The human will is the source of such error. It forces us to go beyond the guaranteed limits of correctness, that is, to judge various ideas when they are not clear and distinct. If we had more control over ourselves, we would wait until the ideas were clear and distinct and then we would never be mistaken. The possibility of such exactness is found in mathematics, because its central ideas are clear and distinct. But with respect to ideas based on sense experience there is always the danger of error, since those ideas may be clear but not distinct.

At this point in his book, Descartes sums up what we can be said to know. The list runs as follows: We can know with certainty, (1) that we exist, (2) that God exists, (3) that God is not a deceiver, and (4) that, because that is so, whatever is clearly and distinctly conceived is true. We have seen that we can be certain of mathematical truths whose ideas are clear and distinct. But beyond them do we know anything? For example, does mathematics actually apply to the physical world? Indeed, *is* there a physical world? Our mathematical ideas are entities that belong to our minds. Do they therefore give us knowledge of external reality? It is here in the text that the famous problem of our knowledge of the external world surfaces. Can we have knowledge of anything beyond the circle of our own ideas?

In the "Fifth Meditation," Descartes addresses this question. He states that though we have clear and distinct ideas of mathematical relations, such that a body which measures ten feet by twenty feet will have a size of two hundred square feet, we cannot be sure that any such body actually exists. But in the "Sixth Meditation" he offers a convoluted proof that such bodies do exist. The argument begins with three possibilities, two of which are eventually excluded, and the third is then accepted.

The argument commences with the statement that we have a natural inclination to believe there is a physical world, and to believe that sense experience gives us access to it. Thus, when I see a tree, I have a natural disposition to believe there is such a tree that exists

independent of my ideas. Still, having such a belief does not conclu-
sively prove that the tree really does exist. Arriving at this juncture in
the argument, he now contends that there are three possibilities.
First, I am myself the cause of my ideas of physical objects, that is,
that there really are no physical objects, and that I am simply wrong
in attributing my experience to a physical world outside of me.
Second, it is possible that it is God that produces such ideas, that no
physical entities exist, and that I am mistaken in thinking that my
experience is correct. Third, there really are physical objects that
correspond in some sense to my ideas, and that I am not in error in
attributing my sense experience to such external sources.

The first of these hypotheses is ruled out on the basis that I have
no awareness of creating my own experience, and that I cannot
make myself experience things when I want to. This suggests that
there exist entities that are at least to some degree mind independent. The second option could be true. God has the power to give
me all the sensations I would have even if there were no physical
objects to which these sensations correspond. (God is at least as
powerful as the evil demon.) God is my creator and has disposed me
to believe there exists an external world. If such a world did not
exist, God would be a deceiver; but since God is not malicious, this
possibility can be eliminated. So what remains is the third possibility,
that there exist external objects which to some extent correspond to
our ideas of them.

The "Sixth Meditation" now asks what we can know about the
external world. We can be sure only of the mathematical properties
of physical objects. Thus, we cannot know with certainty that they
are colored, give off odors, or are textured, since we do not possess
clear and distinct ideas of these qualities. Our knowledge is thus
restricted to a kind of mathematical physics, that is, knowledge of
the properties of extension and motion. These properties, however,
Descartes believed sufficed to explain all natural objects whether animate or inanimate.

What, then, was the ultimate result of this extended six-part
meditation? Beginning with profound doubts, Descartes ended with
the conviction that there are many things we can know with absolute
certainty. It is certain that I exist; that God exists and is not an evil

demon; that all ideas that are clear and distinct are true; that the theorems of mathematics, being clear and distinct, are true; and, finally, that a world external to the circle of our ideas exists. But we cannot know with certainty whether the colors, sounds, smells, tastes, and tactile sensations we have belong to these objects, for none of these ideas is both clear and distinct. Accordingly, our knowledge is less extensive than the ordinary person imagines, but it is more extensive than one might have expected starting with the Method of Doubt.

Three objections to Cartesianism

Apart from the criterial difficulty mentioned above, there are numerous other objections to Descartes's line of reasoning. Let us briefly consider three of them.

(1) The empiricists were later to argue that there are no such things as innate ideas, that is, ideas that are inherent in the human mind and do not derive from experience. Babies, for example, show no signs of possessing such ideas; and indeed on the contrary, most scientific or even anecdotal evidence indicates that every piece of information infants eventually acquire is learned. Rationalists defend Descartes by arguing that empiricists can offer no compelling explanation of how we acquire such notions as equality, circularity, and so forth. In recent years, the celebrated linguist Noam Chomsky has supported this position. He argues that what he calls the "projection phenomenon" cannot be explained on empirical terms. By this notion he means that children and indeed all native speakers can invent new, grammatically correct sentences that they have never heard before. He attributes this ability to linguistic aptitudes that are innate. Interestingly enough, his book is called *Cartesian Linguistics*.

(2) A second objection is what has come to be called the Cartesian Circle. In order to avoid the possibility that an evil demon exists and is misleading Descartes with respect to everything he believes, Descartes proves that God exists. He then argues that clearness and distinctness is the criterion for all certitude, because God is not a deceiver. But since this criterion is arrived at only after the existence of God has been proven, he cannot appeal to this criterion when he presents his proof for the existence of God. Hence, the apparent

proof is circular and begs the question. In effect, it assumes the existence of that whose existence is to be proved.

(3) When the *Meditations* was first published, a series of criticisms by leading philosophers was appended to it. What Descartes was later to call "the objection of objections" was made by two important scientists of the period, Fathers Marin Mersenne and Pierre Gassendi. Descartes was never able effectively to respond to this criticism.

Mersenne and Gassendi contended that Descartes's theory never refuted the Demon Hypothesis. Once one accepted the possibility that such an evil being might exist, then one had to admit that the demon could deceive us about everything. Any arguments that Descartes offered to show that we cannot doubt our own existence might be the result of the demon's efforts. Even the argument proving that God cannot be a deceiver may actually be one of the demon's deceptions. Thus, they asserted that we could never be sure that the truths we are forced to accept are the truths known to God. We have to believe these propositions, but from God's point of view they might be false. Innate ideas may well exist, but how can we be sure that they are also truths about putative things that exist outside of our minds? The Cartesian system might consist entirely of beliefs that we are forced to accept, but which we can never check against an external reality. They concluded that what Descartes has shown is that all we ever know are our own ideas. Every demonstration Descartes offers that clear and distinct ideas must be true is itself only one more idea in our minds. Thus, the Cartesian argument cannot prove that our innate ideas are not mere illusions of the mind.

Descartes responded to this objection, admitting in effect that it was correct. He agreed that we could never transcend the circle of our ideas, and that what we human beings considered to be indubitable may well be false in some absolute sense. But, he insisted, this was not a fatal flaw, since it was man's world that we were concerned with. If we were not willing to accept merely human certitudes, we would have to "shut the door on reason." Thus, his weak response indicates that he was forced to admit that he could not eliminate all possible doubts and achieve the kind of certitude no skeptic could challenge. In the end the Method of Doubt produced challenges he could not meet.

Many commentators in reflecting on the Cartesian philosophy believe that Descartes doubted either too much or too little. As one of them has written:

> If he had ever really accepted the doubts of the *First Meditation*, could he overcome them in order to discover the knowledge that followed in the later *Meditations*?
>
> If he never actually had the doubts, then could he ever be sure that the truths he proclaimed were not open to question? Thus, either he was too much a skeptic to discover rational knowledge, or too little a skeptic to be certain of the knowledge he believed he had discovered.[4]

THE EMPIRICISTS: LOCKE, BERKELEY, AND HUME

Descartes's philosophy, like Plato's, is a form of rationalism. It holds that there is a one-to-one correspondence between our ideas and the mathematical structure of the world. Knowledge is thus a function of a mirroring relationship between reason and certain aspects of reality. On the other hand, sense experience is fragile. The information we derive from the senses is not clear and distinct, and accordingly, we cannot know that any external objects have the properties revealed by sensation. Reason is thus the key to reality and the ultimate source of certitude. Everything we know—that I exist, that God exists, that God is not a deceiver, and so on—is a product of reason.

The British empiricists of the seventeenth and eighteenth centuries—John Locke, Bishop George Berkeley, and David Hume—turned Plato and Descartes upside down. They deprecated reason and emphasized sense experience. For them, mathematical theorems, or what we now call "analytical truths," are "trifling" or "tautological," that is, they do not express significant information about reality. Like Plato, Descartes regarded the human mind as the repository of ideas existing prior to experience. The empiricists thought of the mind as an empty receptable. In Locke's words it is a wax tablet (*tabula rasa*). How does the tablet become imprinted with knowledge? Locke says, "To this I answer in one word, Experience."

The two traditions, starting from Descartes on the one hand, and

Locke, Berkeley, and Hume on the other, seem directly in conflict. The issue has come down to us in the twentieth and twenty-first centuries as the controversy between rationalism and empiricism. In the past three centuries, the empiricist approach to knowledge has become dominant and is the prevailing point of view in Anglo-American philosophy. It is less strong in Europe, where forms of rationalism still play major roles. Yet despite this apparent disagreement, the two traditions have much in common. Since the sources of both can be traced back to Descartes (with an infusion of Platonism), he is often described as the founder of modern philosophy.

It is Descartes who first advanced the notion that the only things we are directly acquainted with are our own ideas. It is this principle that the early empiricists accepted. They also espoused the Platonic/Cartesian thesis that sense experience cannot produce certainty. As a result, they immediately inherited the Cartesian problem of the external world, including its skeptical underpinnings. How can we know on the basis of our subjective experience that anything external corresponds to it? All three of these famous thinkers addressed this issue. It is central to each of their philosophies. Their answers are different, but their assumptions are the same. Despite their emphasis upon sense experience, their conceptual models basically derive from Descartes. Locke purports not to be a skeptic, yet his theory—the so-called way of ideas—leads to a form of skepticism. Berkeley sets out to defeat atheism and ends up by eliminating the external world entirely. Each of us is never able to know more than our own ideas. The first sentence of Hume's *Treatise* is "All perceptions of the human resolve themselves into two distinct kinds, which I shall call Impressions and Ideas." He is thus working with the Cartesian presuppositions. The outcome of his thinking is a mixture of empiricist and skeptical theses. Yet in the end, these thinkers managed to create a new philosophy, even though it retains many of the basic assumptions of its rationalistic adversaries. The variations and innovations on Cartesian themes are thus well worth studying. Let us begin with Locke.

John Locke (1632-1704)

Locke reached intellectual maturity in a period that was both politically and culturally turbulent. His two major works, the *Two Treatises on Civil Goverment* (1690) and the *Essay Concerning Human Understanding* (1689), reflect these events. They were important at the time, and still are, because they contain the founding theories of political democracy and of empiricism, respectively. We shall discuss his political views later. It is his great contribution to epistemology that we shall consider now. Still, to understand each of these works some background is necessary.

Locke was trained as a physician, but he never engaged in clinical practice. Instead, he became the private secretary to the Earl of Shaftesbury, and the tutor of his son. Shaftesbury and Locke both challenged the authority of Charles II during the Restoration period, and consequently had to take refuge in the Netherlands. They· remained there until William of Orange became king of England after the Glorious Revolution of 1688. The Glorious Revolution was the culmination of a nearly century-long struggle by Parliament against the absolute authority of the Tudor monarchs: James I, Charles I, Charles II, and eventually James II, who was forced into exile in 1688. Locke's *Second Treatise* provided a philosophical justification for the right of the people to govern themselves, and is thus the main document from which all defenses of democracy flow.

The struggle against absolutism in England was complicated by incessant and bitter religious wars. Roman Catholicism had been the prevailing religion in England and Scotland for centuries. But in 1533, Henry VIII (1491-1547) broke with Rome after the pope refused to annul his marriage to Catherine of Aragon. During the reign of Elizabeth I, a strong religious reform movement sought to purify the English church of remnants of Roman Catholic "popery." These Puritans were impelled by a spirit of moral fervor to make their lifestyle the pattern for the whole nation. These pressures led to civil war in the middle of the seventeenth century, with the Puritans under Oliver Cromwell on the one side, and the absolutist Tudors, defending the Church of England, on the other.

But revolutionary movements of another sort were taking place at the same time. These were, broadly speaking, "cultural" in a sense of the term that would include scientific and technological developments and their import for a new understanding of human nature. Locke's empiricism provides a conceptual justification for the new science. The scientists of the Royal Society insisted that experiment was *the* modus operandi for discovering how nature worked. The astounding achievements of such innovators as Robert Hooke, Robert Boyle, Isaac Newton, and Thomas Newcomen were enormously important in solving both theoretical and practical problems. These advances gave England commercial advantages over the Continent that they were to maintain for another two centuries. Locke's later writings on education and religion unravel the social and political implications of these developments. They provide the basis for the work of such moral and political reformers as Cesare Beccaria, Jeremy Bentham, and James and John Stuart Mill in the two centuries that followed.

It is the empiricism of Locke that we shall focus on here. The *Essay Concerning Human Understanding*, as explained above, argues that all knowledge derives from experience. What Locke means by "knowledge" is complicated, as we shall see. It differs from the conceptions entertained by Plato and Descartes in certain respects, while agreeing with them in others.

The *Essay* is a long work, difficult to read and difficult to summarize. It is divided into four parts. Book 1 contains arguments against the thesis of innate ideas. (We have already listed the main ones above and shall not discuss them further.) Book 2 contains a theory of the human mind. As we have indicated, Locke takes the mind to be like a blank sheet of paper that experience will cover with writing. Experience is divided into two parts: the observation of external objects and the observation of the internal operations of the mind. For Locke, the mind is not wholly passive. It has active functions, such as being able to combine simple ideas into more complex ones, to be conscious of its own operations: perceiving, thinking, doubting, believing, and reasoning. His description of the mind is basic to the empiricist view that all knowledge comes from experience. The mind has no ideas of its own—no "innate" or "inherent" notions that it brings to or imposes on experience—so its operations are performed only on those things imprinted on it.

Book 3 discusses language, with an emphasis upon the meaning of words; and book 4 discusses knowledge and related cognitive states and processes. We shall skip book 3, which is not primarily concerned with knowledge, and concentrate on books 2 and 4, beginning with the former.

Locke develops two theories therein whose influence in Anglo-American philosophy has never waned. The first we can label "the reductive thesis"; the second, "the thesis of primary and secondary qualities." The reductive thesis was developed to explain how all knowledge derives from experience. The primary-secondary quality distinction is designed to support the reductive thesis by arguing that primary qualities belong to external objects and that these are the sources of the knowledge we have. We shall consider each in turn.

The reductive thesis

As pointed out above, Locke accepts the Cartesian thesis that the only things we are directly aware of are ideas. An idea is thus anything that is present to the mind. His reductive thesis distinguishes simple from complex ideas. It argues that simple ideas arise directly from experience, that is, from contact we have with external objects or phenomena. Thus, the green of grass, the taste of a lemon, the desire for a cup of coffee are what he calls "simple ideas." They are ideas that are not compounded of any others. He also holds that the human mind has some active powers. It cannot create simple ideas but it can compound them to make "complex ideas." Thus, the idea of a dragon is a complex idea. It consists of the body of a snake, the head of a horse, and the wings of a bird. There are no dragons in existence, hence the idea of a dragon could not come directly from experience. But its constitutents can and do. The idea of a dragon is a melange of simple ideas that *do* arise from experience. The reductive thesis thus states that all complex ideas can be reduced to simple ideas, and that these in turn arise from the direct confrontation with the real world.

Locke's influence over subsequent philosophy, whether in epistemology, metaphysics, or philosophy of language, has been tremendous. For example, the philosophy of "logical atomism" developed by Bertrand Russell and Ludwig Wittgenstein in the first half of the twenteth century is a version of Locke's reductionism. Russell and Wittgenstein do not speak of ideas but of words. On such a view, proper names are equivalent to simple ideas. They are names that contain no subnames, and they directly refer to objects such as individual persons. They thus provide the hookup between language and the real world. Atomic sentences are composed of names and are thus like chains, whose links are proper names. Such sentences get their meanings from the relationship of the names to corresponding objects. All complex sentences, and thus the main body of language, can in turn be reduced to atomic sentences. So Russell arrived at the view that all meaningful descriptive sentences derive from experience. The thesis is thus a modernized, linguistic version of Locke's original conception.

Primary and secondary qualities

The distinction between primary and secondary qualities adds a further wrinkle to the reductive view. According to Locke, we can distinguish two different kinds of ideas among those we possess. One is of the shapes, sizes, the solidity, and the motion of objects. These are ideas of what he calls "primary qualities." They differ from the ideas of colors, tastes, smells, and the coldness or warmth of things. These, he calls "secondary qualities." His view is that primary qualities belong to external objects and that secondary qualities belong to the mind, and that it is the primary qualities of things that give us knowledge of their real characteristics. Locke here makes an assumption that subsequent philosophers, especially Bishop Berkeley, challenged, namely, that the ideas of primary qualities arise from properties of the objects themselves. As Berkeley was to point out, this is an inference without justification and indeed is probably nonsensical since there is no way of verifying the claim. We shall discuss this point in more detail later.

Locke's view entails that the real world is not colored and is neither warm nor hot. Such properties belong to the human psyche.

What produces them? The answer is primary qualities. They have the "power" to create "secondary" effects in observers. Hence, shapes, sizes, and motion can produce colors, tastes, and so so. But the latter properties do not belong to the external world; they are subjective and mind dependent. Some contemporary physicists and chemists support this position. They claim that ordinary objects such as chairs, tables, and human beings are composed of collections of atoms moving in space, and that atoms in turn are collocations of charged particles moving rapidly in the space within atoms. Atoms, quarks, and electrons have only primary qualities, but their behavior impinges upon our sense organs and produces colors, heat, desires, and so forth. According to Locke and some scientists, if we could see the world as it actually is we would apprehend only primary qualities: sizes, shapes, solidity, and various motions.

The distinction between primary and secondary qualities gives rise in Locke to another theory—an ancient theory about the nature of change that goes back to Parmenides and Plato. Locke supposes that qualities cannot exist by themselves. Size and shape, for example, must belong to something. They do not float around in space but are properties of some "stuff." Unfortunately, in our experience of the world we do not perceive any such stuff: We only perceive primary and secondary qualities. Locke thus posits the existence of an underlying substance which he calls a "substratum." It is this that "supports" properties and ties them together to form, say, a whole object such as an apple. But experience cannot give us any information about it; so it is the product of reason that explains why and how things change. Of the substratrum, Locke says it is a *je ne sais qua* ("I know not what"). He also speaks of it as "matter."Accordingly, matter is the basis of experience but it is itself not experienced; nonetheless, logic tells us that it must exist. Matter thus functions as a kind of explanatory posit in the theory. This is a view that had a profound influence. Immanuel Kant was to develop a theory about the "noumenal world" that is something like it. And it was also to engender sharp criticisms from Berkeley and Hume. Berkeley was to say that Locke's account of matter was a good description of nothing.

Locke's theory of knowledge

In book 4, Locke distinguishes four species of knowledge: intuitive, demonstrative, sensitive, and probability. Knowledge he defines as "the perception of the connexion of and agreement, or disagreement and repugnancy of any of our ideas." His definition thus rests on the Cartesian model. Knowledge is characterized in the language of ideas; it is these that we are directly aware of. The theory thus requires that there be some tie between the realm of ideas and a suppositious reality that exists independently of them. Locke here seems unaware of the conceptual leaps he is making: He presupposes connections that require argumentation and justification; but these are lacking in the text.

The four species of knowledge differ in degree of strength. His examples of intuitive knowledge are such propositions as "white is not black," "a circle is not a triangle," and "three is more than two." Intuitive knowledge is immediate. One can directly see the connection between the ideas involved. Speaking much like Descartes, Locke says of this knowledge that the "mind is presently filled with the clear light of it."

Demonstrative knowledge is not immediate. Proofs are things that show the mediating connections between ideas, and a clear and plain proof is a demonstration. Demonstrative knowledge is certain but not as evident as intuitive knowledge because of the need to pass through the steps of a proof in order to reach the certainty of the conclusion.

Sensitive knowledge is less certain than intuitive or demonstrative knowledge; it involves the perception "of the particular existence of finite beings without us." Finally, the weakest form of knowledge is probability knowledge. It is the appearance of the agreement or disagreement of ideas with one another. It guides us in those domains of life "whereof we have no certainty." Locke indicates that probability rests on the testimony of others, and comes in degrees that depend on the veracity of the sources. The highest of such are propositions endorsed by the general consent of all people in all ages. They are similar to what Thomas Reid and G. E. Moore were later to call "common-sense propositions." Locke admits that problems arise when testimonies conflict, as they frequently do, but states that there is no simple rule or set of rules that allows one to settle such controversies. The cases must be judged individually and contextually.

Rather than criticizing Locke's views ourselves, we shall turn to the objections voiced by Berkeley and Hume. They are as powerful as any that have been made.

George Berkeley (1685-1753)

Berkeley's three major works—*A New Theory of Vision* (1709), *Treatise concerning the Principles of Human Knowledge* (1710), and *Three Dialogues between Hylas and Philonous* (1713)—were composed before he was thirty. In the most important of these, the *Principles*, he was quick to point out the skeptical implications of Locke's theory. If matter is the fundamental stuff of the universe, and if in principle it is unknowable, then human knowledge is impossible. But clearly we do have knowledge, so Locke's view is just plain wrong. Berkeley therefore set out to correct Locke's approach by developing a more consistent form of empiricism. It presents an account of knowledge strictly based upon sense experience. The resulting theory is antimaterialistic, antiskeptical, and antiatheist. Berkeley sees all of these negative views as arising from conceptual errors, Locke's *Essay* being a major source of such misconceptions. In his *Commonplace Book* (a kind of notebook, containing philosophical musings), Berkeley says of Locke, "Like all philosophers he was in a fog. What is surprising is that he could see anything at all in it."

In effect, Berkeley is arguing that the Lockean theory misdescribes objects with which all of us are familiar. The task of the clearheaded philosopher is to correct such misdescriptions, and set the record straight. We should therefore recharacterize or redefine such things as tables and rocks in terms of their observable characteristics. In the case of a table, we would be describing a set of discernible properties: being square, being brown, being situated in a particular place, and so forth. Berkeley argued that Locke's theory that such properties exist in an unknowable material substratum is nonsense. Since we cannot get behind the curtain of our ideas, there is no evidence, even in principle, to justify such an account. Locke's philosophy thus obfuscates rather than clarifies our picture of reality. This, according to Berkeley, is characteristic of traditional philosophers. Their views tend to mystify rather than to explicate. As he puts it, "We first cast up a dust and then complain we cannot see."[5] His own account tries to avoid creating dust and to present an alternative, accurate picture of the way the world is. This consists in cutting out Locke's talk of matter and just concentrating upon what our ideas tell us about reality.

This way of presenting Berkeley's philosophy makes it sound very commonsensical. Yet because of his acceptance of the Cartesian and Lockian terminology of "ideas" it results in some of the most outlandish claims in the history of philosophy. It leads him to declare that "we eat and drink ideas," and that "armies and elephants exist in the mind." How does his commonsense beginning result in such paradoxical assertions? The answer is that he accepts the Cartesian principle that all we are directly aware of are our own ideas. What Berkeley adds to this principle is the surprising notion that such things as tables, chairs, persons, and the like are nothing but "heaps of ideas."

Berkeley defends his position by a clever argument. The first premise is that trees, houses, and persons are objects perceived by the senses. The second premise is that whatever is perceived by the senses is an idea (this is the Cartesian/Lockian presupposition). The third premise is that all ideas exist in the mind. Therefore, Berkeley concludes that trees, houses, and persons are ideas that exist in the mind. Q.E.D.

Berkeley considers various objections to the argument. Consider the first premise. Suppose one argues that it is false, and that trees, houses, persons, and so on exist when they are not sensed. To this, Berkeley responds that though they may not be sensed by me, they are in principle sensible objects. He thus challenges someone to find an object that exists and in principle is not susceptible to being perceived.

The second premise might be challenged on the ground that we do not sense ideas, but physical objects. Berkeley responds to this by claiming that there are no sensations without ideas, and that it is nonsensical to speak of some additional thing that ideas are supposed to represent or resemble. He thus regards the Lockian notion that behind the world of ideas there is a substratum that exists external to the mind. If these putative external objects exist, they are perceivable in principle, and hence are ideas.

The third premise attacks the primary quality/secondary quality distinction in Locke. According to this premise, all ideas exist in the mind. But, according to Locke, primary qualities exist in an unperceivable substratum. Berkeley regards this as an unintelligible posit. He holds that extension, figure, motion, rest, and solidity are as much ideas as green, loud, and bitter. All are mind dependent. There is nothing special about the former sorts of ideas. Therefore, the Lockean distinction between primary and secondary qualities is spurious.

Berkeley's criticism of Locke is penetrating. He holds that the very concept of matter, as Locke uses it, is self-contradictory. Matter is supposedly unsensed extension, figure, and motion; but since extension, figure, and motion are ideas that we derive from sense experience, they must be sensed. The thesis that unsensed sensations can exist is therefore self-inconsistent.

As mentioned, Berkeley's philosophy is antiskeptical and antiatheist. He thinks skepticism and atheism are conceptually tied together, so in defeating skepticism he is also defeating atheism. In his overall metaphysics, there are three key notions: mind, ideas, and God. The similarities to Descartes's three basic concepts are obvious. Ideas exist but they cannot exist independently of a mind. By their very nature they are mind-dependent entities. Minds are called "spirits" or "souls" by Berkeley. Spirit has two functions: understanding and willing. Understanding consists in the perception of ideas, and will is spirit producing ideas. It is evident, says Berkeley, that no idea, including those of sensation, can exist outside of a mind. This follows not only from the definition of "idea" but also from the definition of "exists." To say that a table exists means that a particular mind, M, is actually now apprehending it, or that some other mind, O, is now apprehending it, or that God is apprehending it. Tables, persons, and rocks do not pop in and out of existence as we close our eyes, because God is always perceiving them.

A limerick by Ronald Knox, with a reply, wittily expresses Berkeley's thesis:

There was a young man who said, "God
Must think it exceedingly odd
   If he finds that this tree
   Continues to be
When there's no one about in the Quad."

REPLY

Dear Sir:
Your astonishment's odd:
   I am always about in the Quad.
   And that's why the tree
   Will continue to be,
Since observed by
               Yours faithfully,
               GOD.[6]

Accordingly, Berkeley's thesis about the existence of tables, persons, rocks, and so on is that *to be is to be perceived* (*esse is percipi*). To say that a table exists thus means that it is either now being perceived or that in principle it is perceivable. Suppose there is a table in the next room that no one is now perceiving. To say that it exists there is thus to say that if a person went into the room and looked he or she would have such-and-such sensations—that is, ideas of squareness, brownness, and so forth.

Berkeley's philosophy taken literally is about as paradoxical as anything that has ever been published. But it can also be understood in a less paradoxical way. When Berkeley says that elephants are ideas, he means that we should describe an elephant in terms of what we actually or might perceive: size, solidity, shape, color, and so forth. This proposition is then converted into one that is even less paradoxical. To say that elephants exist in the mind of *Y* now comes to mean that *Y* perceives an elephant. It does not literally mean that a certain large object of enormous weight actually is present in *Y*'s head. Some commonsense philosophers still object to Berkeley's view on the ground that the existence of an object like an elephant is in no way tied to our perceptions of the animal. But in arguing their case, they would agree that Berkeley's position is less extreme and more plausible than it initially sounds. In later philosophy, a variant of Berkeley's view became widely accepted by tough-minded philosophers called "phenomenalists." They took the view that knowledge is wholly derived from experience and therefore that anything that exists must be described in terms of our actual and possible sensations. J. S. Mill and later Bertrand Russell were proponents of this position.

Berkeley's theory of knowledge is thus simple to describe. For him, knowledge consists in the apprehension of ideas. It is thus minds that possess knowledge. One idea can never know another, since ideas are passive and cannot apprehend other ideas. It follows that minds are not knowable because they are not ideas. Unlike ideas, minds are active. Yet there is some sort of cognitive relationship between minds. We are aware of what another believes or intends to do. Berkeley recognizes this fact. He thus invented a term for this relationship: "notion." We have notions of other minds. There is thus in Berkeley an implicit solution to the Other Minds Problem, which poses the question, Is knowledge of the mind of another possible? For Berkeley, the answer is no; we cannot know other minds. But from that fact it does not follow that human minds are wholly cut off from one another. We possess notions of the mental states and activities of other persons.

Berkeley is thus not a solipsist, that is, a philosopher who believes that only he exists and that everything that he perceives exists only in his own mind. He does describe an intersubjective world that connects humans with one another and with the divine.

In summary, his refutation of skepticism both adheres to and rejects part of the Cartesian model. It adheres to the principle that we have direct acquaintance only with our own ideas and it rejects the notion that outside the circle of our ideas there is a material substratum that we can only access indirectly. By lopping the notion of an independently existing material substance from the Cartesian picture, Berkeley thinks he has eliminated any gap between mind and the world that could be exploited by the skeptic.

David Hume (1711-1776)

Unlike Locke's life, which was spent in the turmoil of the parliamentary opposition to the Tudors, Hume's was comparatively quiet and tranquil. After leaving Edinburgh University at fourteen or fifteen, as was then usual, he was urged by his family to study law, but found it unpleasant and instead read widely in literature, philosophy, and history. In 1729 he had a nervous breakdown that commentators attribute to the intensity of his studies, and from which it took him some years recover. In 1734 he retired to France for three years, studying and writing. The result was a full-fledged philosophical system, *A Treatise of Human Nature*, published when he was only twenty-eight years old. Though he later described this as a "juvenile" endeavor, it is generally regarded as his most important philosophical work. Hume's ambition throughout his life was to become a famous literary figure, and he was enormously disappointed when this work, as he put it, "fell dead-born from the presses." A year later he published the *Abstract*, which attempted in an abbreviated form to explain and defend the doctrines of the *Treatise*. He continued to write extensively for the rest of his career. His major philosophical books were *An Enquiry Concerning the Human Understanding* (1758), which is a more mature version of the *Treatise*; *An Enquiry Concerning the Principles of Morals* (1751), which he described as being "of all my writings incomparably the best"; and *Dialogues Concerning Natural Religion*, published posthumously in 1779. Hume finally achieved the fame he desired with the publication of his six-volume *History of England* (1754–62). When the last of these volumes appeared, James Boswell, the biographer of the celebrated Samuel Johnson, called Hume "the greatest writer in Britain."

In 1763 he became secretary to the British embassy in Paris. He returned to London in 1766, bringing with him Jean-Jacques Rousseau, who had been persecuted for his radical views. Rousseau, who was probably paranoid, suspected Hume of plotting against him, left secretly for France, and spread a report of Hume's bad faith. Hume was annoyed at Rousseau and eventually, though reluctantly, published the relevant correspondence between them entitled *A Concise and Genuine Account of the Dispute between Mr. Hume and Mr. Rousseau* (1766). Scholars who have investigated the controversy are generally agreed that Hume was unfairly treated by the delusional Rousseau.

Boswell, a fervent Christian, was at Hume's bedside when he was dying of cancer, and in his *London Journal* describes himself as being shaken to the core because of Hume's refusal to accept the existence of God with death at hand. That Hume should not recant his previous beliefs is not surprising: To have done so would have meant abandoning the precepts he had followed from his earliest days.

In describing Hume's empiricism below, we shall defer a discussion of his views on religious belief until a later chapter.

Hume's empiricism

Hume's theory is influenced by Locke's. He divides perceptions into impressions and ideas. Impressions are perceptions that enter with the most force and violence. Ideas are "faint images" of impressions. Furthermore, perceptions, impressions, and ideas can be classified as either simple or complex. To every simple impression there corresponds a simple idea, differing from it only in force and vivacity. Simple impressions hook up the senses with the real world, whereas simple ideas connect with the world indirectly, via simple impressions. As he says, ". . . all our simple ideas in their first appearance are deriv'd from simple impressions, which are correspondent to them, and which they exactly represent."[7] In contrast, complex ideas do not necessarily correspond to complex impressions. One can imagine a city whose sidewalks are gold and whose walls are rubies, though one never saw such. However, complex ideas—such as the idea of a city with walls of rubies—can always be reduced to a set of simple ideas. From the fact that there are such cities, it does not follow that the complex idea of one is not based on experience. It can be reduced to a set of simple ideas—the idea of a wall, a ruby, and so on—each of which can be traced back to a simple impression. Thus, Hume's philosophy subscribes to the reductive principle that is a key element in empiricism.

Hume also holds against the rationalists that there are no innate ideas, so that any piece of information the mind receives derives from experience. And, like Locke, he also holds that the mind has the power to combine ideas in various ways, including the formation of complex ideas. But he carries his analysis of mental operations further than Locke or Berkeley. Indeed, his psychological theory is complex. He contends that the mind is guided by three principles: resemblance, contiguity, and cause and effect. Thus, a person who thinks of one idea is likely to think of another idea that resembles it. For example, a person's conception will run from a plant to a bush to a tree, or from a cat to a lynx to a tiger. With respect to contiguity, humans are disposed to think of things that are adjacent to each other in space and time. But it is the concept of cause and effect that is the most important element in his psychological account. Most of the beliefs we have arise from our awareness of causal relationships. We note that phases of the moon cause the tides, that unsanitary conditions cause disease, that fertilization causes plants to grow. The idea of causation is thus fundamental in science and in daily life. But what does it mean to say that *A* causes *B*?

Hume's analysis of causation

Most previous philosophers, from Aristotle to Berkeley, answered the question by saying that causation is a kind of mysterious power that an object possesses and transmits to another object or event. On this view, there is a kind of link or bond—a third thing—between cause and effect. It is this bond that creates a necessary relationship between the cause and the effect. Thus, if the cause occurs the effect must occur. But Hume rejects this analysis. He states that when one looks carefully at the relationship between a particular cause and its effect, for example, a particular fire that causes a particular episode of smoke, one never detects any such bond. All one finds is that fire occurs and then smoke occurs. And this is true of every case of causation.

Hume's analysis starts from an accurate description of causal relationships. A billard ball hits another and causes it to move. One finds in such a case that *A* moves before *B*, *A* comes into contact with *B*, and then *B* moves. Generalizing from this case, Hume states that in all cases of causation three conditions are satisfied: the cause is prior to, contiguous with, and constantly conjoined with its effect. This is to say that a cause occurs before its effect, the two are spatially adjacent, and whenever the cause occurs the effect will follow. Or, in an alternative formulation, to say that *A* causes *B* is to say that if *A* does not occur, then *B* will not occur. But in this descriptive account, there is no mention of a power or bond that creates a necessary relationship.

Given this analysis, which has been labeled the "regularity theory," Hume asks, "Why does one expect smoke to follow if fire is present?" His response: "custom."

It is the regularity of this relationship that gives rise to such an expectation. As he states, "All inferences from experience, therefore, are effects of custom, not of reasoning." It is thus custom, and not reasoning, that is the great guide of life. The causal relationship cannot be traced to an impression that detects a necessary bond between A and B. It is simply the priority, contiguity, and regular conjunction of two events that create a cause-and-effect relationship.

It should be noted that in denying that one can find an impression of a necessary connection, Hume is being a consistent empiricist. He is stating that if there is no impression of a bond between cause and effect there is no reason to believe that such a bond exists. To posit such a connection thus goes beyond the available evidence and is not a justifiable inference. As he says, "All ideas are deriv'd from, and represent impressions. We never have any impression, that contains any power or efficacy. We never therefore have any idea of power."[8]

Hume's theory of mind

This same principle leads him to the conclusion that there is no justification for the traditional philosophical theory that the human mind is a single, cohesive entity, that is, an ego, self, or substance. Descartes, Locke, and Berkeley had all assumed that the mind is a separate and distinct substance. Hume denies this on empirical grounds, for if the mind were such an entity we should have some experience of it. There thus should be an impression of the self or the ego—of some unified object. We should be aware of such a thing when we introspect or look inward.

But this is just what we cannot find. As Hume writes:

For my part, when I enter most intimately into what I call *myself*, I always stumble on some particular perception or other, of heat or cold, light or shade, love or hatred, pain or pleasure. I never can catch *myself* at any time without a perception, and never can observe anything but the perception.[9]

So on purely descriptive grounds, one is justified in denying that the human mind is an entity. But if it is not, then what it is it? Hume answers that it is a set of related impressions and ideas that precede and follow one another. In a wonderful passage, Hume compares the mind to a theatre:

> The mind is a kind of theatre, where several perceptions sucessively make their appearance; pass, repass, glide away, and mingle in an infinite variety of postures and situations. There is properly no *simplicity* in it. . . . The comparison of the theatre must not mislead us. They are the successive perceptions only, that constitute the mind; nor have we the most distant notion of the place, where these scenes are represented, or of the materials, of which it is compos'd.[10]

What Hume is describing is commonly called the "bundle theory of the mind." Hume's view is that the mind is not an entity but a bundle or heap of resembling perceptions. The idea of a self, or soul, or ego arises from the human disposition to "feign" the existence of an ego or self to fill the gaps between succeeding and contiguous perceptions. But there is no such thing. If there were, we would have an impression of it. He concludes his discussion of the mind by saying:

> Thus we feign the continu'd existence of the perceptions of our senses to remove the interruption; and run into the notion of a *soul*, and *self*, and *substance* . . . our propension to confound identity with relation is so great, that we are apt to imagine something unknown or mysterious, connecting the parts besides their relation.[11]

Once again, a strict empiricist finds no impression of a self or ego. Thus, the mind is not to be identified with such an entity. Instead, it is simply a series of connected perceptions that stand in certain causal relationships to one another. He writes:

As to *causation*; we may observe, that the true idea of the human mind is to consider it as a system of different perceptions or different existences which are linked together by the relation of cause and effect and mutually produce, destroy, influence, and modify each other. Our impressions give rise to their correspondent ideas; and these ideas in their turn produce other impressions. One thought chaces another, and draws after it a third, by which it is expell'd in its turn.[12]

As with his theory of causation, so with his theory of mind. Hume is not denying that there is causation or that humans have minds. Instead, he is denying that certain classical philosophical theories about causation and the mind are correct. His view is that by following empirical principles he is giving an accurate account of these matters for the first time.

Hume's distinction between relations of ideas and matters of fact, and the Principle of Induction

René Descartes, Gottfried Leibniz, and John Locke all distinguished two different sorts of knowledge, and philosophers subsequent to them and to Hume have made similar discriminations. Hume thus distinguishes propositions concerning *relations of ideas* from propositions dealing with *matters of fact*. Every piece of knowledge can be formulated as a proposition that falls into one or the other of these two categories. The classification is thus exhaustive of all possibilities. Furthermore, no proposition can belong to both classes, so the classification is also exclusive. Consider the following sentences.

    (1) All husbands are married.
    (2) All husbands are taxpayers.

In reflecting on these two propositions one can *see* that the former can be known to be true without any investigation of the world, whereas the latter cannot. It will require some inquiry into the facts. Sentence (1) is thus a proposition concerning the relation of ideas to one another. The idea or notion of *being married* is part of the meaning or idea of *being a husband*. Once one understands the sentence one can see that it is necessarily true. Its truth is determined by how the ideas (or concepts) contained in it are related to one another.

In contrast, (2) cannot be known to be true merely by reflecting on the meaning of its words. One would have to leave language to ascertain whether it is true. One would have to check tax records, the employment situation of each husband, and so forth. Such a sentence is thus about matters of fact. It is not a necessary truth, since it may be true in some conditions and false in others. It will depend on the facts as to which it will be.

Unlike any previous philosopher, Hume drew an important skeptical inference from this distinction.

First, he states, sentences concerning the relations of ideas do not tell us anything about the world. It is part of the meaning of "giant" that every giant is tall. It is thus a necessary truth that all giants are tall. Nevertheless, its truth does not entail that there are any giants. So what we know in such a case is not something about the real world, but rather something about the relationship between two concepts, namely, those of *being a giant* and *being tall*. In technical parlance, such sentences do not have existential import, that is, they do not imply the existence of anything. Nevertheless, because they are necessarily true, they are certain. The theorems of mathematics are examples of such truths. The sentence "$2 + 2 = 4$" can be determined to be true prior to counting apples, for example. One can see that the two ideas, "$2 + 2$" and "4," say the same thing. One can also see that the theorem is certain.

Second, sentences about matters of fact are established as true or false by direct or inferential perceptual experience. The statement "The tree outside is green" cannot be determined to be true or false merely by understanding it. One will have to look. But even in such a case, one might be mistaken. One's eyesight might not be good, the conditions of visibility might be poor, one might be hallucinating, and so forth. Since any statement based on direct observation might be mistaken, no such statement can ever be certain. Or consider the scientific law that water boils at 100°C at sea level. This is a true proposition. The evidence for it is inferential, that is, based on past experience and on many confirming observations. But the law makes claims that go beyond its evidential base and is about *all* cases of water's boiling. But though past experience has always given this result, it is not necessarily true that water will always boil at that temperature. We can imagine a change in the constitution of the earth such that water would boil at a different temperature. What is true of the past is not necessarily true of the future. Thus, according to Hume, no statement concerning a matter of fact is certain.

But such uncertainty runs even deeper. Consider the thesis that the future resembles the past. Hume calls this the Principle of the Uniformity of Nature (it is also sometimes referred to as the Principle of Induction). It is a basic assumption of science. Scientific predictability depends on it. Yet, Hume states, there is no way of proving it. Any proof would either have to be a rational demonstration or an argument from experience. But neither will do for, as the previous distinction makes clear, from reason, as expressed in relations of ideas, nothing follows about any matter of fact. Therefore, reason cannot be used to prove the principle. If one appeals to past experience, one is assuming the very principle that must be proved, namely that past experience is reliable. The argument would thus be viciously circular. So no rational or experiential proof of the principle is possible. Thus, the belief in the principle cannot be rationally justified. Hume draws a skeptical conclusion from this demonstration: Science rests on an irrational belief.

Hume's skepticism

Hume's theory of knowledge thus engenders a skeptical paradox. Insofar as any proposition is certain it will concern the relations of ideas and will be empty of meaningful content with respect to the world of fact. Insofar as any proposition embeds a piece of knowledge about any matter of fact, it is only probable and never certain. Hume concludes that certainty about the world of fact is impossible. We can never attain certitude about the past, the present, or the future. The theory is thus a form of radical skepticism.

As he says:

> When I proceed still farther, to turn the scrutiny against every successive estimation I make of my faculties all the rules of logic require a diminution, and at last a total extinction of belief and evidence.[13]

Why, then, do we believe that the sun will rise tomorrow, that water will flow when we turn on the tap, and that the wheels of our car will turn to the right when we turn the steering wheel in that direction? Hume's answer is, again, "custom." Past experience disposes us to expect certain consequences from certain antecedent conditions. It is habit that thus gives rise to expectation. But we cannot *prove* on rational grounds that antecedent conditions will always have the same consequences, for example, that the sun will rise tomorrow or that water will boil at 100°C.

Skepticism is thus true. Hume's analysis of the limits of reason has the arresting consequence that on rational grounds we should suspend our belief in the power of reason. But he also points out that custom does not allow us to do so. The exigencies of daily life require action based on belief. So our actions based on common sense and scientific beliefs are essentially irrational; they cannot be justified. As he states, the arguments for skepticism "admit of no answer and produce no conviction." Belief, he concludes, is "more properly an act of the sensitive, than of the cogitative part of our natures."[14]

Criticisms of Hume

Some critics have pointed out that Hume's view is self-contradictory. Here is a philosopher, they say, who argues his case. He reasons logically to the conclusions he wishes to draw. In so doing, he is presupposing the validity of reason. Yet his argument concludes that reason cannot be justified. So how can he accept the skeptical conclusions he arrives at? Moreover, if he is right, how should we organize and direct our lives? His suggestion is that we should follow the dictates of custom. But, his critics say, this answer is inadequate, and indeed is inconsistent with his own practice, which consists in rational, carefully reasoned deliberation. But as advice, this is unacceptable. Ordinary persons recognize an *obvious* difference between lives that are based on reason and those that are not. So they distinguish between good and bad arguments, and between persons who act reasonably and those who do not.

Any view that fails to acknowledge these differences cannot be correct. Moreover, there are standards that discriminate rational from nonrational or irrational conduct. Some of these are found in common sense. At the most sophisticated level they are the criteria of scientific method. They allow human beings to distinguish between opinions that have a foundation in fact and those that do not. Any philosophical theory that runs counter to common sense and scientific practice should thus be rejected.

A second criticism turns on Hume's commitment to the Cartesian principle that we are only directly aware of our own perceptions. Once this principle is assumed (and it is assumed by Hume unreflectively) the problem of skepticism is an unavoidable consequence. There is no obvious way of bridging the gap between our sensations and external objects. That there is an external reality is obvious. Hume himself assumes inconsistently that simple impressions arise from contact with such objects. It is beyond doubt that there are objects and events whose existence does not depend on being perceived. For example, mountains and volcanoes existed long before any form of life developed on the earth.

This is the kind of criticism made by one of Hume's contemporaries, the Scottish philosopher Thomas Reid (1710-1796). Reid argued that Hume's results conflict with what persons of common sense know, namely, that they are directly aware of physical objects such as chairs, tables, and rocks. Thus, any question about the nature of knowledge must acknowledge common sense and avoid starting from Hume's position that we can only know our own ideas. The skeptical problem about our knowledge of external reality is immediately passed by if one assumes this starting point. Whether Reid's point of view begs the question is a much debated matter, even today, but it has had continuing influence. Reid's common-sense philosophy was later to be echoed by G. E. Moore (1873-1958) and J. L. Austin (1911-1960).

It is generally agreed, however, that the most probing criticisms of Hume were made by Immanuel Kant. It is therefore to Kant's views that we shall now turn. Because of the length of this chapter, we shall defer a discussion of his life until chapter 6 on ethics and moral philosophy.

Immanuel Kant (1724-1804)

In his *Prolegomena to Any Future Metaphysics* (1783), Kant stated that David Hume first awakened him from his "dogmatic slumbers." For most of his career, Kant had been a rationalist, influenced by Leibniz and a minor follower of Leibniz named Christian August Crusius. But on reading Hume's arguments about the vacuity of reason, he felt it necessary to reconsider his commitment to the Leibnizian point of view. Kant's most important work, the *Critique of Pure Reason* (1781), takes on this task. It is devoted to "discovering how much understanding and reason can know apart from all experience." Kant's answer is a compromise between a strict empiricism on the one hand, and pure rationalism on the other. His defense of a kind of reason that he calls "transcendental"—in opposition to the "transcendent"—is thus both a response to and a substantial criticism of Hume and indeed of the whole empirical tradition.

Rationalism is the doctrine that pure thought alone can discover truths about reality. Descartes, as we have seen, thought that by a priori reasoning he could prove his own and even God's existence. Hume, in contrast, denied that a priori reasoning had any existential consequences. Kant's philosophy is a via media between these two positions. He agrees with Hume that pure reason is empty of empirical content, but disagrees that all knowledge "arises from" experience. His thesis is that mind, the rational faculty in humans, contributes organizational and classificatory structure to knowledge and, accordingly, that all knowledge contains a component that comes from reason. In a famous phrase, he states that "concepts without percepts are empty and percepts without concepts are blind." So both pure rationalism and pure empiricism cannot account for the knowledge that human beings have. His solution is that both reason and experience contribute something to every bit of knowledge. The *Critique of Pure Reason* is dedicated to showing in detail how this is possible.

The argument involves some technical machinery, and especially the identification of what he calls "synthetic a priori judgments." This rests on two distinctions, that between (1) a priori and a posteriori judgments and (2) analytic and synthetic judgments.

Like Hume, Kant assumes that any specimen of knowledge can be expressed as a judgment (proposition, statement, or declarative sentence). Any such judgment will belong either to category (1) or category (2). For Hume, the two categories are exclusive, that is, propositions expressing a relation of ideas cannot belong to the category of those about matters of fact, and vice-versa. For Hume a priori and a posteriori propositions belong, respectively, to categories (1) and (2), so that it is not possible to have a priori knowledge of any matter of fact. This is what he means in denying that propositions expressing a relation of ideas have existential import.

It is just on this point that Kant's philosophy differs. What Kant characterizes as the Copernican revolution in philosophy is the proof that there can be an overlap in this classificatory schema, in particular between the a priori and the synthetic. As he puts it graphically, his main contention is that synthetic a priori propositions are possible. This is another way of saying that both reason and experience make contributions to knowledge, and in particular that reason plays a substantive role in the knowledge we have of the world.

By an "a priori judgment," Kant means a proposition that is both necessary and universal, that is, one that holds for all possible cases and without exception. Such propositions can be distinguished from those that are "a posteriori"—that is, those that arise from experience. These, he agrees with the empiricists, are never necessary.

The distinction between the analytic and synthetic is similar to Hume's between relations of ideas and matters of fact. The main difference is that Kant's account applies only to sentences in the subject-predicate form. Analytic propositions are those in which the concept of the predicate is "contained in" the concept of the subject. Thus, in the statement "All spinsters are unmarried," the notion of being unmarried is part of the notion of being a spinster. Moroever, the negation of any analytic statement is self-contradictory. In contrast, in synthetic propositions, such as "All bodies have weight," the meaning of the predicate term is not comprised in the subject term. Accordingly, the negation of any synthetic proposition will be self-consistent. (Though, of course, if the original proposition is true, its negation will be false, and vice versa. The point is that the negation of a synthetic proposition is never self-inconsistent.)

We learn from experience that bodies have weight, whereas we can know prior to experience that all spinsters are unmarried. Thus, in determining whether synthetic propositions are true or false we must consult experience'.

Kant's rejection of empiricism, then, lies in proving that synthetic a priori propositions are possible.

Kant contends that we find such propositions in both mathematics and physics. The proposition "7 + 5 = 12" is not analytic because one can know what the terms "7" and "5" mean without knowing that their sum is 12. The proposition is therefore synthetic. But it is also a priori because its truth can be established without an appeal to experience. As Kant writes:

> That 5 should be added to 7 was no doubt implied in my concept of the sum 7 + 5, but not that the sum should equal 12. An arithematical proposition is, therefore, always synthetical, which is seen more easily still by taking larger numbers, where we clearly perceive that turn and twist our conceptions as we may, we could never, by means of the mere analysis of our concepts and without the help of intuition, arrive at the sum wanted.

Synthetic a priori propositions are also found in geometry. We can understand the concept of a "straight line" without knowing that a straight line is the shortest distance between two points. The concept of "being straight," when analyzed, does not include the concept of "being the shortest."This proposition is both necessary and universal, and accordingly it must be a synthetic a priori truth rather than an analytic one. The physical principle "Every event has a cause" is also synthetic a priori. It differs from "Every cause has an effect."The latter proposition is analytic but the former is not; yet it is a universal, necessary truth. It clearly applies to experience, but is determinable as true prior to experience. Hence, it is synthetic and a priori.

Synthetic a priori propositions have their own unique kind of necessity. But how can they be necessary and yet apply to experience? Kant's answer turns on his theory of the human mind. It begins by rejecting the empiricist principle that the mind is passive in the sense that it cannot bring anything new to experience. His view is that the mind brings features to sense experience that do not come from such experience. Among these are the concepts of space and time.

These concepts apply to all information derived from the senses. Any object one sees, for example, is perceived as existing in space and at a particular time. But we cannot acquire the ideas of space and time merely through reflecting on what is given in sensory promptings. Kant argues that to know what is meant by saying that one object is next to another, or below or above another, or to the right or left of another *presupposes* a prior familiarity with space as such. The same reasoning applies to time. Kant concludes that we know prior to experience that whatever we experience will occur in space and time. These features he calls "a priori intuitions." It is these that the mind contributes to the raw data of experience. They are the necessary conditions for ordering and categorizing such experiences. We cannot conceive of events and objects without conceiving of them as extended in space and as happening in time. In that sense, they are the necessary conditions that make ordered experience possible.

The important point is that we could not even recognize or describe any experience without presupposing that it satisfies these conditions. But since these conditions are both universal and necessary, they cannot arise from the senses. As such, they are a priori and yet about matters of fact. We thus have knowledge that is both synthetic and a priori.

The human mind is the source of these "forms of intuition." Hence, whatever we experience—all of our knowledge of reality—is the product of two factors: something that is mind independent (the occurrence and movement of objects and events) and something that is imposed on these objects by the mind. Thus, the mind imposes certain conditions on experience, but it cannot and does not create the contents of such experience.

A commentator has described the Kantian theory in the following way:

> The situation portrayed by Kant is analogous to wearing tinted glasses which cannot be taken off. Anything that we see will be affected by the glasses. If we know the nature of the glasses we can determine apart from any experience that all experience will have

certain characteristics imposed on it by our employing them to see. These characteristics will be universal and necessary. But the contents we experience still cannot be determined by the characteristics that all experience must possess because of our wearing the glasses. It is the task of what Kant called "Critical Philosophy" to study the glasses, that is, the conditions of all possible experience and all possible judgments about experience. It is the task of the particular sciences to study the content of actual experiences.[15]

The result of Kant's research is a new theory of knowledge. According to it, the understanding or reason is not a passive receptor of given sensory information but an active ordering faculty—what Kant calls "the lawgiver to nature." Reason is capable of arriving at a priori knowledge of matters of fact because the natural world as we perceive it is partially a product of the human mind.

Criticisms of Kant

It is clear that the whole system depends on proving that synthetic a priori propositions exist. Kant defends this view by appealing to examples from mathematics and physics. But since Kant's time a deeper understanding of the nature of mathematical and physical propositions has been developed by logicians like Gottlob Frege and Bertrand Russell. On their view, the theorems of mathematics are analytic and never synthetic. They are tautologies, that is, propositions ultimately reducible to the law of identity, for example, for all x, $x = x$. In such a case they are a priori. But when applied, the theorems are synthetic, that is, inferences from experience. In that case, they are a posteriori and never a priori. According to Russell, these findings undermine Kant's view that any theorem of mathematics or physics is both synthetic and a priori. If Russell is correct—and most philosophers now believe that he is—then the Kantian system collapses. Here is how Russell explains the point.

> "Geometry," as we now know, is a name covering two different studies. On the one hand, there is pure geometry, which deduces consequences from axioms, without inquiring whether the axioms are "true"; this contains nothing that does not follow from logic,

and is not "synthetic" and has no need of figures such as are used in geometrical text-books. On the other hand, there is geometry as a branch of physics, as it appears, for example, in the general theory of relativity; this is an empirical science, in which the axioms are inferred from measurements, and are found to differ from Euclid's. Thus of the two kinds of geometry one is *a priori* but not synthetic, while the other is synthetic but not *a priori*. This disposes of the transcendental argument.[16]

The Kantian system was also developed as a response to Hume's skepticism. But, according to critics, it engenders a new form of skepticism, so we are no better off than before. Let us see how this objection plays out.

The Kantian system distinguishes between the properties of experienced objects and the properties of the human mind. The mind has a built-in structure which it brings to the raw data of experience. Whatever we experience must thus *necessarily* conform to the structural properties of the mind. Apart from the glasses analogy mentioned above, one might think about the relationship between the mind and sense experience as follows: Suppose one had a camera that could take only black-and-white pictures. In photographing a friend, say, the friend's appearance would be a function of the properties of the camera. The resulting picture would contain no colors. If the friend were wearing a green sweater, it would appear to be black. The situation is thus similar to Kant's description of the relationship between the human mind and sense experience: Given the structure of the mind, we can only know what things are like as they appear to that structure.

According to his critics, Kant's theory thus seems to entail a kind of modified skepticism. In effect, it states that our knowledge is limited to the way objects appear to the mind and not as they are in themselves. Kant admits that we cannot know what things are like independent of the way they appear to us. In drawing a distinction between the way things are in themselves—what he calls the "noumenal"—as distinct from the way they appear to us—what he calls the "phenomenal"—his view raises the Cartesian problem of whether we can really ever get outside the circle of our ideas. It would appear that we cannot, that we are limited to knowledge of phenomena, that is, to the appearances of things.

Kant's view is, to be sure, not a complete form of idealism, that is, the view that the world is wholly mental. That is the kind of theory advanced by Berkeley, who held that everything is either a mind or an idea dependent for its existence on some mind. Kant's compromise position recognizes that appearances or phenomena are not mind dependent in Berkeley's sense. Their existence does not depend on being perceived; they exist autonomously and in their own right. But what the objects that appear to us are really like we can never know, since they are always conditioned by the mind. In a certain sense, then, Kant's view entails a kind of skepticism about our capacity to access the real world as it actually is.

The Kantian view, and its notion that reality is always colored by the nature of the perceiving apparatus, has been enormously influential. In the nearly two centuries since Kant's death, epistemological theories have for the most part either been forms of Humean empiricism or Kantian rationalism. The kinds of skepticism that such theories entail are thus very common today. But so are the continuing efforts to defend the existence of knowledge and certainty. In the next chapter, we shall look at the debate, as vigorous as ever, as it appeared in twentieth-century philosophy.

NOTES

1. Herbert Marcuse, *One-Dimensional Man* (Boston: Beacon Press, 1964), p. 79.

2. René Descartes, *Meditations on First Philosophy* (1642), trans. Laurence J. Lafleur (New York: Bobbs-Merrill, 1960), p. 21.

3. René Descartes, "The Principles of Philosophy," in *Descartes Selections*, ed. Ralph M. Eaton (New York: Scribner's, 1927), p. 272.

4. Avrum Stroll and Richard H. Popkin, *Introduction to Philosophy*, 3rd ed. (New York: Holt, Rinehart and Winston, 1979), p. 61.

5. George Berkeley, *Principles of Human Knowledge* (1710), introduction, sec. 3.

6. See Stroll and Popkin, *Introduction to Philosophy*, p. 81.

7. David Hume, *A Treatise of Human Nature* (1739), 2d ed., ed. L. A. Selby-Bigge (Oxford: Clarendon, 1978), p. 4.

8. Ibid., p. 161.

9. Ibid., p. 252.

10. Ibid., p. 253.
11. Ibid., p. 254.
12. Ibid., p. 260.
13. Ibid., p. 183.
14. Ibid.
15. Stroll and Popkin, *Introduction to Philosophy*, p. 180.
16. Bertrand Russell, *History of Western Philosophy* (London: Allen & Unwin, 1946), p. 73.

4 THE TWENTIETH CENTURY

Philosophical fashions come and go and often result in new formulations of old problems and new solutions to them. But such "solutions" usually turn out to be variations of older ones, with all their merits and liabilities. The remark is particularly apposite with respect to skepticism. As we have seen, its history is at least two thousand years old, and though fashions change, skeptical challenges, and a variety of responses to them, are still with us as we begin the twenty-first century. A backward glance at the twentieth century reveals that the debate between skeptics and nonskeptics is still as lively as ever. In this chapter we shall look at the views of two prominent twentieth-century skeptics, Bertrand Russell and Jacques Derrida, and two philosophers of an opposite persuasion, G. E. Moore and Ludwig Wittgenstein. In differing ways, Moore and Wittgenstein argued that the acquisition of knowledge and certainty is possible for human beings. An examination of these four views will bring us up to date on that ancient controversy, and will give us a good idea of how things stand today.

BERTRAND RUSSELL (1872-1970)

Life

Russell's life was unusual for a professional philosopher. Like Karl Marx, he was enormously influential both within philosophy and in the broader social community. Perhaps no other twentieth-century "intellectual" attracted more followers and opponents. He has been described as a "genius-saint" by his admirers and as "the greatest heretic and immoralist of our age" by detractors. During the First World War he was an outspoken critic of England's involvement in the conflict. His views were both widely supported and vigorously attacked. In 1916 he was fined £100 and was dismissed from his lectureship at Trinity College, Cambridge. In 1918 he was jailed for six months for his public support of conscientious objection. Interestingly enough, being incarcerated did not affect his philosophical productivity. While in prison he wrote one of his most important books, *Introduction to Mathematical Philosophy*. After the Second World War, along with Albert Einstein and Linus Pauling, he became a major spokesman for nuclear disarmament. The three Nobel laureates were focal points for the worldwide peace movement that erupted in opposition to the development and testing of nuclear weapons.

Russell wrote extensively not only on technical subjects in philosophy, but also on a much broader range of issues, the sort that ordinary persons think philosophers should concern themselves with. In such books as *Principles of Social Reconstruction* (1916), *Roads to Freedom* (1918), *The Practice and Theory of Bolshevism* (1920), *Why I Am Not a Christian* (1927), *Skeptical Essays* (1928), *Marriage and Morals* (1929), *Authority and the Individual* (1949) and *New Hopes for a Changing World* (1951), he discussed nearly all those "popular" matters that the "average man" encounters in daily life: the education of children, the role of religion, the relationships between the sexes, just versus unjust wars, freedom versus organization, and so forth. His attitude toward most of these topics ranged from the liberal to the radical and was coupled with a strong dose of skepticism about the integrity and intelligence of politicians. The strong effects his writings produced were the results of powerful rational argumentation, a brilliant and clear writing style, and a caustic wit. One might characterize him as a twentieth-century Voltaire.

A description of Russell's life would require a whole book, and indeed there exist numerous such biographies, for example, by Rupert Crawshay-Williams, G. H. Hardy, Alan Wood, and Ray Monk. Russell's own memoirs—*The Autobiography of Bertrand Russell*—is a fascinating document. It was published in three volumes between 1967 and 1969. He knew personally and /or corresponded with most of the famous people of his time—T. S. Eliot, Joseph Conrad, Katherine Mansfield, William Gladstone, Pearl Buck, Harold Laski, inter alios. His grandfather Lord John Russell was prime minister of England on two occasions (1846–52) and (1865–66), and Russell himself, as Third Earl Russell and Viscount Amberley, was in direct line of succession to the British throne.

His mother, father, and grandfather all died while he was a child, and he was brought up by his grandmother, Lady Russell. In a characteristically witty and ironical way he describes her as follows:

> My grandmother . . . was a Puritan, with the moral rigidity of the Covenanters, despising comfort, indifferent to food, hating wine, and regarding tobacco as sinful. Although she had lived her whole life in the great world until my grandfather's retirement in 1866, she was completely unworldly. She had that indifference to money which is only possible to those who have always had enough of it.[1]

Russell married four times (Alys, Dora, Patricia, and Edith) and carried on long affairs with a number of women, among them Lady Ottoline Morell, Vivien Eliot (the wife of T. S. Eliot), and the actress Lady Constance ("Colette") Malleson. These relationships are described in detail in Ray Monk's biography, *Bertrand Russell: The Spirit of Solitude*. He was a lecturer at various American universities just before World War II erupted. One of the positions to which he was appointed ended in a tremendous international flurry. In 1939 he resigned as professor at UCLA to accept a position at City College of New York when an enormous protest at his appointment broke out. Here is how Russell describes the situation:

The Government of New York City was virtually a satellite of the Vatican, but the professors at the City College strove ardently to keep up some semblance of academic freedom. . . . An Anglican bishop was incited to protest against me, and priests lectured the police, who were practically all Irish Catholics, on my responsibility for the local criminals. A Lady, whose daughter attended some section of the City College with which I should never be brought in contact, was induced to bring a suit, saying that my presence in that institution would be dangerous to her daughter's virtue. . . . The lawyer for the prosecution pronounced my works "lecherous, libidinous, lustful, venerous, erotomaniac, aphrodisiac, irreverent, narrow-minded, untruthful, and bereft of moral fiber." . . . A typical American witch-hunt was instituted against me and I became taboo throughout the whole of the United States.[2]

The suit against Russell came before a judge ("an Irishman") who decided against him, leaving him without employment. Since he could not obtain funds from England because of the war, he was virtually destitute. He was temporarily saved by Dr. Albert C. Barnes, the inventor of Argyrol and the creator of the Barnes Foundation near Philadelphia. He arranged for a five-year appointment for Russell to teach at the foundation, but Barnes, who was an eccentric, tired of Russell and fired him on December 28, 1942. Fortunately, Russell was able to obtain a contract, with a substantial advance, from Simon and Schuster to publish his new book, *History of Western Philosophy*, which eventually became a best-seller and his major source of income for many years.

With the possible exception of Wittgenstein, Russell was the most influential philosopher of his time. His literary output was incredible. He wrote seventy books, more than two thousand articles, and an estimated forty thousand letters. Ray Monk states that the quantity of writing that Russell produced in his lifetime "almost defies belief." According to Monk, there is now finally a complete bibliography of his work. It consists of three volumes and contains more than four thousand entries. The authors, Kenneth Blackwell and Harry Ruja, spent thirty years gathering the data for it. No similar compendium exists for the secondary literature about Russell. But no doubt, if and when it is compiled, it will be several magnitudes larger.

Philosophy

Russell died in 1970 at the age of ninety-eight. During his long career as a philosopher he changed his mind on various points of doctrine. He began as an idealist, but was converted to realism by G. E. Moore. He was a platonist, and thus a kind of rationalist, in epistemology in his early years, but later disavowed this view and supported a sophisticated form of empiricism. In the philosophy of perception, his views ranged from forms of realism to phenomenalism, and his moral philosophy showed a similar vacillation. Yet, despite these changes, he held a consistent attitude about how philosophical problems should be approached. This, at various times, he described as a "scientific philosophy, grounded in mathematical logic." He never deviated from this general posture, even though at times it led him to modify or abandon views he had held earlier.

As previously mentioned, Russell's writings covered a palate of subjects that included moral philosophy, education, political theory, and a wide gamut of popular themes. Nearly all of these have skeptical overtones. It is impossible to deal with such a vast range here. We shall therefore restrict our discussion to a topic that Russell himself regarded as central, namely, the theory of knowledge. His major books in this area alone include *The Problems of Philosophy* (1912), *Our Knowledge of the External World* (1914), *Mysticism and Logic* (1917), *The Analysis of Mind* (1921), *The Analysis of Matter* (1927), *An Outline of Philosophy* (1927), *An Inquiry into Meaning and Truth* (1940), *Human Knowledge: Its Scope and Limits* (1948), *Logic and Knowledge* (1956), and *My Philosophical Development* (1959).

Russell's epistemology has two main influences, one historical and the other logical. We shall bypass a discussion of the logical influences; they would require another essay by themselves. The historical influences derive from the three British empiricists Locke, Berkeley, and Hume. Their most important effect on Russell was a commitment to sense-data theory, a modern version of the Lockean and Humean theories that what we are directly aware of are impressions and the ideas arising from them. As we have seen, this theory is an inheritance from Descartes, who held that we are directly aware of our own ideas and only indirectly aware of their sources in the external world. It is compatible with this sort of view that nothing might exist outside the circle of our own ideas. To hold such a view would be a radical form of skepticism. This is not Russell's position, as we shall see; but Russell's empiricism also gives rise to a weaker form of skepticism, namely, that even if we have some sort of access to the external world it can never be direct and therefore can never give us certitude about what exists "outside of our minds." This is the nature of the problem that Russell confronts and with which his theories are designed to deal.

The problem arises on the basis of two plausible assumptions: first, that human beings have minds, and second, that there exist objects whose existence does not depend on being apprehended by any mind. Thus, a distinction is drawn between such things as headaches, pains, feelings, and desires, which are thought to be "mental" and which could not exist "outside the mind"; and things like tables, chairs, rocks, and the moon, which are physical and do exist "outside the mind." The "big" question is whether one is justified in believing in the existence of such external objects, given that the only evidence one has for their existence is the occurrence of mental sensations. It is always possible that one could have all the sensations one normally does and yet that these might not correspond to anything external at all.

For theorists of perception there have been historically only three "solutions" to the External World Problem: (1) direct realism, (2) representative realism, or (3) phenomenalism.

Direct realism is the view that at least some of the time we apprehend physical objects just as they are. On this view, when one sees a red tomato, one is directly apprending a physical object. It is the real, independently existing red object that one sees. It is agreed that there are hallucinations and other visual aberrations, but these are regarded as "abnormal." The theory is that, under normal conditions, one sees an object such as a tomato just as it really is. Representative realism, in contradistinction, holds that even in normal cases of perception one's apprehension of the object is always mediated by the sensations one has. Thus, when one sees a tomato, what one sees is the product of a complex set of processes. Light bounces off the tomato, is reflected through the air, and is picked up by the human visual system. This processes the light through the eyes, the cones, the retina, the optic nerve, and is then transmitted to the brain. The brain "interprets" these data and "reproduces" an image of the object. It is not the object but the image that is directly seen. The nature of the object is *inferred* from the image. On such a view, it is always possible that our perceptions may misrepresent the way the world is. This view is *realistic* in the sense that it posits the existence of external objects. Its problem is not that such objects do not exist but how we can acquire acurate knowledge of them.

Representative realism is also called the causal or copy theory, since light bouncing off an object produces a causal sequence whose last event is called "seeing." Presumably, the sensation one has copies the external object.

Phenomenalism rejects both direct and representative realism. It holds that it is meaningless to speak of an existing external object. All we are really aware of are various sensations when we "see" something. According to the phenomenalist, any form of realism goes beyond the empirical data in assuming the existence of external phenomena or events. Instead, such supposed external objects are simply identical with the sense experiences we have or might have. This is essentially Bishop Berkeley's theory. Thus, what one means by a physical object is a set of actual and possible perceptions. To say that one sees a brown table, for example, is just to say that one is sensing a group of data that are brown, square, and that have a certain sort of texture. There is no substratum or underlying material that has the properties of being brown, being square, and so forth. The External World Problem is solved on this view by denying one of the conditions that give rise to the problem, namely, that there are objects that exist independently of our actual or possible perception of them.

Russell consistently rejected direct realism, and throughout his career vacillated between representative realism and phenomenalism. Both theories give rise to skeptical challenges whose general validity Russell accepted. His philosophy of perception is to a great extent an attempt to accommodate such challenges while limiting their impact and scope. Both phenomenalism and representative realism start from a position that Russell felt to be beyond any sort of conceptual challenge. In this sense, his starting point begins from something he holds to be certainly true, namely, that we are aware of certain kinds of basic data. These he calls "primitive data." They give rise to primitive knowledge, and such knowledge is to be distinguished from derivative knowledge, which is based upon the former. Thus, when we have a certain sort of visual experience, for example, of what common sense would call seeing a dog, what we are directly aware of is a complex visual patch: a pattern of color, shape, texture, and size. Russell calls this a "canoid patch." In such a case we are certainly aware of something. But it is a matter of inference, and therefore derivative, to say that what we are seeing is a dog. Thus, to see what we call a "dog" goes beyond what we are actually seeing when we confront primitive data. Misrepresentation of the external object is always possible; hence, our "knowledge" of such an object can never be certain.

In a famous paper, "Knowledge by Acquaintance and Knowledge by Description" (1912), Russell expands and refines the distinction between primitive and derivative knowledge. Now he provides an alternative account of this relationship. As the title of the paper indicates, there is, first of all, knowledge by acquaintance. This is the same kind of knowledge he has called "primitive" or "basic." There is also knowledge by description, which is roughly equivalent to derivative knowledge. Most knowledge is by description. In knowing today that Julius Caesar crossed the Rubicon, what we know derives from descriptions in books, or from statements made by teachers or others, about Caesar. But nobody alive today was ever acquainted with Caesar. Still, knowledge by description rests on certain facts that can be traced back historically to the actual event of Caesar's crossing the Rubicon. Only an eyewitness to the crossing would have knowledge by acquaintance. But it is this sort of knowledge that is the basis of later descriptions. In the end, all knowledge by description thus ultimately depends on, or can be traced back to, knowledge by acquaintance. As Russell puts it:

> The fundamental epistemological principle in the analysis of propositions containing descriptions is this: *Every proposition which we*

can understand must be composed wholly of constituents with which we are acquainted.[3]

This principle is another version of the reductive thesis that we have already depicted in describing the views of Locke and Hume. Its main idea is that all nonanalytic knowledge derives from experience, where "experience" in turn means "sense experience that involves the direct awareness of sense-data."

In adhering to this theory, Russell was rejecting any form of radical skepticism, since he contended that basic knowledge could not be mistaken. However, as soon as inference enters the picture, mistakes become possible; and here is where the skeptic's position must be taken seriously. On Russell's view, we cannot have certainty about the physical world, but only some degree of probability. According to this position, one must accept as a kind of practical knowledge the information generated by science. Such knowledge is never absolutely certain, but is so well established and works so well in everyday life that one is justified in accepting it as true. Russell's skepticism is thus very moderate and in the end represents his commitment to the validity of the information produced by the use of the scientific method.

Russell is a kind of Cartesian in terms of his starting point, and in terms of wishing to discover a foundation for the whole edifice of knowledge that is beyond skeptical doubt. Like Descartes, he asks, "What can we know with absolute certainty?" and his answer is, "Primitive data." But unlike Descartes, he does not think that from such primitive data we can infer certain knowledge about the physical world, or about God, or even about ourselves. Not even from the fact that thinking occurs can one infer that one exists. What is true is that thoughts and doubts exist, but it is a matter of inference that they should be *your* thoughts. To the question, How can there be thoughts you are aware of that are not yours? he offers a theory derived from William James that he calls "neutral monism." This is too complicated to be discussed in detail here, but according to it basic data are neutral but can become mental or physical depending on the kind of causal sequences in which they exist. Thus, they are originally nonmental and nonphysical, and accordingly may exist as neutral events without belonging to any person. Whether this is an acceptable answer is open to question, but at least it offers the possibility that the cogito may not express basic or primitive knowledge after all. Still, whatever status basic knowledge has, it is the foundation from which all other, derivative knowledge arises, including scientific knowledge. Russell's skepticism is thus a version of mitigated skepticism, namely, that some information is more reliable than other information, but that none of it (except for primitive data) can be absolutely certain.

Criticisms of Russell

From a skeptical standpoint both Russell's representative realism and phenomenalism are open to criticism.

The representative realist holds that our mental representations copy or reproduce the external object when we are said to "see" such an object. But the view has a radical skeptical consequence, for it is impossible to compare such a mental representation with the actual object. That is, one cannot remove the mental representation and put it next to the external object to see if they are similar or not. Even worse, one cannot know but instead must *assume*, that there is such an external object. The criticism thus has the consequence that each human being is aware only of his or her own mental sensations. Whether anything "external" exists or, if it does, what it is like cannot be known at all. Hence, we are left with the original problem of the external world that a view like Russell's empiricism was designed to solve.

The phenomenalistic alternative does not fare much better. To insist that physical objects are just heaps of actual or possible sense-data is to say something that is intrinsically incredible. That is, to hold that a mountain or planet is simply a set of sensations is to produce a view that nobody of common sense could take seriously. For common sense, the existence of such objects has nothing to do with their being perceived or thought of. Moreover, even if phenomenalism could be defended on philosophical grounds it would still be subject to a skeptical rebuttal. On the phenomenalist analysis, it is hard to see how perceptual error can occur and, accordingly, how such error could be objectively rectified and corrected. To say that one sees a table is ordinarily taken to imply that one might be right or one might be wrong. But if in any such case one experiences a heap of tablelike sense-data, then the existence of error seems impossible, for there seems to be no way of distinguishing veridical from nonveridical perception. The skeptical riposte to Russell would insist that his phenomenalism has thus ruled out the possibility of error. Since any cogent theory must acknowledge the possibility of error, Russell's view must be rejected. But to acknowledge the possibility of error is, of course, to admit that the skeptical challenge cannot be dismissed.

G. E. MOORE (1873–1958)

Life

Unlike Russell, who was as much a public philosopher as an academic, Moore spent his life almost entirely in university circles. He was thus a "philosopher's philosopher." In the twentieth century, four British philosophers were regarded as exceptionally gifted: Moore, Russell, Wittgenstein, and Austin. The first three were together at Cambridge during overlapping periods. Austin was an Oxonian. But all were active at the same time, mostly before and just after the Second World War. These four philosophers contributed to one of the golden ages in the history of the subject. It is difficult to assess their comparative merits, but there is no doubt that each of them was an original and profound thinker. This is surely true of Moore. He made fundamental contributions to two of the major fields of philosophy: ethics and epistemology.

C. D. Broad, another colleague of Moore's at Cambridge, wrote in an obituary notice, "It is doubtful whether any philosopher known to history has excelled or even equalled Moore in sheer power of analysing problems, detecting and exposing fallacies and ambiguities, and formulating and working out alternative possibilities." Broad also said about Moore, "Apart from his immense analytic power Moore's most noticeable characteristic was his absolutely single-minded desire to discover truth and avoid error and confusion. Fundamentally, he was a man of simple tastes and character, absolutely devoid of all affectation, pose, and flummery." Moore had an immense impact on those around him, much of it stemming from his integrity as a human being and a philosopher. In particular he influenced the Bloomsbury Group, who found in his *Principia Ethica* (1903) a justification for a libertine way of life that involved nonconventional sexual relationships. Many commentators think that this interpretation of Moore's theory rested on a misunderstanding, but there is no doubt that Moore was regarded as a role model by these writers. There are a number of studies written about him, both as a human being and as a thinker. Three of the most insightful and interesting are Leonard Woolf's *Sowing*, John T. Wisdom's "Moore's Technique," and Norman Malcolm's "George Edward Moore."[4]

Moore's autobiography, which appears at the beginning of *The Philosophy of G. E. Moore* (1942), is a charming thirty-six-page essay. Apart from personal details, it is of great historical interest about the state of philosophy in Cambridge from the end of the nineteenth century up to the Second World War. It relates Moore's assessments of such distinguished philosophers as Bertrand Russell, George Stout, Henry Sidgwick, John M'Taggart, James Ward, Frank Ramsey, and Ludwig Wittgenstein. Many of these persons were Moore's teachers. He was an undergraduate, for example, when he attended a tea party, during which M'Taggart, who was one of the dons, advanced the claim that time is unreal. Moore states in his autobiography that this seemed to him at the time and still does "a perfectly monstrous proposition." He states that Russell, who was only a year older, influenced him more than any other philosopher. He first met Wittgenstein when he (Moore) was about forty. Of Wittgenstein he affirms, "I soon came to feel that he was much cleverer at philosophy than I was and not only cleverer, but also much more profound." This he said about a graduate student who at that time was only in his midtwenties.

Moore and Wittgenstein had a complex, ongoing relationship. For a year or two before the First World War broke out and Wittgenstein returned to Vienna to join the Austrian army, they were very close. But during this period, Wittgenstein asked Moore to procure a fellowship at Cambridge for him. Moore tried to do this but failed. Wittgenstein became extremely angry and wrote an intemperate letter to Moore, accusing him of subverting his attempt to become a fellow. Moore did not answer the letter, feeling it was outrageous in tone and content, and simply severed his relationship with Wittgenstein. He cut off all communication until 1929 when Wittgenstein, who had been absent from Cambridge since 1914, decided to return to the university as a Ph.D. candidate. Moore and Russell agreed to serve as his dissertation committee, and Wittgenstein submitted his now-famous (but then mostly unknown) book, *The Tractatus Logico-Philosophicus*, which had been published in 1921, as his doctoral thesis. In his report Moore wrote, "It is my personal opinion that Mr. Wittgenstein's thesis is a work of genius; but, be that as it may, it is certainly well up to the standard required for the Cambridge degree of 'Doctor of Philosophy.'" When Moore retired as professor, Wittgenstein was his replacement. In the *Autobiography*, Moore mentions that he was "glad to think" that Wittgenstein was his successor.

Philosophy

Moore was only thirty years old in 1903, when he wrote two pieces that revolutionized philosophy. The effect of these works continues until today. The first of these was a book, *Principia Ethica*, and the second was a paper, "The Refutation of Idealism." In *Principia* he defended a type of "moral realism," the notion that moral judgments are either true or false. In support of this position, Moore developed a powerful argument against what he diagnosed as "the naturalistic fallacy." The fallacy, according to Moore's account, consists in trying to give a definition of a moral concept, *good,* in nonmoral terms. According to Moore, "propositions about the good are all of them synthetic and never analytic." Thus, such propositions as "pleasure is the only good," or "The good is the desired," are synthetic and hence their predicates do not capture the meaning of "good." The result applies to any "naturalistic" property, such as preference, desire, or utility. The argument concludes that goodness is a simple property and is therefore not definable. Moreover, since physical science deals with naturalistic properties, no scientific account of goodness, and therefore of morality, is possible. There cannot be an "empirical," correct theory of morality on this analysis. The book was important for another reason. In emphasizing the need to clarify the meanings of such key concepts as "good," "the good," "ought," and "right," it began a tradition of metaethics that governed moral philosophy for most of the century.

His "Refutation of Idealism" was the first in a series of papers he wrote during his long career that dealt with perception and knowledge. These papers attacked two doctrines that Moore felt were antithetical to common sense, idealism and skepticism. The "Refutation of Idealism" was wholly concerned with the first of these topics. Moore argued against Berkeley's idealist thesis that every object is a composite of ideas and therefore depends for its existence on being perceived (*esse is percipi*). Instead, he asserted that the act of perceiving must be distinguished from the object perceived. So though the *act* of perceiving a blue patch is mind dependent, there is no reason to believe that the patch or its color is. The notion that a patch could exist unperceived is thus a form of realism, a philosophy that Moore in his later papers continued to assert and that changed the intellectual climate in Anglo-American philosophy, which up to Moore's work had been dominated by various forms of idealism. With this essay, and his later pungent criticisms of constructive metaphysics, Moore did more than any other person to undermine the influence of Kantianism and Hegelianism in twentieth-century Anglo-American thought. As we have seen above, Moore directly influenced Russell in this respect.

Moore's treatment of skepticism

Although epistemology was one of Moore's two main interests, and, as he grew older, his dominant interest, he never wrote a book in this area. In 1953, at the urging of John Wisdom, he published in book form a series of lectures that he had originally given in 1911. The work is called *Some Main Problems of Philosophy.* Though it contains some ideas that are similar to those he was developing two decades later, his later philosophy is much more original and profound. These later writings fall into two (sometimes overlapping) categories: those defending certainty against probabilists, mitigated and radical skeptics, relativists, pragmatists, and conventionalists; and those defending the existence of sense-data. His most important papers in the former category are "A Defense of Common Sense" (1925), "Proof of an External World" (1939), "Four Forms of Skepticism" (1940), and "Certainty" (1941). His major papers concerning sense-data theory are "The Status of Sense-Data," (1913–14), "Some Judgments of Perception" (1918), "A Defense of Common Sense, Part IV" (1925), and "Visual Sense-Data" (1957). This last essay was his last published paper, appearing just a year before his death.

These papers represent a curious collection. In the essays dealing with common sense Moore is basically an anti-Cartesian, and in those defending an unusual version of sense-data theory he is a Cartesian, writing in the tradition of Locke, Berkeley, Hume, and Russell. Though in this sense he can be identified with these writers, it would be a mistake to describe him as an empiricist. To be sure, like the empiricists he rejected any form of pure rationalism, idealism, or speculative metaphysics; but he also rejected the empiricist doctrines that contingent propositions are never certain, and that science and science alone is the key to reality. He is perhaps better characterized as inheriting and developing the commonsense tradition of Thomas Reid, the great eighteenth-century contemporary and critic of Hume. But even this statement would require qualification, since in "Visual Sense-Data," his last paper, he defended a form of the representative realism found in Locke.

"A Defense of Common Sense"

Wittgenstein told Moore that in his judgment this was Moore's greatest paper, an assessment that is widely shared. It is one of the most influential essays written by any philosopher in the twentieth century. It is divided into four parts. The first part describes what Moore calls the "Common Sense View of the World." It is this view that is posed against any form of radical skepticism and which, as the title indicates, he wishes to defend. Part 2 of the paper rejects idealism. Moore states that there is no good reason to suppose that every physical fact is logically dependent on some mental fact. He takes this claim to be part of the commonsense view. Part 3 rejects any form of religion as being part of the commonsense view. He states that there is no good reason to suppose all material things are created by God, or to suppose there is a God, or that we shall continue to exist and be conscious after the death of our bodies. Part 4 is, along with part 1, one of the most discussed pieces of philosophy in this period. In this section, Moore draws a distinction between propositions he knows to be true with certainty (as in part 1) and what he calls the "correct analysis" of such propositions. In this part he discusses direct realism, representative realism, and phenomenalism as theories about the correct analysis of such propositions, and finally opts (though reluctantly) for a form of representative realism. There is a hint of skepticism in this section, since Moore claims that nobody knows what the correct analysis of such propositions is. This part of the paper had an enormous influence in generating what became one of the preeminent ways of doing philosophy among Anglo-American philosophers, namely, the approach later called "philosophical analysis." Let us concentrate on part 1, since this is directly relevant to his rejection of skepticism.

Moore presents the Common Sense View of the World in two steps.

(1) He first gives a list of propositions that he claims to know with certainty to be true. He divides this list into two parts. Examples from the first part are:

- "There exists at present a living human body which is my body."
- "This body was born at a certain time in the past, and has existed continuously ever since, though not without undergoing changes; it was, for instance, much smaller when it was born, and for some time afterward, than it is now."
- "Ever since it was born it has been either in contact with or not far from the surface of the earth, and at every moment since it was born there have also existed many other things having shape and size in three dimensions from which it has been at various distances."
- "But the earth had existed also for many years before my body was born; and for many of these years, also, large numbers of human bodies had, at every moment been alive on it."

An example from the second part is:

- "I am a human being, and I have, at different times since my body was born, had many different experiences, of each of many different kinds: e.g., I have often perceived both my own body and other things which formed parts of its environment, including other human bodies."

Let us call this two-part complex statement "Truism 1."

Moore now states that "I now come to the single truism which, as will be seen, could not be stated except by reference to the whole list of truisms just given in I." He calls this "Truism 2." This states that each of *us* (meaning by "us" the same as "very many human beings") have frequently known propositions about themselves which he stated in Truism 1 he knew about himself. Truism 2 is, then, what he means by the Common Sense View of the World.

Moore makes twelve remarkable statements about these two propositions:

- They are obvious truisms.
- In his own opinion he knows them to be true with certainty.
- They are wholly true.
- What they mean is what is ordinarily meant.
- They entail the existence of physical objects and the reality of physical space.
- They have the property that if they are not true, then no philosopher has ever existed and none could therefore have held that no proposition belonging to Truism 2 is true.
- No philosopher has consistently supported a position incompatible with 2, e.g., by alluding to the existence of other philosophers or the human race the truth of 2 is being presupposed.
- He finds it strange that philosophers should assert propositions inconsistent with what they know to be true.
- He does not know the propositions in 1, and the Truism 2, to be true directly, but on the basis of other propositions that are evidence for them. But he does not know exactly what the evidence is.

- We all know many propositions to be true without knowing how we know them to be true.
- In holding 2 to be true, he is holding the Common Sense View of the World to be *wholly* true in certain fundamental aspects. He also claims that *all* philosophers have agreed with him about this.
- Any philosopher who holds views incompatible with the Common Sense View of the World is thus ipso facto mistaken. He thus implies we can reject any such view once we know it is inconsistent with the Common Sense View of the World.

Moore's essay hit the philosophical world like a bombshell. If no proposition belonging to the Common Sense View of the World is true then it follows that no philosopher has ever existed, and therefore that no philosopher could have held that no such proposition is true. He states that he is more certain that some philosophers have existed and have held some views than any claim to the effect that the Common Sense View is false. He draws the shocking conclusion that any philosophical theory running counter to the Common Sense View can be rejected wholesale without any detailed examination of its arguments.

In this essay, Moore goes on to attack radical skepticism. He asserts that skepticism of that sort is self-contradictory. When a skeptic says, "No human being has ever known of the existence of other human beings," the skeptic is making a statement about human beings and about human knowledge in general. Such a statement entails that the skeptic knows that other human beings now exist and have existed in the past. Accordingly, that person knows the very things which, according to this theory, no human being has ever known. The theory can thus be dismissed as self-refuting.

Criticisms of Moore

The philosophical literature on this paper is so vast that it is impossible to summarize the main arguments for and against Moore's view. Let us pick two criticisms from this gamut of objections.

The first states that Moore presupposes exactly that which is at issue, namely, that he knows a group of propositions to be true with certainty. But this statement is a mere assertion and is not supported by any argument. It is especially suspicious since Moore admits that he does not know how he knows these statements to be true, but states that it is on the evidence of other statements. His further admission that he does not know what this evidence is strikes his critics as equally peculiar. Without such supporting reasons, they say that Moore produces a host of unsupported assertions that we have no particular reason to believe. Like anyone else, Moore could be mistaken that he has spent most of all of his life at or near the surface of the earth. Perhaps, while asleep, he was removed by others from the surface. In that case, he would have been mistaken. More generally, it is always possible that Moore is dreaming that he knows these propositions; and if so, it follows that he cannot know what he claims to know.

The second objection is found in Wittgenstein's *On Certainty*. Wittgenstein states that Moore's so-called truisms are really not self-evident at all, but are peculiar utterances. Generally speaking, Wittgenstein argues, a statement lacks a conceptual point and therefore is a special kind of nonsense if it is used to say something that everyone already knows and which the speaker knows that they know. If, in perfect light and in the company of people who are not suffering from any sort of mental illness, I were to look at a dog and say without any special point being at stake, "That is a dog," I would be saying something that is a species of nonsense. A significant utterance presupposes that the speaker is trying to communicate some information to the auditor that he, the speaker, assumes the auditor does not know. But if the auditor already knows what the speaker knows, and the speaker knows that this is so, then it is pointless to make such a remark. Moore's so-called truisms are like this: to say that one knows that the earth is very old, that there are other human beings in one's environment, and so forth, is to say things everyone knows. These utterances thus do not say anything sensible and accordingly do not constitute a refutation of skepticism. Wittgenstein agrees with Moore that skepticism is mistaken, but thinks that Moore's refutation will not do. Let us now see what Wittgenstein himself proposes.

LUDWIG WITTGENSTEIN (1889-1951)

Life

Wittgenstein was one of the greatest philosophers of his time. An unusual personality, he avoided publicity and spent months, even years, working in isolated places in Norway and Ireland. Yet he had a forceful, charismatic personality that exerted a great influence over others. H. G. von Wright, the author of the famous *Biographical Sketch* (1982), writes about him as follows:

> Just as there were many groundless legends concerning Wittgenstein's life and personality, so there grew up much unsound sectarianism among his pupils. This caused Wittgenstein much pain. He thought that his influence as a teacher was, on the whole, harmful to the development of independent minds in his disciplines. I am afraid that he was right. And I believe that I can partly understand why it should be so. Because of the depth and originality of his thinking, it is very difficult to understand Wittgenstein's ideas and even more difficult to incorporate them into one's own thinking. At the same time the magic of his personality and style was most inviting and persuasive. To learn from Wittgenstein without coming to adopt his forms of expression and catchwords and even to imitate his tone of voice, his mien and gestures was almost impossible. The danger was that the thoughts should deteriorate into a jargon. The teaching of great men often has a simplicity and naturalness which makes the difficult appear easy to grasp. Their disciples usually become, therefore, insignificant epigones. The historical significance of such men does not manifest itself in their disciples but through influences of a more indirect, subtle, and often unexpected kind.
>
> Wittgenstein's most characteristic features were his great and pure seriousness and powerful intelligence. I have never met a man who impressed me so strongly in either respect.[5]

The profound effect that Wittgenstein had on his acquaintances and then later on the entire philosophical world perhaps has its closest parallel in the life of Socrates. As von Wright indicates, he was idolized by those who studied with him. Yet this was a comparatively closed circle, so his reputation and influence for much of his career were only local. Socrates published even less in his lifetime than Wittgenstein did in his—as far as scholars know, absolutely nothing. Yet he was revered as Wittgenstein was by a small coterie of admirers. Unlike Wittgenstein, who was not a public figure, Socrates was widely known to the Athenian public and, through the writings of Plato, was eventually to become a legend for all time. During his lifetime, Wittgenstein published only the *Tractatus Logic-Philosophicus* (1922)—a title proposed by Moore as a substitute for the original German, *Logisch-philosophische Abhandlung*—and a brief paper, "Some Remarks on Logical Form," in 1929. All the works for which he is now famous, *Philosophical Investigations*, *Remarks on Colour*, *Zettel*, *On Certainty*, *Vermischte Bemerkungen*, *Remarks on the Foundations of Mathematics*, *Last Writings on the Philosophy of Psychology*, and *Lectures and Conversations on Aesthetics, Psychology and Religious Belief*, were published after his death. As a result of these studies, his approach to philosophical problems has altered the conceptual landscape of the century. No philosopher has been so intensively studied and imitated. His contributions have transcended philosophy and have had an enormous impact in literature, psychology, linguistics, sociology, and anthropology. He has become the "intellectual cult figure" of the second half of the century.

Despite the isolation in which he lived for so long, his life is fascinating and it is not surprising that there now exists an extensive biographical literature about it. To obtain a grasp of this unusual person one should begin with two recent biographies, *Wittgenstein: A Life. Young Ludwig 1889–1921* (1988), by Brian McGuinness; and *Ludwig Wittgenstein: The Duty of Genius* (1990), by Ray Monk. There are in addition many other works: such as *Wittgenstein*, by W. W. Bartley III, which is a highly controversial biography because of its contention that Wittgenstein was a promiscuous homosexual. There is a novel by Bruce Duffy, *The World As I Found It* (1987), which is a somewhat scurrilous account of Wittgenstein's personal interactions, including those involving Russell and Moore. Norman Malcolm's *Ludwig Wittgenstein: A Memoir* (1984) contains G. H. von Wright's *Biographical Sketch.* Both of these are by distinguished philosophers who interacted with Wittgenstein on virtually a daily basis. Finally, there is Rush Rhees's *Recollections of Wittgenstein*

(1984). This is a collection of essays by persons who knew Wittgenstein very well. For a less flattering portrait of Wittgenstein see the essay by Fania Pascal, "Wittgenstein: A Personal Memoir." Given the complexity of his life we cannot here explore it in detail. But we shall add a few words before proceeding to speak about his philosophy.

Wittgenstein was born in Vienna into a family of Jewish descent. His grandfather had converted to Protestantism and his mother was a Roman Catholic, the religion into which Wittgenstein was baptized. His father was a wealthy industrialist and his mother was a person with a strong cultural background. Nearly all the children were musically gifted. Wittgenstein's brother, Paul, was a distinguished pianist who lost his right arm in World War I and for whom Ravel wrote the "Piano Concerto for the Left Hand Alone."

Wittgenstein's early interests lay in engineering and mathematics. In the summer of 1908 he became a research student in the engineering department at the University of Manchester where, under the tutelage of Theodor von Kármán, he experimented with the use of jet propulsion for airplanes. His reading of Russell's *Principles of Mathematics* of 1903 stimulated his interest in the foundations of mathematics. He approached Gottlob Frege in Jena, asking if he could study with him, but Frege suggested he return to England to work with Russell, who at that time was in the forefront of the field, having (with A. N. Whitehead) just completed the third volume of *Principia Mathematica.* He was at Cambridge for about two years, until the outbreak of the First World War, when he returned to enter the Austrian army.

His military career lasted for the entire war and he saw considerable combat. In 1918 he was captured by the Italians and imprisoned near Monte Cassino. In his rucksack at that time he had a copy of the *Tractatus*, which he had completed during a leave of absence in 1918. Wittgenstein felt that with this work he had solved all philosophical problems, and decided to abandon philosophy for other activities. For the next six years he taught grammar school in a tiny village in Lower Austria, but ran into difficulties with the pupils and their parents and resigned. He then decided to build a house in Vienna for his sister, Gretl. This extraordinary building, very austere and simple, is now a national Austrian monument.

In 1928 Wittgenstein heard a lecture by the Dutch intuitionistic mathematician L. J. Brouwer, which stimulated him to think about the foundations of mathematics and logic again. The result was a decision to return to England and to register as a research student— an ironic situation given that many of his peers already considered him one of the greatest living philosophers. After Moore retired in 1939 he replaced him as professor at Cambridge, but, given his restless character, he was unhappy in a formal academic position and resigned in 1947. From that time until his death he worked at his research. The volume of material he wrote after his return to Cambridge is incredible: According to recent estimates, it amounts to ninety-five volumes, not all of it strictly philosophical, and some of it alternative versions of the same texts. And, as mentioned, none of it was ever published in his lifetime. Wittgenstein could have had no inkling that he would become the most important philosopher of the century.

Philosophy

There is considerable debate by commentators about the relationship between Wittgenstein's early philosophy (i.e., that of the *Tractatus*) and his later philosophy (i.e., those materials he wrote after returning to Cambridge in 1929). The three main works in his later philosophy are *Philosophical Investigations*, *Zettel*, and *On Certainty*. The debate is whether there is general continuity between his early philosophy and the later philosophy, or whether the latter represents a rupture and radical departure from the former. A majority of scholars favor the latter position, though it is often modified by pointing out that some of Wittgenstein's important ideas are the same throughout his career, so that it depends on how much emphasis one puts on these particular elements in any given interpretation of the relationship. A strong argument in favor of the idea that the later philosophy radically differs from the earlier and indeed amounts to a repudiation of it comes from three essays Moore wrote in the early thirties. Moore attended lectures given by Wittgenstein in this period and took careful notes. These essays were published under the title, "Wittgenstein's Lectures in 1930–33." In these lectures Moore quotes Wittgenstein as stating that he had found a "new method" of doing philosophy. The clear implication is that the new method is to be contrasted with his old method, that is, the kind of philosophy he was doing before his return to Cambridge. Here is what Moore writes:

> He said that what he was doing was a "new subject" and not merely a stage in a "continuous development"; that there was now, in philosophy, a "kink" in the "development of human thought," comparable to that which occurred when Galileo and his contemporaries invented dynamics; that a "new method" had been discovered, as had happened when "chemistry was developed out of alchemy"; and that it was now possible for the first time that there should be "skilful" philosophers, though of course there had in the past been "great" philosophers.
>
> He went on to say that, though philosophy had now been "reduced to a matter of skill," yet this skill, like other skills, is very difficult to acquire. One difficulty was that it required a "sort of thinking" to which we are not accustomed and to which we have not been trained—a sort of thinking very different from what is required in the sciences. And he said that the required skill could not be acquired merely by hearing lectures: discussion was essential. As regards his own work, he said it did not matter whether his results were true or not: what mattered was that "a method had been found."[6]

As we shall see below, the new method is essentially contrasted with the method of the *Tractatus*, and amounts to a renunciation of the main doctrine of the latter, the so-called picture theory. On that view, meaning is determined by a one-to-one correspondence between the elements of language and the ingredients of the world. According to the *Tractatus*, meaning is thus a function of a mapping relationship, an isomorphism between language and reality. But the later philosophy disavows that notion: now it is context, use, and the function of linguistic expressions in social interactions that are the sources of meaning. So the two views differ importantly in this respect. Yet one of the philosophical topics about which Wittgenstein's views remained constant is skepticism. Unlike many philosophers, who took the skeptic to be saying something sensible but false, namely, that knowledge and certainty are unattainable, Wittgenstein contended that skepticism attempts to say that which cannot be said and is a special form of nonsense. In the *Tractatus*, for example, we find a clear expression of this point of view. Wittgenstein writes:

> 6.5 For an answer which cannot be expressed the question too cannot be expressed. *The riddle* does not exist.
>
> If a question can be put at all, then it can *also* be answered.
>
> 6.51 Scepticism is *not* irrefutable, but palpably senseless, if I would doubt where a question cannot be asked. For doubt can only exist where there is a question; a question only where there is an answer, and this only where something *can* be said.[7]

The philosophical task on his interpretation is thus not to provide a counterargument to the effect that certainty is achievable, or to attempt to prove, as Moore did, that the external world exists, but rather to show why skepticism is senseless. This point of view is continued in sections 243 to 275 in *Philosophical Investigations*, which contains one of Wittgenstein's most famous "treatments" of skepticism. This is his so-called Private Language Argument. That Wittgenstein is said to be producing an "argument" is perhaps misleading. He is showing, rather, that the Cartesian model of the mind and the skepticism it suggests embody notions, such as that of a private language, which are special kinds of nonsense.

According to the model, each human being is directly aware of his own sensations, such as pains, thoughts, and desires; whereas the thoughts of others are apprehended only indirectly and via the intermediation of one's private sensations. This "model" of the human mind suggests that each of us uses a private language to refer to our own pains, thoughts, and desires. The point of Wittgenstein's analysis is to show that such a conception is incomprehensible. It presupposes that each person could develop his own (let us say) pain language, and only he or she could know what its words meant or referred to. Wittgenstein says that such a conception does not describe a *language* because every language requires that its rules allow for mistakes and the correction of mistakes. But such a "private language" would lack this requirement; one could never know whether one had on different occasions correctly denoted the same sensation or not. So its "rules" would not really be rules. Indeed, if they were, anybody could learn them and thus the language, like any language, would be public. Hence, the notion that there could be such a language is not sustainable. Accordingly, the skeptical idea that each of us could be completely encapsulated in the circle of his or her own ideas is not a sensible notion, and is to be rejected *tout court*. One of Wittgenstein's most powerful points in this connection is that on the skeptic's view one could never explain how human social intercommunication via language is possible, that is, that sensation language is public and is understood by others. When I say, "I am in pain," ordinary persons understand what I mean. That such public discourse is not only possible but is an everyday occurrence shows how deviant the skeptic's view is.

In his last monograph, *On Certainty*, Wittgenstein develops an even more general refutation of skepticism. In this work he focuses on the skeptic as a kind of "obsessive doubter," a person who, via such arguments as the Dream Hypothesis and the Demon Hypothesis, is willing to doubt any claim to knowledge. Wittgenstein now argues that what the skeptic is calling "doubt" is not really a case of doubt at all. Again, that which the skeptic wishes to say using the terminology of doubt cannot be said. As he writes:

> A doubt that doubted everything would not be a doubt.
> A doubt without an end is not even a doubt.[8]

To understand the full import of Wittgenstein's attack on skepticism and its conception of doubt we must describe, even if only briefly, the role that his new method plays in his approach. This new method emphasizes that language gets "its life" from its use in communal interaction. It is a fact that people communicate with one another about an infinite variety of things. The question is: How is such communication possible? Wittgenstein's answer makes use of a new concept, the notion of a "language game." Communication takes place within a language game. This is not a term that is found in the earlier philosophy and its occurrence is taken by many commentators to be strong evidence that the later philosophy represents a deeper and more sophisticated type of thinking than the earlier work. He also describes a language game as a "form of life."

Entry 23 in *Philosophical Investigations* is one of the key passages that explains these notions. Here is what he writes:

> 23. But how many kinds of sentence are there? Say assertion, question, and command?—There are *countless* kinds: countless different kinds of use of what we call "symbols," "words," "sentences." And this multiplicity is not something fixed, given once for all; but new types of language, new language-games, as we may say, come into existence and others become obsolete and get forgotten. (We can get a *rough picture* of this from the changes in mathematics).
>
> Here the term "language game" is meant to bring into prominence the fact that the speaking of language is part of an activity, or of a form of life
>
> Review the multiplicity of language-games in the following examples, and in others:
>
> Giving orders, and obeying them—Describing the appearance of an object, or giving its measurements—Constructing an object from a description (a drawing)—Reporting an event—Speculating about an event—Forming and testing a hypothesis—Presenting the results of an experiment in tables and diagrams—Making up a story; and reading it—Play-acting—Singing catches—Guessing riddles—Making a joke; telling it—Solving a problem in practical arithematic—Translating from one language into another—Asking, thanking, cursing, greeting, praying.
>
> It is interesting to compare the multiplicity of tools in language and of the ways they are used, the multiplicity of kinds of word and sentence, with what logicians have said about the structure of language (including the author of the *Tractatus Logico-Philosophicus*).[9]

By "language game" and "form of life," Wittgenstein means those everyday activities in which all of us participate. This is daily life in which we do such things as tell jokes, solve practical problems, write history, shop, call others on the telephone, and so forth. In each of these activities we are using language in the process of interacting with others. Note that in this entry Wittgenstein criticizes his previous view in the *Tractatus* as being the product of a *logician*, comparing it with the view generated by his new method. His overall notion here is that the Cartesian model, with its subjective point of view and skeptical implications, cannot possibly explain all these differing uses of language. Its viewpoint is first-person only. He is emphasizing with the examples he gives that many of these "uses" are interpersonal, such as giving orders and obeying them, reporting an event, and making a joke and telling it. On the Cartesian picture such uses cannot be explained. Its model is too simple. Indeed, the point of referring to language games is to avoid all types of philosophical model building—i.e., theorizing. Cartesianism is just such a theory. Such theories oversimplify the complexities of daily life and are ultimately misleading with respect to the way the world is. So the basic criticism of the Cartesian model is that it rests on a conception of a *language* that is not a language at all, and accordingly is a conception that lacks sense. And this criticism is then generalized to apply to the skeptic as an "obsessive doubter."

There are two problems with the conception of doubt incorporated in the Cartesian model. The first is that doubting is always considered an inner psychological state. One can thus in principle conceal one's doubts from everyone else. Wittgenstein rejects this view. He shows that doubt is a part of a set of practices similar to the playing of certain games: it is a special kind of language game. It is like playing baseball. One cannot play baseball by simply looking inward—one must instead act in ways that are nonpersonal, following objective rules, and thus functioning as a member of a community. Doubting exhibits many of these same features. Intuitively one may think of doubt as an inward state, something like a felt sensation. But clearly a person could doubt this or that statement without feeling anything at all. Wittgenstein does not deny that sometimes one in doubt may feel something, a certain feeling akin to hesitation, for example. But his point is that it would be a mistake to identify doubting with any sensation. The game of doubting —that is, what people normally do—is quite different. It might consist in examining records, questioning persons, checking newspaper files, and so forth. Such a complex, public process is what Wittgenstein means by saying that doubting belongs to the language game.

Now contrast that open process with obsessive skeptical doubt. Wittgenstein asks us to consider this example:

> It would be as if someone were looking for some object in a room;
> he opens a drawer and doesn't see it there then he closes it again,

waits, and opens it once more to see if perhaps it isn't there now, and keeps on like that. He has not learned to look for things.[10]

According to Wittgenstein, the activity of opening the drawer, looking without finding anything, and *doing it over and over again* is senseless. This is the kind of senselessness that skepticism exhibits. The person looking for an object has not learned how to play "the game of looking." This is a game we all learn from childhood. The point is that after a try or two we realize the object is not there. To do this over and over again is a sign of mental illness. Obsessive (i.e., philosophical) skepticism is like that. Nothing for the skeptic will count as evidence; so no matter what evidence is produced he will continue to doubt. His activity thus lacks point. As Wittgenstein puts it, "skeptical doubt is not a case of real doubt." Real doubt, in principle, must come to closure. But obsessive doubt does not. It just goes on and on. This is why Wittgenstein says it is senseless. On the positive side, Wittgenstein lists many cases where we do know this or that, and can be certain of it. Like Moore, he is thus a defender of certitude, but his approach to skepticism is entirely different. Moore credits the skeptic with having a legitimate and sensible position, but thinks it is mistaken because he (Moore) can assure the skeptic that he does know this or that, and indeed can even prove there is an external world. But for Wittgenstein, Moore is giving too much away. Skepticism does not have to be met by counterargument. It just has to be shown to be without substance. His technique is directed toward showing that nothing has been said by the skeptic that needs be contested.

Criticism of Wittgenstein

Wittgenstein's views have been criticized both from a standpoint of internal consistency and from an external standpoint. With respect to internal criticisms the main objection is that though Wittgenstein disavows theorizing and what he calls "explanation" in philosophy in fact his views amount to exactly such a theory. He is putting forth a view about the nature of philosophy and a counterposition to it. His idea that we must avoid theorizing in philosophy is thus a countertheory and is inconsistent with his professed position. Since this professed position presupposes exactly the view that it claims should be avoided, it cannot be accepted.

These critics point out that in the *Tractatus*, Wittgenstein actually expressed this same objection to what he was doing. In the penultimate entry, he writes:

> My propositions are elucidatory in this way: he who understands me finally recognizes them as senseless, when he has climbed out through them, on them, over them. (He must, so to speak, throw away the ladder, after he has climbed up on it.)
>
> He must surmount these propositions; then he sees the world rightly.[11]

The critics say these comments can be applied to the later philosophy as well. The difference in the early work is that Wittgenstein recognized that he was doing philosophy while regarding philosophy as nonsense. In the later writings, he is theorizing just as most philosophers do, while advancing the view that theorizing is senseless. He is thus, without knowing it, hoist upon his own petard.

A second criticism is external. It contends that Wittgenstein, who wishes to avoid generalization (and theorizing) in favor of particular examples as described in particular language games, is guilty of overgeneralizing. Persons who charge Wittgenstein with this failure are those who favor theory. They might agree with Wittgenstein that there are many bad, even outlandish theories, but from that fact it does not follow that theorizing is always to be avoided. Like all human activities, some theories are better than others. There is thus no reason in principle why in philosophy there cannot be correct theories just as there are in the physical and social sciences. In philosophy one can develop all sorts of theories: for example, about the logical relationships that must hold between statements if arguments are to be sound, about the conditions that must be satisfied if one can be said to have knowledge, about what constitutes a good society, and so forth. Some of these will clearly be better than others, and some may indeed be true. This objection to Wittgenstein thus contends that one should look at each theory on a case-by-case basis to see whether that particular theory withstands criticism or not.

Accordingly, Wittgenstein's wholesale rejection of theorizing must itself be rejected.

JACQUES DERRIDA (1930–)

Life

Our fourth contemporary thinker, Jacques Derrida, is a radical skeptic. But unlike nearly all of the modern skeptics we have examined in this work, his antecedents do not come from the Cartesian tradition. Indeed, like Wittgenstein, he is an anti-Cartesian. His intellectual roots are to be found in the German and Austrian traditions of G. W. F. Hegel, Martin Heidegger, and Edmund Husserl. These philosophers, like Moore and Wittgenstein, were antiskeptics. Though his philosophical terminology exhibits resonances of theirs, his views are in strong opposition to the kind of "dogmatism" he feels they espouse. But Derrida's assault on dogmatism is even wider ranging. He attacks some of the most stalwart defenders of certainty in the Anglo-American tradition as well: Wittgenstein, Austin, and John Searle among them.

Derrida was born in Algeria of a Jewish family, but has spent most of his life in France. He is unquestionably—and in an interesting sense—the most controversial figure we have discussed in this book. Unlike Russell, who generated public opposition to his political views, but whose philosophical credentials were never challenged even by those who disagreed with his various doctrines, Derrida is wholly unknown to the general public. The controversy and opposition to him comes entirely from within the academic community. In part, but to a lesser extent, the opposition is from those who contend he is not a philosopher at all and that, despite his claim to be one, his work belongs to literature or film studies or sociology and not to philosophy. But a still more serious opposition, also generated within the academic philosophical community, challenges the quality of his work itself. Here the claim is that this work is poor, and indeed that Derrida may well be a charlatan, a fake posing as an intellectual. In 1992 Derrida was a candidate to receive an honorary degree from Cambridge University in England. This proposal was greeted with alarm by a distinguished group of philosophers who generated substantial opposition to the idea. Besides contacting colleagues at Cambridge, they expressed their reservations in the press. Here quoted verbatim is the letter they wrote to the London *Times* and which was printed in the May 9, 1992, issue of that newspaper:

> Sir, The University of Cambridge is to ballot on May 16 on whether M Jacques Derrida should be allowed to go forward to receive an honorary degree. As philosophers and others who have taken a scholarly and professional interest in M Derrida's remarkable career over the years, we believe that the following might throw some needed light on the public debate that has arisen over this issue.
>
> M Derrida describes himself as a philosopher, and his writings do indeed bear some of the marks of writings in that discipline. Their influence, however, has been to a striking degree almost entirely in fields outside of philosophy, in departments of film studies, for example, or of French and English literature.
>
> In the eyes of philosophers, and certainly among those working in leading departments of philosophy throughout the world, M Derrida's work does not meet accepted standards of clarity and rigour.
>
> We submit that, if the works of a physicist (say) were similarly taken to be of merit primarily by those working in other disciplines, this would be in itself sufficient grounds for casting doubt upon the idea that the physicist in question were a suitable candidate for an honorary degree. M Derrida's career had its roots in the heady days of the 60's, and his writings continue to reveal their origins in that period. Many of them seem to consist in no small part of elaborate jokes and puns ("logical phallusies" and the like) and M Derrida seems to us to have come close to making a career out of what we regard as translating into the academic sphere tricks and gimmicks similar to those of the Dadaists or the concrete poets.
>
> Certainly he has shown considerable originality in this respect. But again, we submit, such originality does not lend credence to the idea that M Derrida is a suitable candidate for an honorary degree.
>
> Many French philosophers see in M Derrida only cause for silent embarrassment, his antics having contributed significantly to the widespearead impression that contemporary French philosophy is little more than an object of ridicule.
>
> M Derrida's voluminous writings in our view stretch the normal forms of academic scholarship beyond recognition. Above

all, as every reader can very easily establish for himself (and for this purpose any page will do) his works employ a written style that defies comprehension.

Many have been willing to give M Derrida the benefit of the doubt, insisting that language of such depth and difficulty of interpretation must hide deep and subtle thoughts indeed. When the effort is made to penetrate it, however, then it becomes clear, to us at least, that, where coherent assertions are being made at all, these are either false or trivial.

Academic status based on what seem to us to be little more than semi-intelligible attacks upon the values of reason, truth and scholarship, is not, we submit, sufficient grounds for the awarding of an honorary degree in a distinguished university.

Yours sincerely,

BARRY SMITH (Editor, *The Monist*); HANS ALBERT (University of Mannheim); DAVID ARMSTRONG (Sydney); RUTH BARCAN MARCUS (Yale); KEITH CAMPBELL (Sydney); RICHARD GLAUSER (Neuchatel); RUDOLF HALLER (Graz); MASSIMO MUGNAI (Florence); KEVIN MULLIGAN (Geneva); LORENZO PENA (Madrid); WILLARD VAN ORMAN QUINE (Harvard); WOLFGAG ROD (Innsbruck); EDMUND RUNGGALDIER (Innsbruck); KARL SCHUHMANN (Utrecht); DANIEL SCHULTHESS (Neuchatel); PETER SIMONS (Salzburg); RENE THOM (Burs-sur-Yvette); DALLAS WILLARD (Los Angeles); JAN WOLENSKI (Cracow).

The opinion expressed in the letter to the *Times* is not shared universally, even by philosophers. Newton Garver, an eminent philosopher and a judicious critic, says this about Derrida:

The three books published in 1967 were an immediate success and are still read today. Derrida has since published at an awesome rate: the bibliography in Wood 1992 lists 34 books and 269 "texts." The works, as far as we have examined them, are not generally repetitive; on the contrary, the new essays discuss different texts, are constantly interesting, and maintain a stylistic ingenuity that, despite occasional obscurity and exaggeration, makes Derrida one of the distinctive stylists of the French language. One can but marvel at the astonishing productivity. While Derrida's work is difficult to classify, it is widely considered philosophical; furthermore, his graduate training was in philosophy and many of the texts he "deconstructs" belong unmistakably to the traditional corpus of philosophy. Yet philosophers have remained largely aloof.[12]

136 SKEPTICAL PHILOSOPHY FOR EVERYONE

When Garver remarks that "philosophers have remained largely aloof," he is referring to the fact that within contemporary analytic philosophy very little credence or even attention is given to Derrida's work. It is mostly in literature, in film studies, and in sociology that his work is, as one writer puts it, "taken seriously." Yet a distinguished philosopher of language, A. P. Martinich, who is mainly critical of Derrida's work nonetheless finds some aspects of it to be similar to the kinds of analyses typical of analytic philosophy.

As he says:

> He purports to show that supposedly differentiating properties of one term of the dichotomy are also properties of the other term. In this regard, Derrida's deconstructionism is similar to some of the work of W. V. Quine. In "Two Dogmas of Empiricism," Quine deconstructed the analytic/synthetic distinction by showing that each rests upon the empiricists' distinction between fact and meaning and that that distinction is untenable. In other works, he has deconstructed the distinction between philosophy and science. Quine and Derrida are similar in that their deconstructive techniques rely on internal criticisms of technical concepts. . . .[13]

A literary critic, Barbara Johnson, states that Derrida has had a "tremendous impact on contemporary theoretical thought."

Why has Derrida received such radically different evaluations? Let us suggest some answers. These will also set the stage for a discussion of his skepticism.

"Derrida's philosophy"

Since there is such a deep disagreement about whether Derrida is really a philosopher or not, we have put the term "Derrida's philosophy" in quotes at the head of this section. This leaves the debate open but at the same time will allow us to describe those views he holds that represent radical forms of skepticism. Since skepticism is generally agreed to be a philosophy, we shall henceforth speak of Derrida's philosophy without quotes. We shall begin with three features of Derrida's work that set him apart from mainstream analytic philosophy.

The first is that Derrida is basically a textual critic, whereas most analytic philosophers are concerned with problems, such as the Problem of the External World, the Other Minds Problem, the Problem of Evil, the Free Will Problem. They are less interested in the texts that discuss these problems, such as Hume's *Dialogues* or Descartes's *Meditations,* and so forth.

In saying this, we are not suggesting that these texts are of no interest at all; it is rather that the interest in them is subordinate to the problems they raise. With Derrida it is the text itself that counts. It is this to which his deconstructive method primarily applies. Derrida's view that the text is fundamental is captured by one of his most famous and most paradoxical sayings—"There is nothing outside of the text."[14]

A second feature of Derrida's writing is that it contains practically no arguments; or, even worse, if there are arguments they are disguised by his convoluted, punning, inpenetrable literary style. For analytic philosophers, argument is the essence of philosophy. The use of argument is considered virtually to be identical with rationality itself. Argument consists in giving reasons in support of a particular conclusion; in such a case one is acting according to the canons of rationality. But Derrida does not "philosophize" in this way. Consider his remark that there is nothing outside the text. Common sense and most philosophers would say that if the text is a work of fiction this may be true; but if it is a work in history or an autobiography it is not. The text of Thucydides' *History of the Peloponnesian War,* for example, is a document written in the Greek language and as such must be distinguished from the events the author was speaking about, namely a war that was fought between Athens and Sparta in the fifth century B.C.E. To say there is nothing outside the text suggests that no such war ever took place, which is absurd. One should therefore expect some sort of justification for the remark that there is nothing outside of the text. But instead of giving an argument in support of this assertion, here is what Derrida says about Rousseau's *Confessions*:

> *There is nothing outide the text.* And that is neither because Jean-Jacques' life, or the existence of Mama or Thérèse, *themselves,* is not of prime interest to us, nor because we have access to their so-called

"real" existence only in the text and we have neither any means of altering this, nor any right to neglect this limitation. All reasons of this type would already be sufficient, to be sure, but there are more radical reasons. What we have tried to show by following the guiding line of the "dangerous supplement," is that in what one calls the real life of these existences "of flesh and bone," beyond and behind what one believes can be circumscribed as Rousseau's text, there has never been anything but writing; there have never been anything but supplements, substitutive significations which could only come forth in a chain of differential references, the "real" supervening, and being added only while taking on meaning from a trace and from an invocation of the supplement, etc. And thus to infinity, for we have read, *in the text,* that the absolute present, Nature that which words like "real mother" name, have always already escaped, have never existed; that what opens meaning and language is writing as the disappearance of the natural presence.[15]

A third feature of Derrida's approach is that it lacks examples. The works of Moore, Frege, Russell, Austin, Ryle, and Wittgenstein are characterized by an abundance of examples, illustrations, cases. They support conclusions these authors draw. But that is not Derrida's style. As Newton Garver remarks:

> . . . where there is or may be a problem about understanding an abstract concept, such as "perception" or "meaning," Derrida presents other abstractions, not paradigms or clear examples of correct use or appropriate instances. The extended pun about meaning (*vouloir dire*) is based on abstract analysis, as is his comment that there never has been any perception.[16]

Sources of Derrida's philosophy

As already indicated, Derrida's views are influenced by the works of Hegel, Husserl, and Heidegger. These writers tend to have murky, difficult, technical, and impenetrable literary styles. Derrida's mode of writing belongs to this tradition. But there is another source of his views which is equally influential and will allow for some clarification of what he is trying to express. He was influenced by the famous Swiss linguist Ferdinand de Saussure (1857–1913). In his *Cours de linguistique generale* (*Course in General Linguistics*) of 1916, Saussure advanced a thesis about meaning which in analytic philosophy would be called a theory of holistic semantic meaning. According to this point of view, meaning does not reside in single linguistic units such as words or even sentences, but in the language taken as a whole. Quine is a notable, contemporary exponent of semantic holism. In "Two Dogmas of Empiricism," he writes:

> The dogma of reductionism survives in the supposition that each statement, taken in isolation from its fellows, can admit of confirmation or infirmation at all. My countersuggestion, issuing essentially from Carnap's doctrine of the physical world in the *Aufbau*, is that our statements about the external world face the tribunal of sense experience not individually but only as a corporate body.[17]

A similar view is to be found in Saussure, who states that:

> Whether we take the signified or the signifier, language has neither ideas nor sounds that existed before the linguistic system, but only conceptual and phonic differences that have issued from the system. The idea or phonic substance that a sound contains is of less importance than the other signs that surround it.[18]

These quotations illustrate that like Derrida these authors take "a language," "the corporate body," or the "linguistic system," to be the basic repository of meaning. Sentences, ideas, phonemes—i.e., subunits of the corporate body or the system—have meaning only in a parasitic or perhaps symbiotic sense. They obtain whatever meaning they have as parts of larger wholes.

Thus, according to Saussure, language is a social phenomenon, a structured system that can be analyzed both synchronically (as it exists at any particular time) and diachronically (as it changes in the course of time). He also distinguished between *parole*, or the speech of the individual person, and *langue*, or a systematic structured language such as French that exists at a given time within a particular society. The concept of *langue* led to a linguistic theory called "structuralism." It is this theory that exerted an enormous influence on Derrida. It is *langue*, or the whole language, that is the ultimate repository of meaning. Derrida's variation of the theory gives it a stronger interpretation: that meaning does not exist outside of the language. And if the language is considered a kind of "text," then no meaning exists out of the text. He infers that accordingly it makes no sense to speak of anything outside of the text.

Derrida's approach to structuralism makes use of it in the above sense while criticizing it. According to Saussure, there is a sense in which linguistic units have no intrinsic meaning but are "marked off" from other linguistic units in a kind of opposition to them. Language for Saussure is a system of differences rather than a collection of independently meaningful units. Therefore, what distinguishes a linguistic structure and gives status to its elements is a series of conceptual oppositions: good versus evil, being versus nothingness, presence versus absence, truth versus error, identity versus difference, mind versus matter, man versus woman, soul versus body, life versus death, nature versus culture, speech versus writing, and so forth. Derrida accepts this idea but then argues that such oppositions are spurious. He contends that such oppositions give a privileged position to the first term in these contrasts, that is, to man over woman, soul over body, truth over error, and mind over matter. His main point is that his "reading" of texts—his so-called deconstruction of them—is designed to show that it is a mistake to give dominance to the first linguistic unit in such contrasts.

It is at this point we encounter Derrida's radical skepticism. For to say that such theories of dominance are misleading or conceptually incoherent is to say that any given text can be interpreted in more than one way, and with various degrees of explicitness. It follows that there is no such thing as an objective or true interpretation of any text. Any reading must be allowed. Derrida's conclusion is thus in the spirit of the radical skepticism of Protagoras, who affirmed that "man is the measure of all things." This is thus a strong form of relativism with its rejection of absolutes, whether these are absolutes of understanding, meaning, or interpretation.

Criticism of Derrida

Let us set aside some of the criticisms noted above: that Derrida's work does not meet accepted standards of clarity and rigor, that it consists of tricks and gimmicks similar to those of the Dadaists, and that his written style defies comprehension.

But there are two other criticisms, one external and the other internal, that we should mention. First, the notion that nothing exists outside of the text seems to be a linguistic form of what in the theory of perception is called "phenomenalism." This, as we have explained earlier, is a view that Russell held at various times. Most philosophers consider it to be so paradoxical as not to be believable. In the theory of perception, a so-called physical object, is just a heap of actual and possible sense-data. It follows that there is no material world on such a view—only resembling and differing perceptions. Derrida's idea that nothing exists outside of the text seems similar. Even if it is true that meaning does not exist outside of or apart from a language, and that one can think of language as a kind of dissemi-nated text, it still seems unbelievable that nothing but textual mean-ings exist. Surely, words and sentences are often about "external objects," such as persons, places, and things. The criticism, then, is that Derrida seems to be advocating a form of the egocentric predica-ment that we find in strict Cartesianism. On such a view, we cannot get outside of the circle of the text, and there is no reality that exists external to it. The view is thus rejected by realists who claim it is too paradoxical to be given any credence.

A second criticism comes from within Derrida's own system. We can thus label it an "internal" criticism. According to this point of view, Derrida's project—stemming from his interest in Saussurian lin-guistics—is to develop a kind of science of writing, which he calls "grammatology." This science would systematically study the opposi-tions, mentioned above, that linguistic systems incorporate and which give preference to one of the contrasting terms, such as "man" over "woman." But the very idea that there could be such a science as grammatology presupposes the existence of a kind of objective sci-ence or logic that Derrida's approach wishes to challenge. Derrida thus finds himself in the self-defeating position of trying to account for certain systematic errors by means of the very tools which incor-porate (on his account) those very errors. It is thus not possible to show that the belief in truth over error is an error without implicitly believing in the notion of truth. As a critic has written: ". . . to show that the binary oppositions of metaphysics are illusions is also, and perhaps most importantly, to show that such illusions cannot simply in turn be opposed without repeating the very same illusion."[19] This criticism thus claims that Derrida's program is basically incoherent, since it wishes to deny the principles it must assume for its criticisms to get off ground.

CONCLUSION

In this chapter we have attempted briefly to describe some contemporary trends in philosophy in which the debate about the status of skepticism continues to be pursued actively. All these current views are of great significance for all branches of philosophy, since they concern themselves with the nature of philosophical activity itself, and the kinds of questions it is appropriate for the philosopher to raise. As we shall see, though the subject matter is different, similar but not identical assessments of the role of skepticism also arise in philosophy of religion, political theory, and ethics. We shall turn to these fields now.

NOTES

1. Bertrand Russell, "My Mental Development," in *The Philosophy of Bertrand Russell*, 3rd ed. (New York: Harper Torchbook, 1963), vol. 1, p. 5.

2. Bertrand Russell, *The Autobiography of Bertrand Russell: The Middle Years, 1914–1944* (New York: Bantam Books, 1968), pp. 319–20.

3. Bertrand Russell, *The Problems of Philosophy* (Oxford: Home University Library, 1912), p. 58.

4. Norman Malcolm, "George Edward Moore," in *Knowledge and Certainty* (Englewood Cliffs, N.J.: Prentice-Hall, 1963), pp. 163–86.

5. H. G. von Wright, "A Biographical Sketch," in Norman Malcolm, *A Memoir* (New York: Oxford, 1984), p. 17.

6. G. E. Moore, "Wittgenstein's Lectures in 1930–33," in *Philosophical Papers* (New York: Macmillan, 1959), pp. 322.

7. Ludwig Wittgenstein, *Tractatus Logico-Philosophicus* (London: Routledge & Kegan Paul, 1922), entries 6.5–6.51.

8. Ludwig Wittgenstein, *On Certainty* (Oxford: Blackwell, 1969), entries 450 and 625, respectively.

9. Ludwig Wittgenstein, *Philosophical Investigations* (Oxford: Blackwell, 1958), entry 23.

10. Wittgenstein, *On Certainty*, entry 315.

11. Wittgenstein, *Tractatus*, entry 6.54.

12. Newton Garver and S. C. Lee, *Derrida and Wittgenstein* (Philadelphia: Temple University Press, 1994), pp. 173–74.

13. A. P. Martinich, "Analytic Phenomenological Deconstruction," in *Certainty and Surface in Epistemology and Philosophical Method*, ed. A. P. Martinich and Michael James Denham White (Lewiston, N.Y.: Edwin Mellen Press, 1991), pp. 171–78.

14. Jacques Derrida, *Of Grammatology* (Baltimore: Johns Hopkins Press, 1976), pp. 158–59.

15. Ibid.

16. Garver and Lee, *Derrida and Wittgenstein*, p. 193.

17. W. V. Quine, "Two Dogmas of Empiricism," in *From a Logical Point of View* (Cambridge: Harvard University Press, 1961), p. 41.

18. Ferdinand de Saussure, *Course in General Linguistics* (New York: Philosophical Library, 1959), p. 120.

19. Barbara Johnson, *Jacques Derrida: Dissemination* (Chicago: University of Chicago Press, 1981), p. x.

RELIGIOUS BELIEF AND SKEPTICISM

Religious belief and activity go back as far as we have recorded history. Practically every group on the planet has some sort of religious tradition, some type of worship, and some sort of interpretation of the nature of the world and what people should do about it in terms of their religious beliefs.

From the beginnings of philosophy as we know it in ancient Greece, there has been some conflict between religious believers and philosophers looking for rational and scientific explanations of what is going on. Over the centuries, philosophers have been both gadflies, questioning religious beliefs and practices, and explicators, helping to codify and interpret religious beliefs and practices. In the last two centuries, many philosophers have sought to explain the nature and role of religious belief in terms of human nature, human societies, and growing human knowledge of the world. The philosophy of religion can encompass many kinds of inquiries, including those concerned with the special kind of knowledge religious believers claim to have, whether from a book, a message, a prophet, or a unique experience.

We will start our discussion by examining some problems about religious knowledge that arise within the monotheistic religions: Judaism, Christianity, and Islam. These involve claims about what happened at certain times in history, and claims about the special character of the records we have of these happenings, namely that they are *revealed* in certain ways to certain people and are of a different kind or order than other historical information.

Let us start our consideration of this subject by looking at two skeptical philosophical problems that arose during the clashes between the Roman Catholic Church and the new Protestant movements in the sixteenth and seventeenth centuries. Both problems emerge in part from the activities of the great Renaissance humanist Desiderius Erasmus.

Prior to the invention of printing, the so-called revealed messages of Judaism, Christianity, and Islam were known through manuscripts dispersed throughout Europe, North Africa, and the Middle East. With the new printing technique, texts became standardized. It is fitting for our subject that the first printed text in Europe was the Gutenberg Bible. Scholars comparing manuscripts held in various libraries began preparing "critical" editions; that is, editions that purported to establish the correct text of secular and religious works.

At the beginning of the sixteenth century, Erasmus, one of the finest scholars of his time, prepared a critical edition of the Greek text of the New Testament, the book that was supposed to have all-important special religious knowledge for Christians. Erasmus omitted the proof text about the Doctrine of the Trinity, and instead presented a footnote stating that the text did not appear in any of the early manuscripts of the New Testament that he was able to examine, nor was it mentioned by any of the early church fathers writing in the first centuries of Christian history. Erasmus's scholarly observation became a spur to investigate the history of the texts of the Bible that have come down to us, and to question whether we do in fact have an accurate text of what is supposed to be the original Word of God revealed to Moses, the prophets, and the first disciples of Jesus.

Erasmus raised many criticisms about corruption in church practices and in the lives of the clergy, but he did not join the Reformation. It is said that "Erasmus laid the egg that Luther hatched." But Erasmus found that Luther and some of the early reformers were too dogmatic about their views. The Roman Catholic Church pressed Erasmus to take a public stand and he finally did, in a published debate with Martin Luther about the freedom of the will. Erasmus claimed that the question of whether men had such freedom was so complicated and fraught with conflicts that one ought to admit that human beings could not be sure of any answer. They should follow the attitude of the ancient skeptics, suspending judgment on the question, while accepting the teachings of the church nondogmatically.

Luther was furious at his erstwhile friend and insisted that it was all important for the nature and destiny of man that *the* correct answer be found. It was too dangerous to rest undogmatically content with the church's teachings, which might be false. He cried out to Erasmus that the Holy Ghost was not a skeptic, and that humans needed certainty in their religious beliefs since the beliefs were all important in that their salvation depended upon what they believed.

The point at issue between Luther and Erasmus grew in importance as the Reformation developed in Europe. Leading thinkers on both sides saw that the central issue was that each side had a different standard or criterion for determining true religious knowledge. The Roman Catholics had as their "judge of controversies" the pope and the church councils. The Protestants appealed to Scripture and their consciences as the standard by which to measure the truth or falsity of their religious knowledge claims.

The issue so framed is one that we have seen before in the way that skepticism entered into intellectual concerns. Once a conflict of views had been delineated, one needed a criterion by which to determine which of the conflicting views was correct. But then what happens if there is no agreement as to what criterion ought to be applied? And what happens if it can be shown that the stated criterion cannot actually be applied?

The debate about the "rule of faith" and the "judge of controversies" started at the very same time that the ancient skeptical arguments of Sextus Empiricus were rediscovered and published, in the mid–sixteenth century. The first editor and translator of Sextus's *Adversus Mathematicos (Against the Dogmatists)* was a Catholic controversialist, Gentian Hervet, who was the secretary of the cardinal of Lorraine, a veteran of the theological debates with the early Calvinists in France, and a participant in the Council of Trent. In his preface to his edition of Sextus (1569), Hervet said that ancient skepticism was the perfect answer to Calvinism since by showing that nothing can be known, one would see that Calvinism cannot be known!

This skeptical tactic was developed by Michel de Montaigne and his followers and some French Catholic theologians into what they called "a new machine of war" for devastating the Protestants. The Catholic warriors would demand that their Protestant opponents reveal the source and standard for their views. The Protestant would appeal to the Bible, and then the skeptical fun would begin. How do you know which book is the Bible? How do you know what it says? How do you know what it means? How do you know what you are supposed to do about it?

The unhappy Protestant would, according to the Catholic arguers, be reduced to appealing to his inner feelings to justify his answers. And could private inner feelings be sufficient to justify breaking with the Church of Rome and risking eternal salvation? The Catholics stressed that the Protestants had to accept that their criterion of religious knowledge was subjective, within the individual believer. The Protestants accepted this but insisted that the true believer's inner feelings were divinely caused, and hence had objective validity.

The Protestants also insisted that the Catholic criterion of religious knowledge, the appeal to the pope and the decrees of church councils, was just as open to skeptical challenge. After all, the decrees of church councils were known through historical documents, open to the same sort of questioning as that raised about the Bible. How do we know that we have an accurate text? How do we know what it means? And, in one of the wilder points in this dispute over the rule of faith, a Protestant arguer, Jean La Placette, set forth what he called "the incurable skepticism of the Church of Rome." The church members based their faith on what the pope said. But how, he asked, do we know who is the pope? We have heard it said that a man living in the Vatican is the pope, but is he really? All the evidence that could be put forth could be challenged by skeptical questions about the kinds of sense-data, historical documents, and testimony that would be introduced. So La Placette contended that the Church of Rome could have at most only one secure member, the pope himself. But Cartesian doubts could be raised even for him: Was he dreaming that he was the pope? Was he being deceived by some force making him believe he was the pope? And so on.

These disputes about the rule of faith laid bare a philosophical problem for any system of religious knowledge claims, namely, what justifies accepting the claims. Within the Judeo-Christian complex of religious views, the Bible plays a special role. Even its name, "the Bible" indicates this, since the name means "the book" as distinguished from all others.

A new kind of philosophical challenge to accepting the Bible as "a" or "the" source of true religious knowledge started to come under serious questioning during the Renaissance and the centuries thereafter. The invention of printing led to standardizing the text. But it also led to trying to determine what was the *right* text. There were manuscripts in various languages going back to the early Middle Ages. There were obvious differences between the Hebrew text, the ancient Greek translation of the Hebrew text, the Septuagint, the Latin translation, the Vulgate of Saint Jerome, the ancient Aramaic paraphrases that were in use in the time of Jesus, as well as citations in ancient Jewish and Christian writings. Erasmus had shocked his contemporaries with the news that an all-important text, one that stated the Doctrine of the Trinity, was not in the earliest manuscripts of the New Testament or in any citations from early church fathers.

A monumental attempt to standardize the biblical text was the preparation of the Polyglot Bible by scholars at the new Spanish university of Alcalá de Henares. The founder of the university, Cardinal Ximines, decided to underwrite this great project—the publication of the Hebrew, Greek, Latin, and Aramaic biblical texts. It was a printing marvel in three columns—Hebrew on the left, Latin in the middle, Greek on the right—with the Aramaic paraphrase across the bottom of each page. Special printers had to be found to create the fonts and to carry through the project. More scholarly compilation of texts had to take place. Cardinal Ximines gathered together Greek and Hebrew scholars starting in 1506 to examine different manuscripts and to determine the correct text. An enormous amount of money went into the scholarly preparation, the purchase of manuscripts, and the physical printing, which was completed in 1517. One of the Greek experts wanted to put in a footnote about the Trinity passage. The cardinal decided that there would be no footnotes, just the *right* text. He offered to publish, outside of the Bible project, a book by the Greek expert on the problem of ascertaining the right text.

Scholarship over the next centuries found an enormous number of variants in the available Greek and Hebrew manuscript texts, and none of them could be considered originals, or holograph copies. The oldest manuscripts went back to the early Middle Ages, and were obviously historical documents that were copied from other, prior historical documents. One could separate out families of manuscripts which could be traced back—but not as far back as the purported authors, Moses, Ezra or Matthew, Mark, Luke, John or Paul. If one accepted this as the case, then how could anyone be sure that the copies of copies that we now possess are the true accurate texts revealed to Moses, the prophets, and the apostles?

The English Puritans in the mid–seventeenth century tried to eliminate this problem by making it an article of faith that God had preserved the biblical text throughout history, through all of its copyings, and in all of the translations of the text. Modern fundamentalists have also insisted on this. But this still leaves the problem of what, exactly, the correct biblical text is, in light of the thousands of variants; the differences between the Hebrew, Greek, and Latin texts of the same books; and the wide variety of translations in many languages.

A whole industry of scholarly research developed, studying every scrap of parchment, every ancient inscription, every archeological site in Palestine and its environs, in order to find better and better texts. In the twentieth century, the discovery of the Dead Sea Scrolls has provided a wealth of new data for the Bible scholars.

Some daring thinkers in the seventeenth century began exploring certain points in the biblical text that led them to suspect that Moses himself was not the author of the entire five books of Moses, and that the Bible itself may have had more than one author. Isaac La Peyrère, Thomas Hobbes, and Benedict de Spinoza discussed the implications of the fact that the death of Moses and events thereafter are described in Deuteronomy, one of the five books attributed to Moses. Could Moses have described his own death and events that came afterward? Spinoza, in his *Theological-Political Tractatus,* advanced the theory that the Bible should be studied in terms of its context, its possible authors, and the history of the times in which it was written. Spinoza proposed seeing the Bible, the supposed revealed Word of God, as a literary production of some human beings in ancient Palestine dealing with problems of the time. To comprehend their messages, one would need to know the Hebrew of their times, not the Hebrew of the present. Spinoza's contextualization of the Bible involved a great philosophical shift. The central religious document of Western religion could be considered not as divinely given, but as one more achievement of human activities under human circumstances. It then became a compendium of early Hebrew writings about the peculiar situation of the Israelites from the time of their escape from Egypt through the problems of the next several centuries. It was one more history of an ancient people whose relevance for the present remained to be examined separately.

A century before Spinoza, John Calvin had raised the question, How can one tell the difference in kind between the Bible and the history of Rome written by Titus Livy? Calvin pointed out that both books portrayed the histories of a people and described amazing things that had happened to them, which they thought were due to divine influences. But Calvin also insisted that the divine inspiration of the Bible showed itself so that a sincere reader could distinguish the religious nature of the Bible from the secular nature of Livy's history. One was revealed, the other was not. Spinoza contended that there was no evident divine inspiration to the biblical text itself, and that it was just one more contribution to secular literature.

At the same time that Spinoza was denying that there was a special revealed or divine character to the contents of the Bible differentiating it from all other books, a bizarre case from antiquity was being revived to put up the very problem at issue. In the third century C.E., a pagan, Apollonius of Tyana, had lived a life very much like that of Jesus of Nazareth. He had had a miraculous birth, he performed miracles, he was persecuted and killed by the authorities, and his followers expected him to return to earth again. They built churches and monuments to him. A life of Apollonius was written in the fifth century by Philostratus in Greek. In the Renaissance, this text was revived and published. By Spinoza's time, some realized that if one compared the life of Jesus with the life of Apollonius, there was a serious problem in determining that one of them lived a divine life and the other did not. The English deist Charles Blount published an English translation of the life of Apollonius and, in a very, very long footnote, included a discussion between a Jew and a Muslim trying unsuccessfully to find a way of telling whether Apollonius or Jesus was divine. Blount, who was the first to translate Spinoza's text into English, tried to show that there was no way to ascertain that biblical history portrayed some special kinds of events, and so-called Greek mythological writings did not.

If the Bible could then be seen apart from its alleged special religious status, does that tell us anything about religion? Spinoza insisted that the religious-moral message of the Bible was that one should love one's neighbor as oneself, a moral truth that rational people could figure out for themselves without all of the materials about ancient Hebrew history. The biblical form of this moral message was, according to Spinoza, for those who could not philosophize enough and who needed to be taught to obey the moral rule. Hence, biblical religion for Spinoza became a political strategy for keeping the ignorant and willful people in line in order to have a moral society. In fact, Spinoza suggested that Moses, after the Exodus, used religious stratagems to get the ancient Hebrews to accept his laws. He made them think that they were divine laws when they were actually political laws to establish a new society for the Israelites who were then outside of the Egyptian legal system.

In light of Spinoza's naturalistic interpretation of the Bible and its role in human affairs, someone anonymously wrote a book shortly after Spinoza's death called *The Three Impostors, Moses, Jesus and Mohammed, or the Spirit of Mr. Spinoza*. All three religious leaders were portrayed as having created religions in order to secure control of the societies they were in. The religions they created were essentially political programs to control people, a view that had earlier been suggested by Machiavelli and Hobbes. The studies of the anthropology, the sociology, and the social role of religions raise problems about how to connect a particular religious claim of special knowledge with what is going on in society. We will return later to ways in which religious philosophers have sought to connect documents such as the Bible with special kinds of knowledge constituting the essence of religion.

JUDEO-CHRISTIAN ATTITUDES TOWARD RELIGIOUS BELIEF

Before moving forward in time, let us consider some classical problems. In the ancient world we have evidence of two kinds of philosophical attitudes about religious beliefs and systems of the time: one raising questions within the belief systems about the claims being made; and the other criticizing kinds of beliefs other than one's own.

Within the Judeo-Christian religious worlds, one finds both some questioning about the claims of the religions and severe critiques of religious beliefs systems outside of these traditions. One of the amazing features of the Bible that has come down to us is that it includes rather severe doubts of the overall religious claims in books such as Ecclesiastes and Job.

In the latter we are presented with Job, a fine upright man who has followed all of the religious practices of ancient Judaism, and yet finds himself beset with a terrible series of personal tragedies, including the deaths of his wife and family, the ruin of his body and of his personal wealth. So, he and his friends cry out, why should a just man be punished, while all kinds of bad persons flourish?

The Job story poses a basic dilemma for believers in ancient Judaism and modern Judaism and Christianity, as long as the believers accept without question that a deity controls the world and everything that happens in it. In the discussion that comprises the biblical text of Job, all sorts of ways are explored to resolve the problem. Maybe Job is lying; maybe he is secretly wicked. Maybe he violated some divine command. Maybe he had a bad attitude. Maybe he blamed God for his misfortunes. Each of these possibilities is dismissed in the biblical text. And after the debate between Job and his friends, God appears out of a whirlwind to blame anyone who tries to judge the ways of God. God's ways are mysterious to men. Having made a philosophical resolution of the problem—what is known from then on as the Problem of Evil—the biblical discussion ends with the news by the biblical author that Job was right for not questioning God, and his friends were wrong for questioning. Job is then physically rewarded with a wife, a new family, new animals and crops, and a new and presumably better material life for believing without any explanation.

The book of Job is a philosophical shocker in the Bible, the book devoted to expositing God's relation to the world, and to humanity in particular. A fact contrary to the prevailing religious picture is offered throughout the biblical text, namely that the nonbelievers, the godless, often flourish, while the truly pious, religious persons suffer. *Why?* The philosophical question is raised and discussed at length, and then the door is slammed on any answer.

Another book of the Hebrew Bible, Ecclesiastes, seems to present the view of someone who is disillusioned with the ancient Jewish religion: "Vanity of vanities. All is vanity" (Eccles. 1:2). "There is nothing new under the sun" (Eccles. 1:2). The entire book, supposedly written by the High Priest of Jerusalem, is a dirge about the worthlessness and meaninglessness of events and developments in the human world. And when this should be enough to undermine anybody's religious convictions, the author solemnly ends his text, "Let us hear the conclusion of the whole matter. Fear God and keep his commandments, for this is the whole duty of man" (Eccles. 12:13).

The biblical narrative covering the reactions of the ancient Hebrews to a long series of disasters, including enslavement in Egypt, internal wars, capture and exile by the Babylonians, domination by other Hellenistic groups, and finally incorporation into the Roman Empire, led to a most complex series of religious practices and a conviction that the Jews, followers of the *true religion,* would be rewarded and saved by the coming of a political Messiah. Practicing religious Jews spread all over the Roman Empire from Spain,

North Africa, southern France, Italy, Greece, and the Middle East, keeping up their religious duties and awaiting the arrival of the Messiah. A small group of Jews in Palestine in the first century C.E. insisted that their leader, Jesus of Nazareth, was the expected and long awaited Messiah.

New Testament documents indicate that the early Christians sought to cast doubt on the character of Jewish expectations, and to insist that Jesus of Nazareth met the necessary conditions to be the Messiah, and that he would soon return from his demise to meet the sufficient conditions. This sounded extremely implausible to most late-first-century Jews and to Greek pagans. Paul summed up the epistemological situation very sharply in his first letter to the Corinthians,

> For it is written, I will destroy the Wisdom of the wise and will bring to nothing the understanding of the prudent.
> Where is the wise? Where is the scribe? Where is the disputer of this world? Hath not God made foolish the wisdom of this world?
> For after that in the wisdom of God the world by wisdom knew not God. It pleased God by the foolishness of preaching to save them that believe.
> For the Jews require a sign, and the Greeks seek after wisdom.
> But we preach Christ crucified unto the Jews a stumbling block, and unto the Greeks nonsense. (1 Cor. 1:1–23)

Paul saw that the central claim of Christianity would not be accepted by Jews because it did not fit in with what they expected and recognized as divine intervention in the world, and it would not be accepted by the Greeks because they could not understand it or make rational sense of it. So Christianity would have to be accepted apart from Jewish religious traditions and apart from the Greek philosophical one.

In Acts 17, a description is given of Paul's activities in Athens, where he first disputed with Jews in their synagogue and then spoke to a group of Stoic and Epicurean philosophers. He sought to convince them that they could not find God in material objects or statues, but only in the spirit. When the philosophers heard the details of his belief in a resurrected deity, they walked away.

Much pagan criticism of Judaism and of Christianity is just to comment on the strange kinds of customs, and the apparent silliness of the beliefs. Plutarch thought the Jews must regard the pig as a deity since they wouldn't eat it, and that the Christians must have been cannibals if they thought they were eating their deity. Some debates have come down to us from Christian church fathers, indicating some attempt to find common intellectual ground on which to discuss and argue the merits of the differing religious beliefs systems. And in what was to be a most influential series of texts for the Christian Middle Ages, the Alexandrian Jewish author Philo Judaeus developed a Platonic interpretation of biblical religion and offered the slogan that Plato was merely Moses speaking Greek. The creation story in Genesis and the creation myth in Plato's *Timaeus* were equated. With Philo, who wrote in Greek and not in Hebrew, a way of interpreting biblical religion philosophically, principally, and metaphysically began. And this grew and grew in the Islamic and Christian Middle Ages.

So far, we have dealt only with philosophical considerations concerning Judeo-Christian religious beliefs. Before going any further, we must also consider philosophical critiques of religious knowledge that were developed with the pagan world.

PAGAN PHILOSOPHERS AND RELIGION

Greek philosophers, even before Socrates, criticized popular religious beliefs. Xenophanes was reputed to have said that religious beliefs were anthropocentric, and if horses could draw, they would draw horse deities. Anaxagoras had pooh-poohed the possibility of divine natural forces. Greek mythology, with stories about gods eating their children and having wild sexual affairs, were scoffed at.

One of the strongest charges against Socrates at his trial was that he was teaching an un-Athenian religion to his students, and questioning the official religion.

The philosophical critiques of pagan religious knowledge are most strongly developed in the Epicurean poet Lucretius's *On the Nature of Things* and in Cicero's *On the Nature of the Gods*. Both of these works recapitulate ideas and arguments that had been made by Epicurean and skeptic philosophers for centuries.

Epicurus in the fourth century B.C.E. had argued against the possibility of any divine providential events taking place. Everything that happens is the result of the collisions of atoms moving endlessly through a universal void. In this natural physical world, all events physical and human have natural and necessary causes. So there is nothing a deity can or could do.

People who fear the gods do not understand what is actually going on. When they do come to a real understanding, they will no longer be frightened by natural events, and will no longer attribute them to some divine beings.

The Epicurean system as set forth by Lucretius is that of a complete materialist world needing no divine force or forces to explain its origin and nature. It has, over the centuries, remained the model for an antithesis to a religious picture of the world. It was referred to as "the hideous hypothesis of Epicurus." And, in fact, the Hebrew tern for "skeptic" or "unbeliever" in the Talmud is *apikuros*.

Cicero, who had studied at the Platonic Academy in Athens in the period when it was first dominated by Academic skeptics and then by Middle Platonists, wrote two lengthy dialogues presenting the teachings of the school. One is *De Academica,* which goes over the various kinds of skeptical arguments they studied; the other, *De Natura Deorum,* on the nature of the gods, is about the application of these skeptical arguments to religious beliefs. A good deal of Cicero's text looks modern and this is because it was studied extensively in the eighteenth century by deists and critics of religious argumentation such as David Hume. The three disputants in Cicero's dialogue are a Stoic, an Epicurean, and a skeptic, and the disputants in Hume's *Dialogues Concerning Natural Religion* are the historical pupils of Cicero's characters. Cicero's skeptical examination of pagan religion stressed the variation in religious beliefs, the lack of convincing evidence for various religious views, and the lack of warrant for inferring from our actual experience that there must be a providential divine force behind the scenes directing what is going on. Cicero's characters, Stoic, Epicurean, and Skeptics, insisted on the social and political value of religion. No matter how little or how inadequate the evidence for religious claims might be, the accepted religion of a society ought to be honored and accepted for the harmonious good of the political group.

It is interesting to note that both Lucretius and Cicero only dealt with pagan religious beliefs. Apparently Jewish and Christian ones were not seen as important. And at the time, the practitioners of these religions refused to accept the need for a socially acceptable religion. Rather, they insisted on the fundamental importance of their beliefs for the good of the believers and ultimately for the world, even if putting these beliefs into practice in the Roman Empire had an essential disruptive effect on the social order. In fact, early Christians saw their role as revolutionary against a corrupt society.

For our purposes, it is important to note that philosophical questions about religion were raised in antiquity. The monumental victory of Christianity over paganism pushed these questions aside. Greek philosophical ideas were used, especially those of Plato, Plotinus, and Aristotle, to provide an intellectual framework for Christian religious beliefs.

After the early modern discussions, culminating in Spinoza's critique of supernatural religion, there was a turn toward using the achievements of the new science as a way of demonstrating fundamental claims of religion. If one line of philosophical consideration of religion led to Spinoza's critique of religion, another was to bolster religious belief by stressing that its central contention, that a divine being who created the world exists, and that the best information about the natural world developed by modern science constitutes decisive evidence in this regard. In one of the psalms it is said "that the firmament showeth his handiwork" (Ps. 19:1).

In the century of the scientific revolution, the discoveries of the great mathematical order in the heavens and of the mathematical laws of physics on earth showed that the world around us was designed perfectly and must have been so designed by an intelligent designer, or God.

The proof of the existence of God, by the argument from design, appeared in ancient times in Aristotle and in the writings of the Stoics, but it gained its greatest currency and appeal as a result of the great physical and astronomical system of Sir Isaac Newton: "Nature and nature's laws lay hid in night. God said, let Newton be! and all was light."[1] Newton set forth the most complete scientific system for explaining how physical motions take place on earth and in the heavens, guided by the principle of universal gravitation. And, as Newton explained, the system had to be perfectly designed or the planets would crash into one another. Hence, the Newtonian system exhibited the great design scheme and constituted the very best argument from design.

SCIENCE AND THE ARGUMENT FROM DESIGN

This form of the argument from design, put forth by many philosophers, scientists, and theologians in the seventeenth and eighteenth centuries, was subject to a withering criticism by the Scottish philosopher David Hume in his *Dialogues Concerning Natural Religion*, published in 1779, three years after his death. Hume carefully separated revealed religion, which might claim to have special access to knowledge about God and his motives and actions, from natural religion, which gained its knowledge of the existence and nature of God from observations of the natural world. Hume presented his case in the form of a dialogue between three philosophers, a skeptic, a believer, and a follower of the argument from design. By using the dialogue form, which Hume took over from Cicero's *On the Nature of the Gods*, the subject could be debated without Hume himself having to express heretical or blasphemous views in his own name. (In fact, the question of which of the characters, Philo, Demea, or Cleanthes, actually speaks for Hume is still being debated by Humean scholars.)

Cleanthes offers the standard formulation of the argument from design:

> Look around the world, contemplate the whole and every part of it: you will find that it is nothing but one great machine, subdivided into an infinite number of lesser machines, which again admit of subdivision to a degree beyond which human sense and faculties can trace and explain. All these various machines, and even their most minute parts, are adjusted to each other with an accuracy which ravishes into admiration all men who have ever contemplated them. The curious adapting of means to ends throughout all nature resembles exactly, though it much exceeds, the production of human con-

trivance—of human design, thought, wisdom and intelligence. Since therefore the effects resemble each other, we are led to infer, by all the rules of analogy, that the causes also resemble, and that the Author of nature is somewhat similar to the mind of man, though possessed of much larger faculties proportioned to the grandeur of the work which he has executed. By this argument *a postieriori*, and by this argument alone, do we prove the existence of a Deity and his similarity to human mind and intelligence.[2]

The heart of the argument from design is to insist that the more we know about the physical, the chemical, and the biological aspects of the world, the more we see Nature as orderly and patterned. The more we study Nature, the more we are impressed by the intricate relationships of the parts of the universe to the whole, and by the general plan of the universe. Having said all of this, the next step is that we realize that the order and design that we find in the world greatly resembles the order and design that we find in human artifacts. Houses are built so that the parts, the door, the window, the floor, are perfectly adjusted to function together. A watch is perhaps a better example, where even the smallest parts are designed to function with the larger ones in order to make the whole watch work.

In the cases of human-planned objects, we can see how wisdom, thought, and intelligence are the causes of the result. So, we can also infer that what appear to be planned events and objects in the natural world should have similar cause or causes, namely, an intelligent deity who is the author or cause of the effects in the universe. And since the amount of order and design and complexity in the natural world far exceeds what human beings are capable of, then the cause of the universe must involve a much greater wisdom than humans possess.

With the progress of science since Hume's day, more and more refined versions of the argument from design are offered by people who know about cellular and molecular biology, about the latest findings in astrophysics, about advances in understanding subnuclear particles, and about advances in knowledge of how the brain works. Many more intricate kinds of order are being discovered, from the furthest reaches of modern astronomy to the tiniest features of the subatomic world. So the suggestion that it is all planned keeps being restated in terms of the latest scientific discoveries. The order that followed after the big bang and the kinds of evolving features of living beings, from the simplest and most ancient to the most complex and most recent, provides new material for new presentations of the argument from design.

Over two hundred years ago, Hume raised some basic difficulties about the merits of the argument from design and about what it could prove at best, which still seem to have great force. Hume's skeptical personage, Philo, first pointed out that the analogy between how human artifacts are made and how worlds are made is not really a good one. In the case of human activity, we often observe the connection between human planning and design and the finished product. We see architects planning houses and carpenters building them. "But surely you will not affirm that the universe bears such a resemblance to a house that we can with the same certainty infer a similar cause, or that the analogy is here entire and perfect. The dissimilitude is so striking that the utmost you can here pretend to is a guess, a conjecture, a presumption concerning a similar case."3

In the case of human planning and its results, we have experienced both the planning and the designed outcome. However, in the case of nature, we have no experience about the planning or the cause, only of the effect. And the effects do not closely resemble human-caused ones. The cause or causes of natural events may be radically different from the causes we know of in human affairs:

> For aught we can know *a priori*, matter may contain the source or spring of order originally within itself, as well as mind does; so there is no more difficulty in conceiving that the several elements, from an internal unknown cause, may fall into the most exquisite arrangement, than to conceive that their ideas, in the great universal mind, from a like internal unknown cause, fall into that arrangement.4

As we continue to see, the latest findings of scientists lead to a form of human vanity, that of assuming that the tiny part of the universe that we know about and live in operates by the same sort of causality as we humans engage in, *and* that these same causal principles are the ones in operation in the entire universe, about which we have no information at all.

So Hume had his skeptical spokesperson, Philo, ask:

> And will any man tell me with a serious countenance that an orderly universe must arise from some thought and art like the human because we have experience of it? To ascertain this reasoning it were requisite that we had experience of the origin of worlds, and, it is not sufficient, surely, that we have seen ships and others arise from human contrivance. . . .
>   . . . Can you pretend to show any such similarity between the fabric of a house and the governance of a universe? Have you ever seen nature in any such situation as resembles the first arrangements of the elements? Have worlds ever been formed under your eyes, and have you had the leisure to observe the whole progress of the phenomenon from the first appearance of order to its final consummation? If you have, then cite your experience and deliver your theory.[5]

So Hume contended that the fundamental thesis of the argument from design, that there is a great resemblance between the effects of human planned activities and effects in nature which leads one to expect that the cause of human artifacts and thought must be like *the* natural causal agency, is not really convincing. In Hume's *Dialogues*, the defender of the argument from design, Cleanthes, answers "that it is by no means necessary that theists should prove the similarity of the works of *nature* to *art* because this similarity is self-evident and undeniable."[6]

So Hume, for the sake of the discussion, was willing to accept Cleanthes' claim temporarily, and then sought to show that even if there actually were a strong resemblance between the human and the natural works, there would still be serious and basic defects in the argument if it is intended to establish the existence of a divine being.

The more the religious arguers contend that the similarity in the effects shows a similarity in the causes between human and natural effects, the less they would be able to come to the traditional religious conclusions about the nature of God:

First, by this method of reasoning you renounce all claim to infinity in any of the attributes of the deity. For, as the cause ought only to be proportioned to the effect, and the effect, so far as it falls under our cognizance, is not infinite, what pretensions have we upon your [Cleanthes'] suppositions to ascribe that attribute to the divine being?

Philo went on to develop the further consequences of this sort of reasoning:

Secondly, you have no reason on your theory for ascribing perfection to the Deity, even in His finite capacity, or for supposing Him free from every error, mistake or incoherence in His undertakings. ... At least, you must acknowledge that it is impossible to tell, from our limited views, whether this system contains any great faults or deserves any considerable praise if compared to other possible and even real systems. Could a peasant, if the *Aeneid* were read to him, pronounce that poem to be absolutely faultless, or even assign to it proper rank among the productions of human wit, he who had never seen any other production.[8]

Even the most recent astronomical discoveries of the formations of galaxies millions and billions of light years away from earth still leave the question about whether these creations are well done, brilliantly done, poorly done, mediocre, accidental, or whatever.

So Philo went on in developing this point:

But were the world ever so perfect a production, it still must remain uncertain whether all of the excellencies of the work can justly be ascribed to the workman. If we survey a ship, what an exalted idea must we form of the ingenuity of the carpenter who framed so complicated, useful and beautiful a machine? And what surprise must we feel when we find him a stupid mechanic who imitated others, and copied an art which, through a long succession of ages, and multiplied trials, mistakes, corrections, deliberations, and controversies had been gradually improving? Many worlds may have been botched or bungled throughout an eternity, ere this system was struck out, much labour lost, many fruitless trials made, and a slow but continued improvement carried on during infinite ages in the art of world-making. In such subjects, who can determine where the truth, nay, who can conjecture, where the probability lies, amidst a great number of hypotheses which may be proposed, and a still greater which may be imagined?[9]

We are told now by the most eminent astrophysicists that our universe is the result of the big bang about 15 billion years ago. And, as Hume suggests, for all we know, this may have been the twentieth, the fortieth, the four hundredth big bang attempt to create a decent workable universe. We keep hearing that all sorts of violent events are taking place, or have taken place at various distant places in this universe. So this one, too, may be a botched one.

The more we try to infer the nature of the universe causer from the similarity of the effect, the universe, to human production, the more we would be led to think of the causer of the universe as like a human being, only more so. This anthropomorphizing of the deity would lead to a theology that bears no resemblance to any of the major religious traditions.

On the other hand, if we deny any similarity between the universe causer and human beings, then the less the argument from design gives us any basis for drawing any conclusion about the nature of the deity.

Hume had Philo sum this up:

> To assert or conjecture that the universe arose from something like design, but beyond that position he [Cleanthes, the user of design argument] cannot ascertain one single circumstance and is left afterwards to fix every point of his theology by the utmost license of fancy and hypothesis. This world, for aught he knows, is very faulty and imperfect compared to a superior standard, and was only the first rude essay of some infant deity who afterwards abandoned it, ashamed of its lame performance; it is the work of some dependent, inferior deity, and is the object of derision to his superiors; it is the production of old age and dotage in some superannuated deity, and ever since his death has run on at adventures, from the first impulse and active force which it received from him.[10]

Obviously one can invent many possible scenarios in keeping with the argument from design in terms of the alleged similarity between what is found in the order of nature and what happens in human productions. Any scenario, explanation, or hypothesis that accounts for the degree of order that we do, in fact, find in nature is as satisfying as any other, if one accepts the argument from design.

Hume went on, from pointing out that the argument from design could lead to the humanizing of the deity, to pointing out some even more undesirable consequences for religious believers. The analogy between the order of nature and human productions is not the only one that is suggested by what we find in surveying the world. There is also a resemblance to the order that arises out of the biological activities of both plants and animals. So Hume has Philo assert,

> I affirm that there are other parts of the universe (besides the machines of human invention) which bear still a great resemblance to the fabric of the world, and which, therefore, afford a better conjecture concerning the universal origin of this system. These parts are animals and vegetables. The world plainly resembles more an animal or a vegetable than it does a watch or a knitting-loom. Its cause, therefore, it is more probable, resembles the cause of the former. The cause, therefore, of the world we may infer to be something similar or analogous to generation or vegetation.[11]

If that is the case, the whole natural world may have within it inner principles of development like those of plants and animals. If that is so, one would not have to infer an intelligent designer of nature. Instead, one could infer some sort of internal self-regulator, such as is found in plant seeds, that guides and orders their development.

If it is objected that there is no evidence for the biological-order hypothesis, Hume agrees, but points out there is no better evidence for any other hypothesis. In what we observe of nature, there are patterns of order in nature. Some of these resemble, to some extent, the effects of human productions, *but* some resemble still more what results from biological organization. So Philo stressed that from our imperfect and limited experience, we are really unable to make a probable conjecture concerning the cause of everything:

> But if we must fix on some hypothesis, by what rule, pray, ought we to determine our choice? Is there any other rule than the greater similarity of the objects compared? And does not a plant or an animal, which springs from vegetation or generation, have a stronger resemblance to the world than does any artificial machine, which arises from reason and design?[12]

Hume then carried his attack further, suggesting that for all we know of the world, a purely materialistic or a chance explanation could do as well as any other. The ancient atomic theory of Epicurus, which explained everything as due to "the fortuitous concourse of atoms," could account for the order that we find. It could be pure chance that the atoms combine and collide in such a way that we perceive an ordered world. In fact, Hume pointed out, if one threw several thousand iron filings into the air, they would come down in a pattern or design. But we would not say that what we see is due to any ordering or designing principle. The so-called ordered universe may, thus, be the result of pure chance or accident, and not of any intelligent design.

Having dissected the argument from design and showing that it does not prove, or even make plausible, what it claims to be the case as regards an intelligent designer of the world, Hume went on to show that the argument also does not tell us anything about the moral character of whatever deity there may be. Even if one accepted the analogy between human and divine affairs involved in the argument from design, this still would not lead us to a conception of a morally just and good deity. If the world designer is supposed to be like a human designer, then we would have no particular reason for inferring qualities of goodness and justice in the world designer. Consider all the awful aspects in the natural world, like earthquakes, tornadoes, tidal waves, floods, the terrible effects of El Niño and La Niña, as well as the way different parts of nature seem to be at war with one another. From all of this, would we, or should we, infer that the natural world was designed by a good and just intelligence?

As Hume had Philo put it,

> Did I show you a house or palace where there was not one apartment convenient or agreeable, where the windows, doors, passages and stairs, and the whole economy of the building were the source of noise and confusion, fatigue, darkness, and the extremes of heat and cold, you would certainly blame the contrivance without any further examination. The architect would in vain display his subtility, and prove to you that, if this door or that window were altered, greater ills would ensue. What he says may be strictly true, the alteration of one particular, while the other parts of the

building remain, may only augment the inconveniences. But you would still assert in general that if the architect had skill and good intentions, he might have formed such a plan of the whole, and might have adjusted the parts in such a manner as would have remedied all or most of these inconveniences. His ignorance, or even your own ignorance of such a plan, will never convince you of the impossibility of it. If you find any inconveniences and deformities in the building, you will always, without entering into any detail, condemn the architect.[13]

So, if one applies the same reasoning to the case of the natural world, one would have to ask, "Is the world considered in general and as it appears to us in this life, different from what a man or such a limited being would *expect* from a very powerful, wise, and beneficent deity? It must be strange prejudice to assert the contrary. And from thence, I conclude that, however consistent the world may be, allowing certain suppositions and conjectures with the idea of such a deity, it can never afford an inference concerning his existence."

Thus, given the way the natural world looks to us, we have no real basis for concluding that it was designed by a good and just deity. It might have been designed by a deity that was amoral, neither good nor bad, neither just nor unjust; or by two opposing deities, one good, one bad, opposing each other. (This is called the Manichean hypothesis.) If we had additional information apart from what the world looks like, then we might be able to come to a better conclusion. But if all of our knowledge is from observation of the world we live in, then we are not able to decide about the moral characteristics of the deity or deities.

After this strong criticism of the argument from design, Hume concluded that although the argument is based on an unsound analogy and is logically unconvincing, it nonetheless is forceful and even persuasive to the extent that reasonable persons will agree "that the cause or causes of order in the universe probably bear some remote analogy to human intelligence." But we have no means of extending this claim to uncover any characteristics of the cause or causes of world order. We can construct all sorts of hypotheses, but if we base ourselves solely on what we observe, we have no way of extending our knowledge of the cause or causes.

Hence Hume, at the end of the eighteenth century, offered a very strong critique of the argument from design about the limits of our knowledge of a deity based on it and on our empirical observations about the world. Nonetheless, along with the progress of science, new versions of the argument from design are offered, principally contending that the very force of the evidence, the vast interconnections from the furthest reaches of the universe to the tiniest sub-subatomic particles, shriek at us that this world has been designed. Scientist theologians like the Jesuit Pierre Teilhard de Chardin have presented forceful versions based on twentieth-century scientific discoveries. Such presentations do not answer Hume's criticisms, but indicate that they are less than fully convincing. But, as Hume pointed out, what does all the detail about the constitution of the natural world tell us about any possible deity?

Two kinds of responses to Hume have been central to further considerations in the philosophy of religion: one, that there are other kinds of evidences of the existence and nature of God; and two, that religious belief is not *based* on arguments and hence is not affected positively or negatively by the merits of any types of philosophical argumentation.

THE COSMOLOGICAL AND ONTOLOGICAL PROOFS

In the first group we will briefly look at some other kinds of arguments that have been offered, namely the cosmological and the ontological ones, and at other kinds of possible evidences to support a religious point of view.

The cosmological argument starts from the accepted view that every event has a cause. Then, must not the universe, the cosmos, itself have a cause? Scientists are tracing back observed effects to causes, and causes of causes. Can one do this indefinitely, or must there be a first cause?

Aristotle, who first presented the cosmological argument, contended that the universe has been going on indefinitely in the past and will continue to do so into the future, but that there has to be a cause for the universe itself, a first cause or reason why everything happens as it does. Aristotle's view is different from that of present-day cosmologists who have been tracing back known astronomical events to the big bang explosion some 15 to 20 billion years ago. In this case the big bang is an initiating event for the physical universe as we know it. However, we can still ask, What caused the big bang?

The claim of Aristotle, Moses Maimonides, Saint Thomas Aquinas, and others is that the first cause must be uncaused, (otherwise there would be an endless regress of causes and causes of causes), and yet be the reason why everything else happens. For Aristotle, who did not believe in a created universe, the first cause is not part of the temporal sequence of causes and is not the first creative event such as that described in the very beginning of Genesis: "In the beginning God created heaven and earth." But all argued that if there were no first cause, then there could be no second, third, and so on, and thus there could be nothing going on. Since there is something taking place and it must have a cause, we can reason that there must be a first cause either in time or in a metaphysical sense.

The cosmological argument was subjected to very serious criticism by Hume and by the German philosopher Immanuel Kant, with the result that most modern philosophies of religion that grew out of Hume's skepticism and empiricism and Kant's critical philosophy have rejected the argument. It is, however, accepted by the Catholic Church as an official and decisive argument for the existence of God.

Hume's theory of knowledge severely criticized the kinds of knowledge that we think we gain through causal reasoning. If a cause is something that has the power to produce an effect, and our knowledge of causes and effects comes from experience, do we ever actually have any experience of the causal power? Or is it that we just observe successive events? If there were a necessary causal connection between events, this would mean that we could demonstrate from the cause that the effect must follow. But Hume insisted anything that is conceivable is possible, and so we can conceive of the event or effect occurring without the cause. And so there is no necessary connection.

In fact, Hume argued, we can conceive of the world, the cosmos, as self-existing. The supporters of the cosmological argument do not ask what is the cause of God, and then reply God is the cause of himself. Okay! But then why cannot the world be the cause of itself? Why cannot the causal agencies be contained within the material world itself? What in Hume's day was called "the hideous hypothesis of Epicurus," that the world is just the fortuitous concourse of atoms striking each other, is also a possibility.

Hume also contended that the maxim "Every event has a cause" is not self-evident or demonstrable. Our causal knowledge is gained only through experiences, and in fact, just consists in noticing recurring sequences of events, so that when we observe one, we expect the other. This, then, is simply a psychological way we look at the world, and not metaphysical way it necessarily has to be.

Immanuel Kant, who developed his critical philosophy as a way of dealing with the skepticism in Hume's analyses, claimed that causality was one of the categories we necessarily used to order our experiences. But we do not know whether or not the causal category applies to cases beyond all possible experience.

The cosmological argument is a direct effort to do causal reasoning beyond all possible experience. A sign that this is not fruitful, according to Kant, is that contradictory results ensue where we have no experiential control. Arguments can be developed to demonstrate that the world must have a beginning in time and arguments just as good can be developed to demonstrate that the world is eternal. These paralogisms of pure reason, as Kant called them, indicate that we are operating in a nebulous area where we have no way of telling what may or may not be true. So, unfortunately, the cosmological argument gets us nowhere.

A third kind of argument for the existence of God is the ontological argument that contends that one can demonstrate the existence of God solely from the definition of God. No other information is needed or involved. This argument was first introduced by Saint Anselm of Canterbury in the twelfth century, and again presented in somewhat different form by Descartes and by Spinoza. Anselm had first insisted that everyone knows that God exists and only a fool denies this, though even the fool knows in his heart what is the case. If God's existence is denied, then one can point out that, by definition, God is that being than which none greater can be conceived. If God does not exist, then we can conceive of a being greater than

God, namely, one with all of God's perfections, that also exists out-side of our minds. To exist in reality is obviously greater than to exist just in a mind.

Descartes spelled this out in greater detail in the "Fifth Medita-tion" when he said,

> The existence of God ought to pass in my mind as being at least as certain as I have, up to this time, regarded the truths of mathe-matics to be, which have only to do with numbers and figures, although that might not be seen at first to be perfectly evident, but might appear to have some element of sophistry. For being accus-tomed in all other things to make a distinction between existence and essence, I easily persuade myself that existence perhaps may be separated from the essence of God and thus God might be con-ceived as not existent actually. But nevertheless, when I think more attentively, I find that existence can no more be separated from the essence of God than the essence of a rectilinear triangle can be sep-arated from the equality of its three angles to two right angles, or, indeed, if you please, from the idea of a mountain, the idea of a valley, so that there would be no less contradiction in conceiving of a God, that is, of a being supremely perfect, to whom existence is wanting, that is to say, to whom there was wanting any perfection, than in conceiving a mountain without a valley.[14]

Spinoza's version is more compact:

> God, or substance, consisting of infinite attributes, of which each expresses eternal and infinite essentiality, necessarily exists. The evidence for this proposition is that if one denied it, then conceive, if possible, that God does not exist. Then His/Her Essence would not involve existence. But that is absurd. It is a contradiction in terms of the definition of God. Therefore God necessarily exists.[15]

In each of the versions we have offered of the ontological argu-ment, the same fundamental theme appears. If we examine our con-ception of God as the perfect being, or that being than which no greater can be conceived, we will realize that one kind of perfection that is involved in the very definition of God is his/her existence. No other human concept is such that its definition entails its existence. Existence is not one of the defining properties. However, the concept of God includes being an existent being. So it is alleged that just from the *idea* of God, we can ascertain that he/she *must* exist, in the same way that we can tell from the definition of a triangle that the sum of its interior angles is 180°.

This sounds fine, but is it convincing? If someone was very worried, desperately worried, about whether God actually exists, and was presented as an answer with the ontological argument, would this suffice to allay the person's worries? As Saint Thomas Aquinas observed in the thirteenth century, the ontological argument would be convincing *if* one antecedently knew that God exists. It would make one aware of the special nature of God compared to any other being, namely, that his/her essence entails existence; or that God is a self-caused being in contrast to everything else, which must have a cause other than itself.

In the eighteenth century, Hume (briefly) and Kant (in great detail) spelled out what they saw as the fundamental flaw in the ontological argument, namely, that existence is not a predicate like other properties. Hume observed that everything we conceive of, we in fact conceive of as existing. Kant pointed out that adding existence to a concept does not enhance or change the concept. The concept of a hundred thalers contains the same amount of money when thought of as existing or just as thought of. So existence is not a property that can be added or subtracted from anything. The idea of God as a perfect being is not increased by thinking of it as existing. Thinking of *the idea of God* and thinking of *the idea of God as existing* are the same. Hence, Kant contended, we cannot build an ontological bridge between our ideas and reality by predicating existence on them. Existence is not like a color, a taste, or a smell that can be added or subtracted from an idea.

The ontological argument at best, according to this analysis, reveals only that God can be so defined that necessary existence is part of its definition. But that only tells us the consequences of one kind of definition and tells us nothing about what in fact exists in the universe.

The critiques of Hume and Kant of the purported arguments to establish the existence of God have pretty much ended this kind of quest for rational evidential proofs of God's existence. Some critics went even further, insisting that Hume's and Kant's analyses should lead to showing that theology is actually a meaningless subject. The logical positivists in the twentieth century proclaimed that concepts only had meaning in terms of experience, and propositions about them only in terms of how they might be verified. The key concept of theology, "God," did not refer to any public experience. And claims about what God can or cannot do, or has or has not done, cannot be verified in experience.

Believers were not overcome by such an attack and, after the initial shock of the positivist's presentation, have been working out a negative defense, namely that the positivists cannot eliminate the possibility of there being a supernatural force or person. In Sir Karl Popper's terms, they cannot falsify religious knowledge claims, even if they cannot be verified. No amount of negative analysis of theological concepts and theological claims rules out completely what the religious person thinks is going on. So one finds in recent analytic philosophical discussions of the philosophy of religion a group of people who are religious believers, using the techniques of twentieth-century analytic philosophy to argue that the religious person's claims cannot be totally disproved. Some, like Alvin Plantinga, have tried to show that the force of the ontological argument has not been overcome by Hume's or Kant's critiques, and that some modern reformulation is possible. Others, like George Schlessinger, have used the battery of analytic techniques to argue that one cannot disprove the possibility of the immortality of the soul, and other such religious knowledge claims. Of course, this negative view does not provide evidence for the religious views, either.

Another type of negative defense of theism is one that is being put forth currently by fundamentalists and neoconservatives against those whom they label "secular humanists." These, they claim, base all values on human views, following the doctrine of the Greek sophist Protagoras, that man is the measure of all things. It is then asserted that for the secular humanists, man is the measure of all values. This, it is alleged, would lead to the view that values are relative, and there would be no absolute values.* What is put forth as

---

*In chapter 6, it is shown that the situation is much more complicated and that there are many other possibilities between sheer relativism and absolutism.

the consequence is that in order to avoid the curse of relativism, one has to opt for an absolute value system, and that such a value system is provided by the Bible, supposedly guaranteed by God himself.

This attempt to avoid relativism by appealing to the argument from catastrophe is open to many of the skeptical themes we discussed earlier. If the absolute value system is said to be the one in the Bible, are we so certain what this system is? The Bible has been read in many different ways. To take just one item, the commandment "Thou shalt not kill" looks simple and straightforward. Yet it has been interpreted to allow killing in self-defense, in defense of one's country, in defense of allowing the execution of criminals by the state, and so on. Which is the correct interpretation? And what is absolute, if so many circumstances can be taken into account that, in fact, justify the opposite of the apparent sense of the commandment?

Another skeptical problem is deciding what set of supposed absolute values to accept. The Bible encompasses a wide-ranging set of possibilities in the Judeo-Christian tradition. What about absolute value claims of other traditions—Islam, Buddhism, animism, and Hinduism, to name a few. The variety of claims to absolute truth raises the problem of finding a way of judging which claims, if any, are true.

Thus, the appeal to the alleged catastrophe of relativism may not really present us with another secure option.

FIDEISM

A religious person at this point may be very irritated at our discussion because religious belief does not depend on accepting the logical soundness of certain arguments or on compiling various kinds of evidences. Most believers have never heard of these arguments, yet they believe. Some believers insist that they believe on the basis of faith, and not on the basis of arguments or evidences. This view is called "fideism," contending that our religious knowledge is not and cannot be founded upon rational or empirical evidence; instead, it ought to be based solely on faith. It has been set forth in the seventeenth century by Blaise Pascal, in the eighteenth century by J. G. Hamann, in the nineteenth century by Søren Kierkegaard, and in the twentieth century by the conservative Calvinists and the Christian Reconstructionists. It has become a leading explanation, if not a justification of religious belief.

Blaise Pascal (1623–1662), the brilliant seventeenth-century mathematician and scientist who became an ardent spokesperson for religious commitment, insisted that he believed in the God of Abraham, Isaac, and Jacob, not the God of the philosophers. The arguments about the existence of God, like those of Descartes, at best could only establish the existence of the God of the philosophers, not a God worthy of belief.

Pascal insisted that a careful examination of the nature of human reasoning would reveal that they are all open to serious skeptical problems. Our very nature makes it impossible for us to discover if our reasonings are true, false, or uncertain, so we are led by nature to be complete skeptics. But at the same time we find that we have to believe.

After his religious experience, Pascal made his first retreat to the Port-Royal monastery of the Jansenists. In his retreat, he worked on a project he had called an apology for religion. This was set forth in the form of *pensées*, or "thoughts." He kept the *pensées* on slips of paper, and had them classified by topic. He never completed the work, and ever since his death there have been different editions of the *Pensées* seeking to put the material in the form the author presumably desired. A central theme is that of the skeptical limits to human being's ability to find certainty and the need to rely on faith instead. In a famous passage, Pascal wrote,

> The main arguments of the skeptics . . . are that we possess no certainty concerning any principles apart from faith and revelation except as we perceive them naturally within ourselves. But this natural intuition is no convincing proof of their truth, because we have no certainty apart from faith as to whether man was created by a good God, or a wicked demon, or by chance, and these principles are true, false, or uncertain depending upon our origin. No person is certain, apart from faith, whether he is awake or asleep.[16]

Thus, according to Pascal, the skeptics have shown that everything we think we know is uncertain. However, he pointed out, we find ourselves drawn by nature to believe all sorts of things. We find ourselves torn between an intellectual skepticism that makes everything doubtful and a natural dogmatism that leads us to believing many things.

So, Pascal went on,

> [W]hat then should man do in this state? Should he doubt everything? Should he doubt whether he is awake, if he is being pinched, or if he is being burned? Should he doubt whether he is in doubt? Should he doubt his own existence? We are not able to go as far as that, and I put it down as a fact that there never has been a completely thorough-going skeptic. Nature sustains our feeble reason and keeps it from raving to that extent.
>
> Should he then assert that he is in possession of certain truth— he who when pressed at all, can show no title to it, and is compelled to let go his hold upon it.
>
> What a chimera then is man! What a novelty! What a monster, what a chaos, what a contradiction, what a prodigy! Judge of all things, imbecile worm of the earth; depositary of all truth, a sink of uncertainty and error, the pride and refuse of the universe!
>
> Who will unravel this mess? Nature refutes the skeptics, and reason refutes the dogmatists. What then will become of you, O men, who try to discover by your own natural reason, what is your true condition? . . .
>
> Know then proud man, what a paradox you are to yourself. Humble yourself, weak reason, be silent foolish nature; learn that man infinitely transcends man, and learn from your master what is your true condition of which you are ignorant. Hear God.[17]

From the perspective of his religious experience, Pascal devoted more than half of the *Pensées* to presenting "proofs of the Christian religion." These are not intended as decisive or demonstrative arguments. They are items that might convince those who want to be convinced, but would not convince others. It was a matter of spiritual temperament as to whether one was inclined to believe or disbelieve. In neither case was there sufficient evidence to convince one of belief, or to justify disbelief.

In a famous section of the *Pensées* called "The Wager," Pascal contended that even though there was insufficient evidence, a prudent person would bet on the God hypothesis. Pascal was the leading expert of the time on the mathematical theory of probability. He put the problem of belief as a gambling one: Is it better to bet that God exists, or that he/she does not? If God does not exist, then it does not matter theologically whether one believes he/she does exist or does not exist. But if God does exist, it can make all of the difference in the world if one has bet that God exists, or has not so bet. Hence, Pascal suggested that any prudent man—or good gambler—would bet that God exists because one has everything to gain and nothing to lose if he/she does not exist. (But, as critics have pointed out from the moment the *Pensées* first appeared, this does not tell anyone what sort of God to bet on, and does not deal with the multiplicity of options within the religious hypothesis.)

Pascal's fideism outlined the inability of reason to provide a basis for religion and indicated that one had to rely on faith. A more extreme fideist, contemporary with Pascal, the French Catholic bishop Pierre-Daniel Huet (1630–1721), saw Pascal as not skeptical enough. Huet attacked the wager argument as pretending that some kind of evidence exists. Instead the bishop advanced a complete version of classical Greek skepticism, and said religion rested on faith alone. As an example of how far he carried this position, he was asked by the church to look into the case of a Jesuit scholar in his diocese who had obtained a doctor's degree with a thesis that contended that there was no evidence for any religious belief, and that Christianity was the least probable of all religions. Huet talked to the Jesuit and found they agreed completely. After all, if Christian belief was based on faith alone, there should be no evidence for it. And with no evidence for it, it would be less probable than other religious claims.

This insistence on the total irrationality of religious belief was spelled out in more shocking and maybe perverse form by the French Protestant thinker Pierre Bayle (1642–1706), the son a Calvinist pastor in France. During the persecution of the Protestants, most of their schools were closed, so young Bayle was sent to the Jesuit school at Toulouse. There he was quickly converted to Roman Catholicism by skeptical arguments directed at Calvinism, "the machine of war." Shortly thereafter, Bayle applied the same arguments to Roman Catholicism, and unconverted himself by skeptical arguments. Under French law of the time, it was a capital offense to convert from Catholicism to Calvinism, so young Bayle had to flee. He went to the Calvinist university in Geneva, Switzerland, then became a teacher in the last Protestant academy in France, and then had to flee again when Louis XIV revoked the legal status of the Protestants. Bayle went to the Netherlands where he became a teacher in Rotterdam and a polemical writer against all sides. His greatest work was his *Historical and Critical Dictionary* (1697), which explored all sorts of theories in philosophy, science, and theology and showed that they were "big with contradiction and absurdity." He leveled the full force of skeptical argumentation, old and new, at thinkers from ancient times to the present. His constant theme was that reason was not able to reach any certain conclusions in any areas of human intellectual interest. Therefore, one should suspend judgment and turn to faith.

Bayle's contemporaries, especially some in his own church, the French Reformed Church of Rotterdam, doubted the sincerity of his appeal to faith, and some even doubted that he had any religious faith. They foresaw that Bayle's many arguments against everything would provide what Voltaire called "the Arsenal of the Enlightenment" and would lead people to disbelief.

Bayle tried to defend himself in a series of clarifications in the second edition of the *Dictionary* (1702). In these, he spelled out more forcefully the relationship he saw between skepticism and religious belief.

Skeptical arguments, as he showed through his writings, undermine any positive knowledge claims in philosophy, science, or theology. The true and believing Christian should not be dismayed because, as he said, the ship of Jesus Christ was not made to sail off rational or philosophical shores. From the outset it was to be believed in spite of arguments against it. Pure faith is faith based on no evidence, rational, probable, or otherwise. This blind faith could not be challenged. But Bayle's opponents saw this as a way of making religion seem ridiculous if it was to be accepted in the face of all opposition. They suspected that Bayle's life-long defense of this extreme fideistic position was just a smokescreen to cover his unbelief. Although Bayle cited and discussed Pascal as having similar views to his own, his opponents noted that Bayle made no profession of any particular religious articles of faith or belief. He fought against theologians both Catholic and Protestant; against, as he said, everything that is said and done. But he offered no positive faith. This has led to an almost three-hundred-year-long argument about what he really believed.

Whatever Bayle did, in fact, believe, one kind of effect of his skeptical attack on everything as a prelude to faith was to inspire a somewhat similar attitude in David Hume, who was studying Bayle's texts from early on. When Hume went to France in 1734 to write his monumental *Treatise of Human Nature*, the books he took with him were the four folio volumes of Bayle's *Dictionary* and the four volumes of Bayle's other works. One view Hume took from Bayle is the concluding remarks of Philo in the *Dialogues Concerning Natural Religion*, "that to be a philosophical skeptic is the first and most essential step to becoming a true and believing Christian." Most readers, then and now, doubt that Hume ever advanced from being a philosophical skeptic to becoming any kind of religious believer. Most readers have seen him as a deist or an agnostic. However, one of the most forceful fideistic thinkers of the late eighteenth century saw him as "the greatest voice of orthodoxy." The German religious thinker J. G. Hamann (1730–1788), a religious philosopher from Königsberg, spent some time in England as a merchant. There, he came to know Hume's writings and was especially struck by the supposedly most irreligious ones, the essay "Of Miracles" and the *Dialogues*. Hamann was a good friend of Immanuel Kant, the philosophy professor at Königsberg, and discussed Hume's views on religion with him and even translated the first and last dialogues as an effort to make Kant see the merits of Christian belief. After reading Hume's attack on any evidence that might be offered for believing in miraculous events where Hume had claimed, no doubt ironically, that any reasonable person who believed in miracles must feel a miracle going on within himself that subverts all reason and understanding, Hamann made his famous remark, "Lies, fable and romances [novels] must needs be probable, but not the foundation of our faith." Hamann saw skepticism as presented by Hume and by Socrates, when he insisted all he knew was that he knew nothing, as preparations for the faith. Real faith was not based on evidence, rational or scientific.

Hamann's fideism had an immense effect on the Danish thinker Søren Kierkegaard (1813–1855). He had been studying the German rational philosophy of the time and the historical critical studies of the Bible. When he encountered Hamann's sharp remarks on reading Hume, and encountered Bayle's fideism as well, he began working out a new approach to finding certainty. Kierkegaard presented his ideas in a series of writings ranging from philosophical essays, stories, religious rhapsodies, and religious polemics. The works are credited mostly to a series of pseudonymous authors who represent various sides of man's quest, and some works are signed by "S. Kierkegaard." This makes interpreting Kierkegaard a real puzzle. In his earliest, most philosophical writings, one finds the development of a complete irrational or antirational fideism. The first of these is an unfinished writing, *On Why All Is in Doubt*, attributed to Johannes Climacus. This name was probably chosen as a reference to an actual neo-Platonic thinker in late Hellenistic times who composed *The Ladder to Paradise*, which was what Kierkegaard was seeking. In the first work, starting from the news that the new philosophy (that is, from Descartes onward) begins in doubt. The author adopts a policy of doubting, and finds no way of overcoming doubt through the various philosophies of the last two centuries. In 1841 Kierkegaard published *Philosophical Fragments, Or a Fragment of Philosophy*, authored by Johannes Climacus. On the title page, the questions are raised as to whether it is possible to find a historical point of departure for an eternal consciousness, whether such a historical point of departure can have more than historical interest, and whether it is possible to base eternal happiness upon historical knowledge.

Kierkegaard began the discussion by considering the argument offered by Socrates in the Platonic dialogue *Meno*. There, it was argued that knowledge cannot be learned. If one learned what one did not already know, how could one recognize it? If one learned what one already knew, then nothing was being learned. The solution offered by Socrates was that one did not learn. What appeared to be gaining knowledge was actually recollecting. One had all knowledge at the outset, but had forgotten.

Kierkegaard suggested instead that one starts in ignorance, total ignorance. No amount of information or reasoning can lead one to knowledge. So if one gains knowledge, it must be by miracle.

From the human point of view, we can never get out of our complete ignorance by studying nature, by history, or by reason. Kierkegaard accepts the criticisms of all of the arguments of the existence of God. He also regarded the collection of historical evidence about Christianity as just gathering gossip on a world scale. What one wants to know is the source of knowledge, the source of enlightenment. But nothing can be learned unless the enlightener is found. He/she/it cannot be found by any historical human means. In fact, Kierkegaard presents the situation in a story about the powerful king who wants to marry a beautiful maiden, but only if she loves him for himself and is not at all seduced by his power. So he has to disguise himself completely so that there is no way she can guess who he really is.

The epistemological disguise, Kierkegaard suggests, is to make the crucial knowledge to be found a complete, total paradox that defies reason. Kierkegaard has Johannes Climacus call it the "Absolute Paradox," namely, that the Eternal has existed in history. We, with our natural faculties, can only prove that this is impossible—yet only if this has happened. Even though impossible, can we gain contact from a historical point of departure with the Eternal, and would certainty flow from such a contact?

So what do we poor mortals do at this impasse? In *Fear and Trembling*, attributed to one Johan de Silentio, Kierkegaard discussed what it is to have faith, blind and complete faith. Such faith cannot be based on any evidential considerations; it can only result from taking a leap into faith. Using the biblical story of Abraham and Isaac, Kierkegaard depicts Abraham as the true knight of faith. He lives totally in his belief. He is told by God that he is to sacrifice his only son, Isaac, and that he will be the father of a mighty nation. Without hesitation he is prepared to do it and is relieved of the terrible action by God. The knight of faith lives in fear and trembling, but acts as faith dictates.

But how does one tell when and where to leap and what to do? If there are no clues, no matter how slight, to guide one, it always has to be a blind action. Although Kierkegaard cast the story in terms of Christian belief, presumably any belief could become the result of a leap into faith. Some such leaps, Kierkegaard recognized, could be disastrous if one gave oneself over to what he called "demonism." But no warning signs exist to separate faiths that will prosper post facto from those that will lead to destruction.

Further in line with his antirational stance, Kierkegaard in his last work, *The Attack on Christendom*, to which he signed his own name, bitterly attacked those who accept Christianity as an easy and nice belief. They have performed the modern miracle of changing wine into water. Instead of seeing that the hardest thing is to be a true and believing Christian, they have made it as a simple matter of birth, or filling out forms, or receiving drops of water. Kierkegaard, at the end, saw himself as a one man movement to challenge accepted Christianity in order to force people to become believers.

Early in the twentieth century his picture of the total irrationality of belief was joined to Friedrich Nietzsche's claim that "God is dead," at least as a meaningful force in human affairs. This has led to forms of existentialist philosophy in which the crucial element of human existence is choice, even when there is no evidence whatsoever what choice to make or avoid. Human existence becomes meaningful only post choice. Man has the "dreadful freedom" that any choice is possible, and has total responsibility for the effects of one choice. For most existentialists, the choice is completely a human affair. Hence, the view has been seen as a form of atheism. Others have coupled it with religious choice, and have developed forms of religious existentialism.

A quite different kind of fideism has been developed from very conservative Calvinists in the Dutch Reformed Church, and by an Armenian American thinker, Rousas J. Rushdoony, in the movement called Christian Reconstructionism. Some Dutch Calvinist theologians in the late nineteenth century balked at using Enlightenment measures of reason and science to evaluate religious views. An American Dutch Reformed teacher, Cornelius van Tyl, developed what he called a Christian epistemology to oppose that of secular thinkers. Rushdoony studied philosophy at the University of California, Berkeley. He later encountered van Tyl's writings, and in a volume of tributes to van Tyl he published his first statement, "By What Standards?" Raising the fundamental question of the Greek skeptics, he asked how one determines what standards to apply to basic beliefs. And, following van Tyl, he urged opting for biblical religion, rather than science or philosophy, as one's source of truth. One had to start somewhere and there was no reason to accept one set of standards rather than another.

Rushdoony went further than van Tyl in insisting that the Bible be used as the sole basis for law in the United States and in the world. Originally he claimed in his seminal book of 1964, *The Idea of the American Republic*, that the original Massachusetts Bay colony was based on a covenant with God, and accepted as the only basis for regulating their society, and their law that which God had told them in the Bible. This society, based on English common law and the Bible, flourished until the American Revolution and the establishment of the United States of America, which introduced the whole structure of a secular society, with all sorts of nonbiblical features such as a national bank, a federal government, and a public school system. The secular society became more and more permissive and unbiblical. The Christian Reconstructionist message is not just a statement of fundamentalist biblical faith, but also a plan for political action to recreate the biblically guided state that presumably existed before the American Revolution. Rushdoony and his friend Howard Phillips set up a political party, the U.S. Taxpayers Party, that runs candidates, usually Phillips himself, for the presidency of the United States. Their platform is to make U.S. law consist only of biblical law. In political terms, they see this as mandating the elimination of the Federal Reserve Bank, the Internal Revenue Service, income tax, and monetary instruments other than gold and silver. They also propose eliminating the public school system and introducing biblical punishments for crimes such as adultery. As one might imagine, they do not gain many votes at national elections, but they have been making headway in electing like-minded people to local school boards, library boards, city councils, state legislatures, and even a few to the U.S. Congress. In 1999 Senator Bob Smith of New Hampshire announced that he was resigning from the Republican Party and that he would stand as the U.S. Taxpayers candidate for president of the United States in 2000.

The Christian Reconstructionists encourage parents to teach their children at home or in religious schools that are not supervised by the secular government. They have been pressing for the teaching of "creation science" in school. Their superconservative program has provided a road map for other religious conservatives. The influence of Christian Reconstructionism is far beyond its numbers, and, as an intellectually based view, it sees no need to argue for its basic outlook. Everyone has to start with some act of faith, and proceed from there.

In the nineteenth century the American pragmatist philosopher William James wrote an essay, "The Will to Believe," analyzing the human drive to believe and the function of fundamental beliefs in human intellectual lives. James saw the belief situation in somewhat the terms that Pascal did. Belief became crucial when it became forced and of monumental consequences for the believer. The belief situation only became serious when the proposed belief was a living one, that is, a belief that required one to take a stand. Thus, for most people there is no living belief option about whether one should worship Zeus or Athena. For most of us, whether we do or do not believe makes little difference in our lives. Many of the seemingly forced options deal with such social and political issues: Should we go to war? Should we ban public ownership of guns? Should we accept unborn children as full-fledged human beings? For many of us, these are living issues and in terms of our actions, they lead us to a series of commitments and even lifestyles. A belief becomes monumental for us if it transforms our ways of living.

In James's analysis, he was trying to separate seemingly frivolous options with monumental possibilities from those that shape ways of living. Should I become an astronaut? If I did, it would certainly transform the way I live now and in the future. But in light of my physical condition, it is no living option at all.

With regard to living and forced options, how does one decide what to believe and act upon? James was a kind of fideist in that he did not think one could find basic principles to justify beliefs. Within his philosophy, the test of a belief would be how it worked for the believer. Some beliefs are not functional for the believer in that his or her life becomes unsatisfactory as he or she tries to live within that belief system. A belief system constitutes a way of life. For James, there are two kinds of believers, tough-minded and tender-minded.

The tough-minded do not see the need to believe in forces above and beyond the experienced natural world and are satisfied that all questions about human affairs can be answered by scientific investigation. They are agnostic or atheistic. They may leave the questions of religion unanswered or unanswerable, except as questions about the psychology of believers. A contemporary of James's, James Henry Leuba, wrote *The Psychology of Religious Mysticism*, in which he sought to show that so-called mystical experience was due to faulty operations of the human glandular system.

James, an important experimental psychologist in his own right, classified himself among the tender-minded. His father had been a leader of the Church of the New Jerusalem, founded by Emanuel Swedenborg. William James found himself unable to accept the religious and theological principles of his father's church, but he nonetheless saw the values of religious belief for certain kinds of people who felt the need to hope that there were forces or agencies beyond the natural world that might be guiding or helping the development of human experience. He did not give any real specificity to what the tender-minded might believe. This openness leaves a very wide range of possibilities.

The Jamesian approach is basically to avoid any investigation of whether beliefs people may hold are true in any more than a pragmatic sense; that is, that they work for the individual.

Others have sought to analyze the character of religious belief in more than psychological terms. Martin Buber examined a very wide range of kinds of religious belief, from Western monotheism to many kinds of Eastern religions. Buber stressed the centrality of feelings of interpersonal relations in religious experience. Instead of experiencing an "It" (an object) one experiences an "I-Thou" interaction. A greater and greater feeling of connection with a world, "Thou," becomes the focus of religious experiences.

Both James and Buber, in pointing to an amorphous religiosity, put the character of it in psychological and sociological terms outside any of the traditional terms of the major religious traditions. Judaism, Christianity, and Islam could be recast in Jamesian or Buberian terms, but in so doing, the entire historical content would disappear. The same result occurs in a movement of modern biblical theologians.

Applying a method of "demythologizing" to biblical religion, they have found much if not all of it can be understood in terms of ancient myths and myth patterns. In the very influential study by the German theologian Rudolf Bultman on the Gospel According to John, practically the entire content of the work was demythologized and relegated to ancient beliefs and writings no longer relevant. What was left for the modern reader and the modern believer was the God encounter, which could not be specified or located in a passage. The encounter that formed the basis of a religious outlook was not explicable in metaphysical terms, or easily transformable into the creed or set of beliefs of an existing traditional church.

What all of this indicates is that much of the discussion and analysis of religion by modern specialists, building on the developments in psychology, sociology, anthropology, rather than theological arguments, tries to find what Kierkegaard called "an historical point of departure for an eternal consciousness," that is, something in human experience that constitutes the religious dimension. Putting the quest in these terms, the actual historical religious churches and creeds become of little importance except as places where modern persons can find comfort or companionship in being religious.

While the analysis of religious belief and of arguments for the existence of a divine being seem to yield few positive results, the number of people in the United States who participate in religious activities and consider themselves believers in something increases. And this not just an American phenomenon. In the former Soviet Union, where for over seventy years the government forcefully attempted to eradicate religious belief, there has been an explosion of people turning to religions old and new. One of the matters that has to be taken into account, too, is that in the modern scientific and technological age, among the religious groups making the greatest number of new adherents are fairly recent ones like the Church of Latter Day Saints, the Seventh-day Adventists, the Chabbad movement in Judaism, as well as the Reverend Sun Myung Moon's Unification Church and the Hare Krishnas. Is this to be explained by political and social scientists, by psychiatrists, or are the new adherents finding another kind of evidence other than what the philosophers have been examining up to now? In view of the emergence and interest in new forms of religious expression as well as a serious movement of secular people to adopt some of the religious practices of their ancestors, or of religions hitherto outside of their experience, further explorations in the philosophy of religion will have to examine what sorts of reasons people now give for adhering to their beliefs, and what they are actually believing. To what extent do these new beliefs and practices depend on historical documents and on past theological positions? The religious revival in the second half of the twentieth century and its effect upon many intellectuals point to further studies in the philosophy of religion.

NOTES

1. Alexander Pope, "Epitaph Intended for Sir Isaac Newton" (1730), in *The Poems of Alexander Pope*, ed. John Butt (New Haven, Conn.: Yale University Press, 1963).

2. David Hume, *Dialogues Concerning Natural Religion and the Posthumous Essays*, 2d ed., ed. Richard H. Popkin (Indianapolis: Hackett, 1998), dialogue 2, p. 15.

3. Ibid., p. 16.

4. Ibid., pp. 17–18.

5. Ibid., pp. 21–22.

6. Ibid., dialogue 3, p. 23.

7. Ibid., dialogue 5, p. 35.

8. Ibid., pp. 35–36.

9. Ibid., p. 36.

10. Ibid., pp. 37–38.

11. Ibid., dialogue 7, p. 44.

12. Ibid., p. 45.

13. Ibid., dialogue 11, pp. 68–69.

14. René Descartes, "Meditations on First Philosophy—Fifth Meditation," in *Philosophical Works*, ed. G. R. Ross and Elizabeth S. Haldane (New York: Dover, 1955).

15. Benedict de Spinoza, "Ethics," in *The Chief Works of Spinoza*, ed. R. H. M. Elwes (New York: Dover, 1955), book 1, prop. 1.

16. Blaise Pascal, "Pensées," in *Pascal Selections*, ed. R. H. Popkin (New York: Macmillan, 1989), #434 Brunschvicq ed.; #131 Lafuma ed.

MORALITY AND SKEPTICISM

Introduction

Moral reflection arises at an early age and continues to play an integral role throughout one's life. Even though most persons are not philosophers in the technical sense of the term, anyone who reflects about the problems that arise in daily life is a philosopher to that extent. Suppose before World War II a certain American citizen, let us call him "John Smith," had been a pacifist but also strongly believed that genocide was wrong. When Hitler came to power and began to exterminate the Jews, and the United States went to war against Germany, Smith faced a moral dilemma. If he refused to fight, genocide would continue. If he joined the army, his commitment to pacifism would be compromised. It seems that two compelling ethical principles were in conflict. Given that dilemma, what should he do? What would be a reasonable decision? Indeed, is a reasonable deci-

sion possible when fundamental principles conflict? How can he justify whatever decision he arrives at? Reflections of this sort are the
raw materials from which classical and contemporary ethical theories
are made. The ordinary individual may merely be trying to solve a
particular problem and may do this by settling on a particular course
of action in specific circumstances. The professional philosopher's
aim is more general: It is to know what constitutes the good life for
any human being, and whether there is *always* a right course of
action in any set of circumstances to achieve that goal. The set of
principles or rules to answer these questions is traditionally called a
"moral theory."

It is important to understand how the term "theory" is used in this
context. Let us begin by comparing and contrasting scientific and
philosophical theories. There are, of course, many types of philosophical theories, and moral theories are a special kind. We shall
therefore want to make some further distinctions in describing them.
Both scientific and philosophical theories attempt to connect widely
different phenomena via an explanatory principle or a set of such
principles. A single scientific principle, the Law of Gravitation,
explains why an apple falls toward a heavier body, why the tides
advance and recede regularly in relation to a coastline, and why the
moon does not drift away from or fall into the earth. The Greek
philosopher Thales also looked for such a principle to explain a host
of diverse happenings. He noted that water, a fluid, hardens in
severely cold weather, and becomes a vapor when exposed to high
heat. He also observed that if one digs deeply enough into the
ground water bubbles up, and if one cuts persons or plants, the surfaces that are exposed are wet. His explanation of these diverse phenomena rested upon the thesis that everything is composed of water.
Using this principle he could account for the existence and behavior
of a spectrum of substances.

Moral theories also look for universal principles to explain widely
different forms of human conduct. People may act in all sorts of ways
and yet all such actions may correctly be described as just. Once
again, the ethicist looks for an underlying principle that will explain
why they are all instances of justice. An example of such a principle
would be the Principle of Utility, the maxim that an action is just if it

produces a preponderance of happiness over unhappiness for the greatest number of persons in the long run. In looking for a fundamental principle that will account for differing phenomena, moral theory resembles scientific theories and the sort of materialistic theory that Thales developed.

But moral theories differ from both of the above types in two important ways. First, the principles such theories attempt to find are what are called *normative*, in contradistinction to scientific principles, which are *factual*. The difference is easy to explain. Many persons fail to repay debts. That remark is a statement of fact. It describes how some persons actually behave. But the principle that persons *ought to* repay debts is not factual. From the truth that some persons do not repay debts it does not logically follow that they should do so. That statement transcends the factual and requires a special kind of proof justifying such an action. Here is an example of such reasoning: A debt is an obligation, and thus a kind of contract. Whenever possible contracts should be fulfilled. They should be fulfilled because that practice would produce a preponderance of happiness over unhappiness. Happiness is clearly more desirable than unhappiness. Therefore, human actions should be directed toward achieving happiness. Repaying debts is such an action, and therefore one should always repay debts. The conclusion that one should repay debts is justified by appealing to a moral statement, namely, that actions should be directed toward maximizing happiness. Notice that such a proof is not provided by collecting more facts, but by giving supporting reasons justifying the conclusion, that is, that one should always repay debts. The proof is conceptual in nature. It is a product of a special kind of argumentation called "moral reasoning." Moral theories attempt to find fundamental explanatory principles that are normative in character. Using such normative principles, they can then explain what a person must do to act morally, and why such a person is always justified in acting morally.

One can distinguish between factual and normative statements in a somewhat different way. It is true that there is a class of moral pronouncements that look like factual statements; but, despite this appearance, they are not factual. If one says, "Stealing is wrong," that judgment looks as if a certain fact is being described, just as if one were to say, "Stealing takes place in the United States." But there is a difference. The latter is a factual assertion. One can confirm or disconfirm it by gathering data based on observation and experiment. But the affirmation "Stealing is wrong" is not verifiable or disconfirmable in the same way. Why is this so? To many ethicists, the answer is that there is no observable or quantitative property in the world called "wrongness." If one were to list all the things one could perceive, wrongness, rightness, obligation, or goodness would *not* be in that list. Science, as a factual discipline, deals with the observable and the quantifiable, with such attributes as being blue, being square, and having a certain weight. But moral theories deal with features of human conduct that are neither observable nor quantifiable. This difference is emphasized by the moral skeptic. Scientific judgments can lead to a consensus because they are about observable data. In the moral realm, according to the skeptic, there are no such observable data, and this is why there are irresolvable moral disagreements.

The second difference between moral and most other types of theories is that the former are generally connected with practical action. Though they may be quite abstract in some respects, they invariably contain a practical component about the goals of human life, and what principles would justify actions directed toward such goals. Science does not deal with such ends or with obligatory, practical action. The fact that bodies fall at a certain rate of acceleration does not entail anything about how they should or should not fall, or about how human beings should act once they become aware of this law. So science is not a normative discipline concerned with the justification of practical action. In our earlier example, John Smith confronted a moral dilemma. Should he or should he not join the armed forces? Whatever his choice, it amounted to a decision having practical consequences about what he should do. The question he was asking himself, in effect, was, How can I justify acting in this way rather than in that? Moral theories are designed to help persons like John Smith make such decisions.

We can summarize: In general, then, a moral theory, like all theories, is a broad-ranging, consistent explanatory system; its special features are that the data it deals with—goodness, rightness, and the like—are not observable, and that its principles attempt to resolve questions about the justification of moral decisions and practical conduct. Since the time of the Greeks, the effort to formulate a theory of this sort has been the main challenge for the ethicist. In this chapter we shall consider some important views of this kind.

As we have seen in earlier segments of this book, skeptics have raised doubts about the possibility of arriving at knowledge of any sort. This same attitude is very much part of their outlook in the moral domain. The skeptic not only challenges the views of particular theories, but doubts that any correct theory is possible. The great advocates of moral knowledge, past and present, have been very much aware of these penetrating doubts, and their views are designed to forestall or accommodate them. Since the time of the Greeks, a lively debate has taken place between these two contending forces—a debate that continues today—between those who believe that it is possible to find a set of defensible moral principles and those who doubt that this is so. Let us call the former group "moral dogmatists." The word "dogmatist," as used in this context, does not mean that these persons are obdurate or unreasonable; it simply means that they believe that positive theories applying to the moral life are possible. Their opponents we can call "skeptics." They cast doubt on what the dogmatists assert. As we shall see, there are many forms of moral skepticism. Therefore, let us look at this contest. We shall begin by considering the fundamental structure that any moral theory must exhibit. Let us call this structure the "Moral Model." It is an abstraction, of course, and differing moral theories will fill in the schema in their own specific ways. But by exploring this abstract structure, we shall be in a better position to understand and evaluate the merits of specific dogmatic approaches and the skeptical challenges to them.

The Moral Model

The model has two fundamental features that we mentioned above, but let us spell these out in more detail: (1) It asserts that moral principles are universal and hold without exception, and (2) it is a form of classical foundationalism. In this second respect, it looks for an

underlying principle, like the Law of Gravitation, to explain and justify all moral conduct. Let us consider these principles in order.

(1) Most ethicists have argued that moral principles hold universally. A contrasting view is Aristotle's, namely, that moral principles
hold for the most part. According to the model, moral principles
require that in all relevant situations conduct must consistently conform to the principle. To say that such universal prescriptions do not
admit of exceptions is to say they are indefeasible, that is, that they
cannot be annulled or mitigated in any way. A defense of this idea is
to be found in Kant's "On the Supposed Right to Lie from Altruistic
Motives," where Kant argues that there are never any circumstances
in which one is justified in telling a lie.

(2) The second feature of the moral model is its *foundationalism*. This is connected with the first feature. It presupposes that
moral principles are universal and hold without exception, but it
goes further than the first in drawing a distinction between different
levels of moral principles. It thus argues for a hierarchy of principles,
whose basis is a *single* foundational principle. All other principles
logically depend upon, and can be justified by, an appeal to the fundamental principle. Because it is basic, the fundamental principle is
not supported by evidence, reasons, or any other moral principles.
To use a phrase of Wittgenstein's, "It is just there like your life."

Here is how the model describes the role played by principles in
cases of moral deliberation: Suppose one holds that cheating is
always wrong, and suppose that a moral skeptic challenges this
claim. A philosopher who subscribes to the model may defend his
position in one of two ways. He may argue that the prohibition
against cheating is a basic principle of morality, and that nothing further can be said in its behalf. Or, if he holds that it is not basic, he
will claim that it can be derived from a deeper principle. Suppose the
deeper principle in this case is the Principle of Utility. This principle,
as mentioned above, entails that cheating is wrong because in the
long run it will lead to a preponderance of unhappiness over happiness. If the skeptic now challenges the Principle of Utility, a proponent of the model again has two options: He can claim that it is basic
or that it rests on a still deeper principle. The eventual outcome of
the process of responding to obsessive challenge is the model of

moral reasoning. It holds that all moral reasoning will ultimately rest upon a principle that lies beyond justification or evidential support.

The Principle of Utility is one example of the kind of fundamental tenet that the model embodies, but there can be—indeed there are and have been—many different principles, each of which is taken to be fundamental. Thus, a Kantian would reject Utility as fundamental in favor of the categorical imperative, and there might even be different versions of the categorical imperative, each of which is singly taken to be fundamental. The important point is that a particular maxim is held to be fundamental by its adherents. We shall discuss these differing views later in the chapter.

Like scientific theory, the model offers a synoptic view of the role played by principles in explaining diverse phenomena. But its special search is for the deepest principle that ties together and justifies a wide range of moral decisions, beliefs, and conduct. It is an admirable quest, but the skeptic will argue that it is replete with irresolvable difficulties.

Assumptions of the model

In addition to these two main characteristics, the model embodies four assumptions. These are not assumptions that support whatever principle is taken to be fundamental—since what is fundamental is not supported—but are ingredients upon which the whole model rests. Let us look at these now:

(1) Adherents to the model presuppose that it is possible to identify accurately those cases or situations to which moral reasoning applies. It is assumed that there is something special about these cases and the reasoning that concerns them. In particular, it is assumed that such cases have sharp boundaries and this is why they allow for easy identification. Truth telling or lying or selfish behavior are such cases. There are no intermediate cases: Either one is telling the truth or one is not; either one is selfish or one is not. Because they have sharp boundaries, the fundamental principle allows one to arrive at certain kinds of judgments about them. As we shall see, the skeptic will question this assumption.

(2) The model assumes, as we indicated earlier, a radical division

between factual judgments and moral judgments. This is classically described as the "fact/value distinction." If something is a factual judgment then it cannot be a value judgment, and vice versa. It is a factual judgment that many people smoke cigarettes. That they should or should not do so is not a matter of fact but an evaluation of their conduct. This difference is usually characterized by saying that moral judgments are normative as distinct from descriptive. There is a parallel distinction drawn in logic. Logical theory is directed toward developing rules that define valid reasoning. How people actually reason is a factual matter, something that could be described by psychological theory. But how they should reason in order to avoid mistakes is a normative question, and it is this sort of issue that logical theory attempts to resolve. In a similar way, how people act is a factual matter; how they ought to act is a normative consideration. Moral theory is thus normative or evaluative and not purely factual.

(3) The third assumption is connected with the preceding. The moral model assumes that there are two different kinds of moral judgments: assessments and prescriptions. This is a linguistic or conceptual distinction and is normally taken to be exhaustive. Assessments have a descriptive tinge, though they are not wholly descriptive in the way that factual statements are. They are descriptive in the sense that they may claim it to be a fact that someone is untrustworthy or selfish; yet they generally presuppose in making such claims that being selfish is morally reprehensible, so they typically carry with them evaluative resonances. Philosophers may also ask whether lying is always wrong or whether suicide is always wrong. The answers to such questions are assessments of the activities of lying and suicide and thus go beyond the descriptive. In contrast, prescriptions are judgments about the merits of pursuing certain courses of action: whether they are desirable or undesirable, obligatory or nonobligatory, or right or wrong. The actions in question may be particular or general. The model thus distinguishes between practices, such as lying, and cases—for example, a lie told on a particular occasion. The model holds that all judgments of both types derive their force through appeals to the fundamental principle.

(4) In explaining such omnipresence, the model distinguishes between *tacit* and *express* appeals to the fundamental principle.

Here it draws an analogy between practice and theory. One can engage in moral conduct or behavior without having the fundamental principle in mind, just as one can engage in cogent reasoning without having logical principles expressly in mind. Moral practice is frequently the product of habit and is, in such cases, generally unreflective or tacit. But the model holds that such unreflective practice always presupposes the existence of the fundamental principle, and that in cases where a justification of practice is required, the appeal to the principle is then made explicit or express.

It thus assumes that access to the fundamental moral principle is possible, and this in turn assumes that some degree of reflection is necessary in order to identify a fundamental moral principle. The unexamined life, according to the model, cannot therefore be a moral life.

The power of the model

Why is the moral model so compelling to philosophers? If one compares and contrasts how animals interact with other animals, with how humans interact with other humans, it is plausible to hold that nothing like a moral sense, that is, an ethical life, exists among the animals. No animals could understand the concepts of habeas corpus, lying, divorce, or genocide. The development of a full-fledged moral outlook seems to be the highest product of the evolutionary scale on earth and to be exemplified only in human interactions. These interactions concern the way that humans feel they should treat others and be treated by them. Such treatment is embedded in traditional practices, such as the respect for others, and these practices in turn are recognized to function as an implicit set of principles. From this set of practices, explicit codifications are eventually developed—for example, the Ten Commandments—and from these, higher-order principles, such as the categorical imperative, are in turn formulated. From that process the moral model also seems to follow. It seems to follow that there is a hierarchy of principles, some depending on and derivable from others, that govern human moral interactions. From that implication it seems plausible to infer that there must be some foundation to this system of rules or principles. But if there is such a foundation, the foundational element itself cannot depend on other principles for its support. This is what it means to say that it is foundational or basic. This whole train of reasoning, or perhaps something like it, is what lies behind the model and is one of the sources of the powerful attraction it has for philosophers.

Five skeptical challenges to the model

First, as indicated earlier, the theme of justification is an important aspect of the model. Justification takes two forms: the justification of (a) of assessments and prescriptions, and (b) practices and cases. According to the model, the process of justification ultimately derives from a single fundamental principle, which itself is said to be beyond justification. If it could be justified it would not be fundamental; to say it is fundamental is just to say that it depends on no other moral principle. Yet the skeptic points out that if the principle that is ultimately appealed to in this process is beyond justification, the moral model is inconsistent. There is something paradoxical in insisting that all moral behavior must be justified while employing a justifying principle which itself cannot be justified. According to the skeptic, the situation is similar to the following: Suppose a person claims to know with certainty that p is true, but cannot give supporting reasons for this claim. Suppose one were to say, "I know with certainty that Smith is in his office, but I can't tell you how I know that." Such a person is saying something common sense would not accept. How can one assert that one knows without being able to justify his claim to know? To demand a justification while using a principle that itself cannot be justified thus violates common intuitions about what constitutes rationally coherent discourse. The skeptic thus concludes that the moral model is conceptually incoherent.

Second, there is a related difficulty. The moral model differs in one respect from foundationalist views in other domains of philosophy, for example in logic and epistemology. The problem is this: In each of the great moral systems, such as utilitarianism or Kantianism, the status of its putative foundational element has been challenged. This is not generally true of nonmoral schemes. In most axiomatic logical systems, such as that developed in *Principia Mathematica*

(1910–1913) by Alfred North Whitehead and Bertrand Russell, the axioms are obviously true and one cannot think of counterexamples to them.

One can illustrate the point as follows: One of *Principia*'s five axioms is called the Law of Commutation. In logical notion it reads: $(p \equiv q) = (q \equiv p)$. In arithmetic it would translated as $(1 + 2) = (2 + 1)$. In English, it says that the statement "p is equivalent to q," is equal to the statement, "q is equivalent to p." It is impossible to think of any exception to this principle; it is a logical law that holds universally. But the same cannot be said of any of the candidates for foundational status in the moral realm, such as the Pleasure Principle, the categorical imperative, or the Principle of Utility. The objections to all such candidates are legion. The Principle of Utility holds, for example, that a law is just if it produces more happiness than unhappiness for the greatest number of persons in society in the long run. But this principle has some obvious counterinstances. It implies, read strictly, that an innocent person can be put to death if his or her demise would produce an excess of happiness over unhappiness for most persons in the long run. Common sense would deny that killing an innocent person in order to maximize social happiness captures the intuitive meaning of justice.

The skeptical inference drawn from such counterexamples is that because arguments against a putative foundational moral principle can always be developed, any such principle will itself require justification and therefore cannot be basic. The moral model leads to an infinite regress of supporting reasons and thus collapses of its own weight. Accordingly, it cannot be accepted as a correct account of moral reasoning.

Third, the skeptic points out that in certain situations so-called universal moral principles may conflict. If that is so, it is impossible to act on either maxim and thus impossible to act morally. Consider the famous example that Plato gives at the beginning of the *Republic*. One is not supposed to tell a lie in any circumstances, and one is never supposed to inflict harm upon the innocent. These are assumed to be universal moral principles. But suppose a madman approaches you with a weapon in hand, asking for the whereabouts of a female friend of yours whom he threatens to kill because he does not like her.

The friend has done no wrong and hence is innocent of any offense. If you tell the truth, that is, inform the insane person where your friend is, you will be endangering her. If you refuse to tell, or if you lie, you will be violating the injunction that you must always tell the truth. If you do the one you will be guilty of abridging the other.

The basic difficulty with any moral system that employs "all" (or its equivalents) in an unrestricted way is logical. It is subject to a famous paradox developed by Bertrand Russell. Any system of rules that gives rise to Russell's paradox is self-contradictory. Let us illustrate the point in its logical form and then show how it applies to the moral model. Here is a simple version of the paradox: Suppose one asserts that all rules have exceptions. Let us call the rule "All rules have exceptions," *R*. Assume *R* is true. If so, it follows that there are exceptions to *R*, and hence, *R* is false. Assume *R* is false. Then there are no exceptions to *R*, and *R* is true. Thus, *R* is both true and false. Now any system in which *R* is both true and false is logically inconsistent and can be rejected. Russell's paradox arises because the word "all" is used in an unrestricted way. If one held that "all the rules belonging to chess" have exceptions, this statement would not give rise to Russell's paradox, since it is not a rule that belongs to chess. But the paradox does arise for the Moral Model since it uses "all" in an unrestricted way to speak about moral contexts. To hold that in all contexts one must speak the truth, or that in all contexts one must not gratuitously inflict pain is to use "all" in this unrestricted sense. Such a system can be shown to be inconsistent, that is, one can derive from it both the statement that one should never lie and its negation. It follows that the system is vacuous and that none of its principles can give substantive advice about how to act in particular moral situations. From this analysis, the skeptic draws the consequence that human beings cannot live by moral principles if they have the universality and unexceptionability the Moral Model ascribes to them.

Fourth, the skeptic emphasizes the relativity of moral practice. Many societies are governed by different moral rules. For example, in most contemporary Western societies incest is strictly forbidden; yet in the twenty-fifth Egyptian dynasty the male rulers were required to marry their sisters on the ground that all other persons were inferior. By Western standards, this was a justification of the practice of incest. For every code that a given society assumes to be universal, one can find another where it is either rejected or ignored. In the Judeo-Christian tradition the "Sabbath" is held to be a day of rest; but for the Jews that day of the week is Saturday and for the Christians it is Sunday. Moreover, the very concept of a "Sabbath" has no application in many societies, for example, in Japan. The skeptic claims that if moral principles are relative to a given society, no moral principle holds universally and, accordingly, that the Moral Model is wrong. One of the main supporting arguments for this skeptical conclusion is that there is no underlying material reality for morality as there is for science. As we explained earlier, moral predicates such as "good" or "right" differ in their status from such scientific predicates as "blue," "square," and "weighing forty pounds."

Fifth, the skeptic holds that every moral principle is capable of being undone in the face of particular cases. Take the following example. It is often held that equal crimes deserve equal punishment. A corollary of this maxim is that it would be unfair to kill one man for stealing a loaf of bread while giving another man a mere warning not to repeat the action. Yet if we look at actual human practice, we can see that this principle is constantly violated. If it is found that one of the persons is an habitual criminal who is often engaged in violence, whereas the other is a first time offender who has stolen the loaf because he has lost his job and wishes to feed his family, the courts will treat these persons differently. Common sense agrees and says that such differential treatment is justified. The skeptic points out that any supposed universal moral principle can be defeated by particular cases. Take the supposed prohibition against torture, for example. One can easily construct a case—say, in a military situation—where torturing an enemy soldier to elicit information can be justified on moral grounds. The skeptic thus concludes that the Moral Model cannot be defended.

The dogmatic rejoinder

Though these are powerful arguments, the dogmatist is not easily defeated. A compelling rejoinder to the skeptic is possible. Let us consider some of these now.

(1) The dogmatist disagrees with the skeptic's view that no successful theory is possible by pointing out that there are such theories in many different fields of human endeavor: in linguistics, sociology, psychology, and literature, as well as in the special sciences, such as biology and chemistry. Why, then, should there not be successful theories about moral conduct? Furthermore, the dogmatist emphasizes that some successful theories are normative. Modern logical theory is a good example. It deals with the principles of correct reasoning, that is, with rules that never permit the derivation of false conclusions from true premises. These rules are not descriptive of how persons *actually* reason, but are recommendations as to how they *should* reason. There are also similar normative theories in linguistics. These concern both syntactical and semantic correctness. A case in point would be the rule that mandates that a plural noun must be accompanied by a plural verb. Ordinary speakers often violate such rules, and it is normative grammar that explains why they are mistaken in their speech habits. Nearly all sports depend on normative rules. In baseball, for instance, a ball hit outside of the chalk lines is ruled a foul. Such rules determine the correctness of play. There is nothing peculiar, then, about having normative theories whose content is human conduct, that is, how persons should behave as moral agents.

(2) Like all theories, moral theories have many advantages over unreflective practice. While it may be true that logical theory gives an account of valid reasoning that may bear little resemblance to how most persons actually think, it is a mistake to infer from this fact that logic is epistemically and pragmatically irrelevant to human practice. An example may help to make the point transparent. The ancient Bablyonians are known to have carried out extensive surveys and measurements of land. These activities were technological achievements, not highly infused with theory. Yet a geometric theory, like that of Euclid, explains why their measurements did (or did not) result in success, as well as explaining many things about space, figures, and measurements that the Babylonians never could have achieved. A theory may also reveal inconsistencies in our everyday practice. This is certainly true in the moral domain. Persons may advance specific claims on different occasions about what it is right

or wrong to do in each of those situations; yet, when generalized, these claims may turn out to be inconsistent. A good theory can not only diagnose the reason or reasons for such inconsistency, but can also rectify its errors. Consider utilitarianism, for example. We know on the basis of direct experience that persons tend to avoid pain. Yet why they should goes beyond the mere instinctive and requires an explanation. This is something that utilitarianism provides. It articulates what is implicit in such instinctive behavior into a consistent moral view—a view that allows for an extension of the conception of a moral agent to nonhuman beings, such as animals.

(3) For the dogmatist, the skeptical objection that fundamental moral principles, such as the categorical imperative or the Principle of Utility, cannot themselves be justified is not a serious complaint. Explanation must come to an end in every field. In logic, for instance, the axioms are basic in just this sense. An axiom by definition is not provable within the particular system that employs it as a base. Indeed, if every explanatory principle itself required further explanation, one would have an infinite regress of explanations, which would entail that no particular explanation could ever get off the ground. As Wittgenstein says in *On Certainty*: "At the foundation of well-founded belief lies belief that is not founded."[1] This comment can be taken as generally true. It neutralizes the skeptical objection that the moral model rests upon a justificatory principle that itself cannot be justified.

(4) Perhaps the strongest skeptical challenge derives from the doctrine of moral relativism. As we have seen, this skeptical position rests on two contentions: (a) That societies differ radically with respect to the moral principles they hold sacred, and (b) that relativism arises in the moral domain because there are no observable features, such as goodness or rightness, that allow for objectively true judgments such as we find in science. The dogmatist rejects both (a) and (b). With respect to (a), the dogmatist denies that there is such a radical divergence of moral practice as the skeptic claims. In every society, for example, rape and murder are not tolerable. Though admittedly there may be disagreement about particular forms of behavior, these may not be really fundamental. To obtain the sort of cohesion that a society requires, every association of human

beings must emphasize the importance of certain principles: for example, truth telling against lying and the treatment of other human beings according to the Golden Rule, which states that each person should treat every other human being as he or she would like to be treated. The categorical imperative of Kant, which states in one of its formulations that each human should be treated as an end and not as a means, is simply a generalization of the Golden Rule. In referring to such underlying principles, the dogmatist is stressing that every society must accept certain rules in order to form a cohesive assemblage. The same idea is to be found in the writings of Wittgenstein. In a famous passage he states, "In order to make a mistake, a man must already judge in conformity with mankind."[2] With respect to (b), the dogmatist states that there are many disciplines that deal with nonobservable entities or features and yet obtain objectivity and agreement in judgment. Mathematics and logic are good examples. Numbers are usually treated as abstract entities (i.e., as distinguished from symbols or marks or sounds, they are not observable entities) and yet there can be unanimity about the results using numbers in all sorts of complicated calculations. The fact that goodness, rightness, and oughtness are not observable does not entail that statements and theories about them cannot lead to a consensus or to other forms of objectivity.

It seems from these responses that the dogmatist has made a good case for the Moral Model. It also seems that the skeptic has made a good case against it. Perhaps one cannot come to a resolution about the merits of the Moral Model by considering it in this very general and abstract form. It may be, for example, that it is particular versions of the model that are more compelling or, alternatively, more easily disposed of. Let us therefore look at some of the most important of these conceptions (i.e., moral theories) and the skeptical objections to them. We shall start with the ancient period, dealing with the views of Socrates, Plato, and Aristotle; follow it with a discussion of religious ethics; and then conclude with two modern theories: Kantian ethics and utilitarianism.

SOCRATES, PLATO, AND ARISTOTLE

Socrates

The earliest, most general moral theory in the Western philosophical tradition is to be found in the writings of Plato (427–347 B.C.E.). Whether this theory is actually Plato's or Socrates' is a scholarly question much debated, but impossible to decide authoratively given the available textual evidence. As we explained in chapter 2, Plato's writings are in dialogue form rather than being expository treatises. They feature a central character, named "Socrates," who was a kind of conceptual gadfly in Athens. He is depicted by Plato as an inveterate interrogator of others, asking profound questions about a host of subjects. Many of these concern moral matters: what justice and piety are, whether virtue can be taught, and whether the good life is identical with a life of pleasure.

Socrates was born in 469 B.C.E. and died in 399. The documents deriving from his philosophical predecessors are few in number and are mostly fragments. These snippets do contain references to ethical matters but none of them is extensive enough to constitute a complete theory. Such a theory is first found in the Platonic dialogues. Apart from these early materials, nearly all the information we have about pre-Socratic thinkers comes from later writers and is thus mostly secondhand. The earliest such commentator is Aristotle, who was born fifteen years after Socrates' death. Two other important scholars were Hippolytus and Diogenes Laertius, both of whom wrote much later, in the third century C.E. From their accounts it seems that the pre-Socratics (Thales, Anaximander, Anaximenes, Pythagoras, Heraclitus, Parmenides, Empedocles, and Democritus, among others) were primarily interested in cosmology rather than in moral speculation. At some point in the fifth century, there was a radical shift in Greek philosophy from scientific to moral and political considerations. Many scholars assert that Socrates was the main source of this change, even though Plato in the *Phaedo* reports Socrates as saying that as a young man he was primarily interested in cosmological questions. Still, if we accept the Platonic dialogues as accurate descriptions of the kinds of issues Socrates raised as he wandered around Athens, we can infer that moral and political questions eventually replaced his naturalistic speculations.

But in even referring to Socrates' views, many scholars urge caution in making definitive judgments. This is because, as far as is known, he never wrote anything. As we indicated in chapter 2, the main sources of contemporary information about his life and doctrines come from three sources: (1) the twenty-four to twenty-six "authentic" Platonic dialogues in which Socrates is either a main speaker or a significant participant (a list that excludes *The Laws,* in which he is not among the dramatis personae); (2) three works by the historian Xenophon—*Apology*, *Symposium*, and *Memorabilia*; and (3) two plays by Aristophanes, *The Clouds* and *The Wasps*. These three sources give us widely divergent portraits of Socrates, yet from them one can elicit significant pieces of information about him. They indicate that he was married, had children, and served in the Athenian army, and that he moved around Athens, posing difficult questions to its citizens. The literary evidence also indicates that he was convicted on charges of impiety and corrupting the young, and was then executed, forced to drink a draft of poisonous hemlock.

Plato was born in 427 B.C.E.; Xenophon, in 430; and Aristophanes, in 448. Both Plato and Xenophon became disciples of Socrates when they were teenagers. Plato's *Apology*, *Crito*, and *Phaedo* describe the trial and death of Socrates in 399 B.C.E. and are thus depictions of events occurring when Plato was twenty-eight, Xenophon thirty-one, and Aristophanes forty-nine. Both Plato and Xenophon were devastated by his execution, and bitterly resented the leaders of the Athenian democracy (Anytus, Meletus, and Lycon) who prosecuted Socrates. Their writings describe a great man, a kind of philosophical saint, whom they and many others worship. Aristophanes, on the other hand, is more critical. He lampoons Socrates as an unworldly cosmologist in *The Clouds*, presenting him as one who reflects on "the things beneath the earth and the things in heaven," and who views merely human affairs with smugness and contempt. He also suggests that Socrates denies the existence of the gods, which is one of the charges brought against him in his trial two decades later. In *The Wasps*, produced in 422 B.C.E., Aristophanes satirizes the followers of Socrates and, by implication, Socrates himself. He describes peculiar people who wander around Athens, "wear long hair, go hungry and wild, socratize—and carry sticks." In saying that these persons "socratize," Aristophanes is clearly being critical of the individual he takes to be their mentor.

These writers, all of whom knew Socrates personally, provide a variegated picture of the man. From these sources, three things of importance emerge for the historian. First, it is clear that Socrates was a prominent personality in Athens, and because that is so, their depictions, though differing, must have been reasonably accurate or they would have been discounted by the many Athenians who were acquainted with him. This is even true of Aristophanes' comic portrait. It must have captured something that the Athenians could recognize in Socrates, even if it was humorous distortion. That works like the *Apology* and the *Phaedo* are at least roughly historical accounts of the trial and death of Socrates is thus beyond reasonable doubt. Second, these divergent portraits reveal that Socrates exercised a powerful effect on younger persons. Third, they also indicate that his teachings were so ambiguous as to give rise to contradictory understandings among those he influenced. As the post-Socratic history of Greek philosophy, lasting some six centuries, reveals, he was interpreted by Plato as a moral dogmatist, by Aristippus as a hedonist, by Antisthenes and Diogenes of Sinope as a Cynic, and by Pyrrho as a moral skeptic. Curiously enough, each of these schools of philosophy traced its views to Socrates. But if they differed so widely, how is this possible? Since our interest in this work is mainly in skepticism, it is this post-Socratic development that we shall concentrate on in what follows.

Doctrine versus method

If we jump ahead two millenia to the philosopher Wittgenstein, who died in 1951, we may be able to answer the question, How did Socrates' inquiries lead to such different philosophical traditions and interpretations by later thinkers? As we explained in chapter 4 many commentators have depicted Wittgenstein as the philosopher most closely resembling Socrates. Socrates published nothing in his lifetime; Wittgenstein published only one book and a paper. (His posthumous works are gradually being published and are estimated to run to more than ninety volumes.) Like Socrates, Wittgenstein was surrounded by a coterie of dedicated student admirers, among them many persons who later became famous philosophers in their own right, such as Norman Malcolm, Rush Rhees, Elizabeth Anscombe, and Gilbert Ryle. These persons idolized him and helped spread his reputation, a reputation which, while he was alive, made him a kind of cult figure whom many individuals imitated, even down to his manner of speaking. This was also true of Socrates. Yet if one asks, "What exactly did they teach?" or "What were their main theories and doctrines?" one finds it difficult to say. With Socrates this problem is compounded because the main evidence we have for his so-called views comes from the Platonic dialogues, and it is not clear whether Plato is reporting what Socrates actually said or is simply expounding his own views using the persona of Socrates to do so. Moreover, the philosopher that Plato describes, called "Socrates," speaks in a very elusive manner, asking questions and seldom offering positive answers. It is thus difficult to extract an explicit doctrine or theory from such descriptions.

With Wittgenstein we have a similar conundrum. His later philosophical works are especially puzzling. They are products of an unusual, highly aphoristic writing style without much discursive prose or explicit argumentation. He admitted that he could not write a systematic treatise and described the contents of his notebooks as "sketches of landscapes." The philosophical purpose of this collection of arcane remarks is often not clear, even to exegetes of the Wittgenstein texts.

Socrates and Wittgenstein have another characteristic in common. It is clear that each thought philosophical problems were unique and, accordingly, not easy to solve. Each invented a special way of approaching such difficulties. Rather than offering solutions, their practice indicates that they both apply a special method designed to bring out the oddity of philosophical questions, and it is thus the method that is in the forefront of their attention, rather than explicit solutions. These unusual approaches raise the question, What is the point of struggling to develop a special method if it doesn't result in solutions? A possible answer is that both wish to teach those confronting a philosophical problem that it is a mistake to look for a precise or neat solution. They seem to be suggesting, though in oblique ways, that one needs a different kind of understanding of what is at stake in such a problem, and that the method will assist in arriving at such an understanding. Of course, the Socratic and Wittgensteinian methods are entirely different, but in both cases it seems that it is the method that counts. Wittgenstein, for example, said his method required a sort of thinking that was very different from what is required in the sciences, and he said that the required skill could not be acquired merely by hearing lectures; discussion was essential. As regards his own work, he said it did not matter whether his results were true or not. What mattered was that a method had been found.

Socrates, as we have seen, was an obsessive questioner. He would surely have agreed with Wittgenstein that discussion is the name of the philosophical game, and that was indeed the practice that he followed. His whole life was spent in discussion: in asking questions, in turning an issue—such as "Can virtue be taught?"—around and around so that it could be viewed from various perspectives. This is what Wittgenstein did as well. Socrates would have also agreed with Wittgenstein that philosophical questions are radically different from scientific questions, and that is why one has to develop a special technique for dealing with them. In the *Apology* he states that he is the wisest of men because he knows that he knows nothing. This, said while on trial for his life, was one of the sources of the skeptical tradition that arose after his death. In the early Platonic dialogues, such as the *Lysis*, *Charmides*, and *Euthyphro*, Socrates never arrives at a positive answer to such questions as "What is piety?" and "What is friendship?" thus reinforcing the impression of a skeptic at work. Scholars generally believe that it is Socrates, rather than Plato, who first surfaced the idea that if these problems are resolvable it is only if a unique method can be invented to deal with them. In the early dialogues Socrates seems to be struggling to develop such a method, but without being able to make it explicit. Rather, it is Plato who extends and deepens the Socratic approach and eventually gives it an articulate form. As so developed, it is known as the "dialectical method," and by the time of Plato's greatest work, the *Republic,* it is firmly in place. Let us see how Plato's moral philosophy emerges from the use of this technique and then how the skeptics attacked the results he achieved.

Plato and the dialectical method

The simplest answer to the question, "What is the dialectical method?" is that it is a search for a definition of a concept. But this simple answer has to be expanded before its full import can be understood. In philosophy, the term "definition" has three common uses. In one of these a definition is an abbreviation of a term. In the sentence "A robber stole the gold," one could substitute the word "thief" for the word "robber" while maintaining the same meaning for the whole sentence. One might do this for stylistic reasons. But in substituting one verbal expression for the other one is not explaining what a robber or a thief is—and that is the sort of thing Plato is looking for. A second use of the term is sometimes called an "explication." It is quite frequently used in those cases where a vague, ordinary language word, such as "democracy," requires a precise meaning. The point of such an explication is to enhance or improve the ordinary usage of the term. But this is not what Plato's dialectical method is attempting to achieve. He wishes to understand what certain concepts, "justice," "piety," and "responsibility," really mean. In short, he is looking for what philosophers call a "real definition." This is an attempt to explain what a given concept means, and the point of such an explanation is to arrive at an understanding of the nature of the object or thing the definition is speaking about. Thus, if one wishes—as Plato does at the beginning of the *Republic*—to find out what justice really is one way of doing this is to find a real definition of the concept of "justice." The supposition of the method is that there is a one-to-one correspondence between a real definition and that feature of the world that the definition describes. Let us explore Plato's procedure for a moment to see how it works.

The *Republic* opens with a discussion between Socrates and a number of his associates and followers about the nature of justice. What is it? What is it to be just? A series of answers from his auditors follows. Cephalus, the first of these, suggests that justice is the same thing as returning debts and always telling the truth: "honesty in word and deed," as he puts it. But Socrates points out that if a madman, weapon in hand, stated that he wished to kill a friend of yours, innocent of any crime, and demanded to know where the friend was, it would not be just to tell him the truth. The point Socrates is making by this counterexample is that the concept "justice" and the concept "honesty in word" do not mean the same thing. Therefore, one has not discovered the nature of justice by the definition that Cephalus gives. Alternative answers are then proposed by Polemarchus, Thrasymachus, Glaucon, and Adeimantus, and each is shown by a counterexample to be inadequate. Later, Socrates will offer his own definition and we shall explain what that is below.

But now let us look more carefully at the discussion to elicit from it what is meant by a real definition—and in this way we shall be able to explain the nature of the dialectical method.

First, there is a concept to be defined. Suppose this is the concept of justice. Let us call this the "definiendum." Second, there is an effort to explain what the definiendum means by finding a synonym for it. Suppose the synonym is "giving each person his due." Let us call this the "definiens." The presupposition of the process is that if the definiens and the definiendum are exactly synonymous then one will understand the nature of the entity being defined, in this case what justice is. Now what conditions have to be satisfied for the definiens and definiendum to be synonymous? This is what Socrates in the early dialogues was never able to specify. At most, he was able to show that the definienda being offered for words like "piety" and "friendship" were not synonymous. It is Plato who takes a further step and specifies the requisite conditions. Looking back at his procedure from a contemporary standpoint, we can say that he was looking for a set of necessary and sufficient conditions that exactly capture the meaning of a concept. Consider the following example. Suppose one wishes to find the meaning of the concept "brother," where this term is used in such contexts as "x is the brother of y." As so used, the sentence entails that at least two persons are involved. Now clearly, if x is the only child in a family, x cannot be a brother. It is a necessary condition of x's being a brother of y that x be a sibling (i.e., there must be at least one y who is a child of x's parents). Therefore, being a sibling is such a necessary condition. But it is not a sufficient condition, since x and y may be female. Therefore, it is also a necessary condition of being a brother that x be male. If we now combine "being a sibling" and "being a male" then the concept "brother" can be exactly defined as "male sibling." Such a definition is not merely a verbal exchange of one term for another; it also explains precisely what it is to be a brother. And it is this kind of definition that Plato is looking for in the *Republic* with respect to the concept of "justice." Indeed, his entire moral philosophy is an effort to find the real meanings of all the basic moral concepts.

We are now in a position to begin to understand the nature and purpose of the dialectical method. It has the following four features:

- First, it involves someone's putting forth a definiens for a particular concept (i.e., for a definiendum).
- Second, there is a challenge by someone (usually by Socrates in the Platonic dialogues) as to whether the definiens is synonymous with the definiendum.
- Third, a way of showing that the two are not synonymous is to find a counterexample to the definiens. Given such a countercase, it follows that the definiendum and definiens are not synonymous. In the instance cited, Socrates shows that a person can be just while refusing to tell the truth or even by lying. Therefore, justice cannot mean the same thing as telling the truth.
- Fourth, by trying one proposal after another, and in the process eventually neutralizing each counterexample, one may eventually arrive at that set of necessary and sufficient conditions that constitute a real definition of the concept under consideration. The dialectical process is thus something like zeroing in on a target. When no further counterexamples can be found, one has finally hit the center of the target and arrived at the exact meaning of the definiendum. The outcome of this process is an understanding of the the nature of item that the concept defines.

This brief summary explains the method. But there are at least three other important aspects to the process that connect it to Plato's moral philosophy.

It will be noted at the outset that the procedure attempts to discover the common property or set of properties that all examples falling under the concept possess. Consider the concept of "brother," for example. In Plato's terminology he is looking for the *idea* or *form* that *all* brothers and *only* brothers possess. In an alternative vocabulary, we can say that the process is directed to finding the essential nature of what it is to be a brother. It will be noted that the dialectical process deprecates the importance of examples in its search for a common property (i.e., form or essence). Plato is not interested in how this particular brother differs from that particular brother but rather what they, and all brothers, have in common. Particular examples or cases are useful only as means for discovering such a common feature. Again, it will be noted that the dialectical method is a conceptual investigation. It does no good to point to a particular person and say, "There is a brother." Using visual or tactual or auditory information or evidence will not produce the answer. One cannot *see* that a person is a brother in the way that one can see that a person is wearing clothes. The senses will never capture the essence of an entity or thing. It is only via the use of reason that such an outcome is possible. Accordingly, one must transcend the evidence provided by the senses and use reason to accomplish this task. This is why Plato is traditionally labeled a "rationalist."

It is this kind of rationalism that is the basis of his moral philosophy: To discover the nature of any moral notion thus requires the use of reason.

Plato's moral philosophy

Plato's moral theory is complicated. A full explanation ideally would refer in detail to his epistemological, metaphysical, and political ideas, as well as to those that are strictly ethical. We shall try to simplify here. Let us take these aspects of his theory one at a time, beginning with his theory of knowledge. As we have just explained, the dialectical method of searching for a real definition applies to moral notions such as "justice," and "goodness," as well as to such nonmoral concepts as "brother," "blueness," or "circularity." Knowledge consists in the apprehension, via the dialectical method, of a form. In any such a case, one knows what it is to be a brother, to be pious, to be just, and so forth. In the particular case of "justice," for example, its definition is "internal harmony." A just person is one whose three psychological faculties (reason, spirit, and the passions) function harmoniously. A just state is one whose three classes (rulers, warriors, and workers) work smoothly together. Real definitions thus achieve knowledge. This is the epistemological aspect of Plato's philosophy.

Let us now turn to Plato's metaphysics, his theory about the nature of reality. This is a two-worlds doctrine that draws a contrast between the real world and the world of appearance. Both contain various kinds of objects, but the objects are different. Those in the real world do not change and are not apprehensible by the senses. Numbers and forms are the constituents of the real world; images and visible objects, of the world of appearance. One cannot see, touch, or hear the forms, just as one cannot see or touch the property that all brothers have in common. But this common property (form) is a real entity. What one can see are individual human beings, "visible objects" in Plato's terminology, some of whom may be brothers. But the senses cannot discern brotherhood per se. Plato contends that because they are subject to change, visible objects are not fully real. They belong to the world of appearance. Accordingly, one's awareness of such objects, via sense experience, never produces knowledge; at most, it produces opinion or belief.

It is thus possible to have knowledge only of those unchanging invisible entities he calls "forms" or "ideas." As we have explained earlier, by "idea" Plato does not mean anything psychological. Being a brother is a real property that various individuals possess, not a psychological entity such as a belief or opinion. These common properties do not belong to the sensible world, and because that is so, these features cannot be accessed through sense experience, but only through reason. Plato's metaphysics is thus intimately connected with his epistemology and bolsters the latter's rationalism.

The moral theory is an immediate consequence of his metaphysical and epistemological views. His metaphysical outlook leads him to the position that moral rules have an objective validity that in no ways depends on men's tastes, opinions, or preferences. His epistemological view supports this theory. If one has knowledge of the form of justice, for example, it follows that there is one and only one morally correct way of behaving. This suggests that moral principles, such as "One must repay debts" or "One must never lie" or "One must not commit adultery," have the same kind of objectivity that mathematical and scientific principles do. Just as the theorem that $2 + 2 = 4$ does not depend for its truth on anyone's opinion, a moral law, such as "Gratitude is due to benefactors," holds universally and is independent of personal opinion or belief.

One can have moral knowledge of such principles, of course, only if one grasps the forms denoted by such moral terms as "justice," "piety," and "right." To this absolutist and objectivist epistemological/metaphysical system, Plato adds another component that is strictly ethical. He holds that if a person has moral knowledge, that person will always act justly or rightly. This is so because justice and rightness—indeed all the positive moral virtues—are in everyone's interest. Hence, if one knows what is good or just one will also act so as to achieve it. Plato is careful to distinguish between what one *thinks* is best for oneself and what is *really* best for oneself. If one has knowledge, then one will not be deceived into thinking something will be in his or her interest when it is not. One interesting consequence of this thesis is that evil behavior is always a function of ignorance. People act immorally when they lack knowledge of what is in their real interest. As he says, "No one errs wittingly." To this relationship between knowledge and right action, Plato adds another ingredient: that acting morally or rightly will always produce happiness. The moral view is thus a form of *eudaemonism*, the thesis that the good life is a happy life. The main elements in his moral philosophy can thus be outlined as follows:

(1) If an agent, x, has knowledge, x will act rightly.
(2) Right action (e.g., to do what is just) is always in the interest of the agent.
(3) Whatever is in the interest of the agent will make the agent happy.
(4) Therefore, if x has knowledge, x will be happy.

The theory as explained so far needs to be supplemented by a brief account of Plato's political philosophy. He takes a negative position with respect to the question of whether *everyone* can acquire knowledge. His view is that most people cannot. He holds to this position on what might be called "genetic" grounds. People differ intrinsically in their abilities: some are naturally faster runners, some are stronger, some are more intelligent, some are more gifted musically than others. Accordingly, Plato contends that only some possess the capacity to acquire knowledge. To be able to do so requires a high degree of intelligence and a sterling moral character. But most human beings are dominated by their senses; they live in, and are content to live in, the world of appearance. Accordingly, they lack the intelligence and moral stature to rise above the kind of information the senses provide. Therefore, only a few out of the entire human population are sufficiently rational to acquire knowledge. This does not mean for Plato that those who cannot acquire knowledge cannot live a just or happy life. Even if they lack the intelligence to acquire knowledge, they might, as as result of their upbringing, be persons with virtuous habits. But given new situations and severe temptations, especially those arising from the desire for money or the temptation to promote the interests of family members, they may deviate from a truly moral life. It is only if a person possesses knowledge that he or she will be *guaranteed* to lead a good life.

But this then raises a different question: Is it possible for *anyone* whatsoever to acquire knowledge and hence necessarily to act rightly? Here Plato's answer is a cautious yes. It depends not only on the individual's intelligence and character but also on the kind of upbringing he or she has had, that is, on how that individual has been reared from infancy. The description of this training program is the essence of Plato's political theory. He believes that by selecting intelligent persons, both men and women, and exposing them from infancy to an intensive intellectual and moral educational curriculum, they can acquire knowledge. And if they do, they will act justly. Plato argues that this "elite" group should then be made the rulers of society, since they will know what is in the real interest of its members. Successful participants in effect will become philosophers, persons who have knowledge and wisdom, and who, once in power, will pass just laws and will themselves act justly. As he states in a memorable phrase, "The ideal state will come into existence only when kings become philosophers and philosophers become kings."

Plato's moral theory thus identifies the good life with a life of happiness, and happiness with the harmonious functioning of the tripartite aspects of the individual soul, and of the three classes that constitute a society. But whether such a society can be brought into existence is for him problematic; since it is not certain that anyone can successfully complete the extensive and strict training program he describes in the *Republic*.

Skeptical responses to Plato

The skeptical challenges to Plato's moral theory are numerous and powerful. Let us consider three of them.

First, Plato's outlook rests on the thesis that if a person knows what is right or good in a given set of circumstances, that individual will never act immorally in those circumstances. According to this principle, men always aim at what they believe to be just or right. But, the skeptic says, if they do, then how can we account for the obvious fact that people often act immorally? Plato's answer, of course, is that such behavior stems from a lack of knowledge. The skeptic agrees that this is sometimes so—a person may experiment with a drug not knowing that its long-range effects are deleterious. But although this may be the case, there are innumerable cases where people have solid knowledge that what they are doing is both immoral and not in their best interest, and yet they continue to act in that way. All sorts of criminals know full well that what they are doing is wrong and yet they do not refrain from engaging in such acts. Persons use alcohol in excessive amounts. They know all the medical facts about the damage that alcohol can do and yet they continue to drink for the transient pleasure they obtain. The skeptic concludes that if Plato's thesis is interpreted as a psychological account of how human beings always behave it is palpably false.

A second skeptical criticism is technical, but very deep. Plato assumes that if one arrives at a real definition of a concept, one will know what the entity is that the concept describes. The skeptic points out that this formula is misleading. It suggests that knowing the meaning of a concept immediately entails that there exists an entity that corresponds to the concept. The skeptic continues the criticism by saying that real definitions, like all definitions, do not carry existential implications. From the fact that we can arrive at a real definition of the concept "giant," it does not follow that any entity exists that is a giant. A giant is defined as a "legendary manlike being of huge stature and great strength and of more than mortal but less than godlike power." This definition exactly captures the meaning of the concept, but from that fact it does not follow that there are any giants. Likewise, from the fact that one can arrive at a definition of "justice" it does not follow that there is an entity, *justice*, which exists in a suprasensible realm. The Platonic thesis that the world of reality consists of such entities is thus the wildest kind of metaphysical fantasizing. The important point is that if there is no such realm, then the further Platonic thesis that knowledge consists in the direct apprehension of forms is also spurious. The skeptical criticism is that if we were to accept the Platonic schema and their compelling objection to it, there would be no such thing as knowledge. And this conclusion, as skeptics, they entirely welcome.

A third skeptical criticism denies the Platonic claim that moral laws have an objectivity that is independent of people's tastes and preferences. According to Plato, there is, in any set of circumstances, a morally correct way of behavior, which can be discovered through the exercise of reason. Thus, for Plato, moral issues are always capable of rational resolution. Through the use of reason one can always determine which moral rule aplies to a given mistake. The skeptic denies that moral principles hold universally and that all moral dilemmas are capable of rational resolution.

Plato's mistake, according to this objection, arises from assimilating moral problems and scientific problems. The latter are in principle always solvable by the use of reason, but this is not true of moral dilemmas. Suppose a woman wonders whether she should have an abortion. Medical science can give her certain facts that may be helpful to her—about the dangers in such cases and so forth. But the personal decision she must take is not determined by the scientific evidence. In the final analysis, the skeptic says, the issue is not decidable on purely rational grounds, though they may play some role. The decision is much more complicated and will depend on a number of factors: one's upbringing, feelings, preferences, tastes, and other determinants. Thus, Plato's rationalism is to be rejected. For the skeptic, it is a case of overintellectualizing human problems. As one skeptic has said, "It is just what one would have expected from a professor who founded an Academy."

Aristotle

There is a direct line of philosophical influence from Socrates to Aristotle. Aristotle, who was born in 384 B.C.E. and died in 322, never knew Socrates, who was executed in 399. But Socrates was Plato's teacher and Plato was Aristotle's teacher. At the age of about seventeen, Aristotle became a student in Plato's Academy and remained there for twenty years, until the death of Plato in 347 B.C.E. Aristotle is clearly aware that he is part of a continuing tradition; in his writings he discusses both Socrates and Plato. He often uses the phrase "we Platonists." It is thus not surprising that his moral philosophy has deep affinities with Plato's. Aristotle's thought stresses the role that reason plays in determining the good life; it is eudaimonistic in the sense of regarding happiness as the fundamental goal for which human beings should strive; it emphasizes the need to develop virtuous habits; and he acknowledges the existence of the forms, though with a different emphasis than we find in Plato.

Yet despite these close resemblances, it also differs profoundly from his teacher's theory. It is far less hostile to pleasure as a fundamental component of the good life; it holds that the senses also give information about reality, and accordingly is more empirical and less rationalistic; it puts more emphasis upon practical reason—i.e., the need to be concerned with daily conduct—and it is opposed to the Platonic conception that moral laws hold absolutely and universally. Most important, it is less hostile to skeptical challenges; indeed, it is clever in incorporating skeptical ideas into its system and by so doing to minimize their deflationary effect. It would be positively wrong to think of Aristotle as a skeptic, yet his philosophy, when compared with Plato's, contains discernible antidogmatic strains. In order to unpack this intricate doctrine and to see its relationship to skepticism we shall start from his metaphysical and political theories.

Aristotle's metaphysics

Aristotle is the first historian of philosophy. At the beginning of the *Metaphysics* he gives an account of his predecessors, starting with Thales. Like them, he is intrigued by the problem of change and attempts to accommodate two different intuitions: first, that something must remain unchanged when anything changes; and second, that change is real. His struggle to provide an explication of the notion of change is one of the central themes of the *Metaphysics* and his solution is encapsulated in the celebrated doctrine of the "four causes," which maintains that change always proceeds "from potentiality to actuality," as Aristotle puts it. In spite of this forbidding vocabulary, the idea it expresses is not difficult to grasp. According to Aristotle, all change can be fruitfully explained as the gradual development of the innate characteristics a thing possesses. For instance, an acorn has certain inborn capacities, dispositions, or tendencies that slowly manifest themselves as the acorn changes into an oak tree. The tree that results from this process represents the fulfillment (or "actualization") of these inherent traits (or "potentialities"). This is a doctrine that a biologist rather than a physicist might develop, and it is not surprising that Aristotle, the greatest biologist of antiquity, should have been its proponent.

Most scholars think that he generalized his biological investigations into a synoptic view about the nature of all change. In living organisms it is plausible to hold that change is development, that is, that it begins with a simple entity, say, a seed, and over time develops a mature structure that may not resemble its origin at all. Of course, its development might be arrested by unfortunate events—say, if the acorn is eaten by a bird. But if all goes well, the acorn will realize its innate capacity to become a tree. In more modern biological language, a primitive entity, an acorn, has a certain genetic structure and, if everything proceeds without serious interruption, that genetic structure will result in a fully developed oak tree.

The genetic concept allows for scientific prediction. Although one may not be able to predict from an acorn exactly what shape the tree will finally have, one knows that it will not develop into an elm tree, or into a mouse. Thus, the species to which a primitive entity belongs determines, within limits, exactly what kind of thing it will become. As Aristotle viewed these biological facts, it seemed to him that each thing, whether living or inanimate, has a proper goal or end which it will attain, all things being equal. In the case of an acorn, it is to become an oak tree. What is the end in the case of a human being?

Aristotle's answer is that there is something called "human nature," which has two components. All human beings are animals. Like chimpanzees, ants, or spiders they require food, drink, and shelter as they move through the cycle from birth to death. But at the same time there is something unique about humans. This unique feature is the *soul* (i.e., what we would today call the *mind*). This feature expresses itself in a variety of ways that no beast can imitate: in the development and use of language, in the capacity for reasoning, in a sense of the past and the future, and in the ability to develop theories about the nature of the world. The ultimate goal of human development is thus bipolar. There is a goal that humans share with animals—to move from infancy to adulthood. There is a goal, however, that is not possessed by the brutes, and that is to be rational. Aristotle sums up his speculations about human nature by saying that the *essence* of man (his final goal) is to be a *rational animal*.

Aristotle's moral theory is thus based on this fundamental insight. In his view, no specification of the good life will be satisfactory that does not take the dual nature of human beings into account. The good life must be one that is specifically good *for such unique animals*. Since they are rational, the good life must be conducted in accordance with reason. In saying this, Aristotle is not implying that the good life is identical with a life of reason, but he does insist that unless such rational capacities are fully exercised, it cannot be a good life for humans.

His moral philosophy depends not only on this metaphysical outlook but also on his political theories. Human dispositions cannot be realized in isolation. From the moment of birth each human being depends on others—to survive a lengthy infancy and adolescence and to learn to participate in those communal features that distinguish mankind from the beasts: the ability to speak a language, to feel remorse, guilt, and gratitude. For Aristotle, human beings are social animals and it is only within the larger scope of a community that full development into adulthood can occur. As he says in a famous apothegm, "He who is unable to live in a society, or who has no need, because he is sufficient for himself, must either be a beast or a god."

In the light of these doctrines, what is Aristotle's depiction of the good life for human beings? Unlike Plato, who tried to deduce the answer by the use of reason alone, Aristotle adopts a commonsense, inductive approach to the issue. He observes the behavior, practices, and customs of everyday folk and infers from these data that people of common sense invariably attribute a single characteristic to lives that they describe as "good." That characteristic is happiness. So Aristotle claims that the correct answer to the question, What is the good life for human beings? is that it is a happy life.

But this answer is only a preliminary response to the question, since people may mean different things by "happiness." Some think such a life is one of sensual gratification, others say it is the acquisition of wealth, others assert it is one of fame. Aristotle thinks that the role of the philosopher is to look beyond these kinds of facile comments to see if there is a deeper answer to the question. His aim is to explain more carefully and more clearly what the common man intends when he says that a good life is a happy life. The *Nicomachean Ethics*, which is the chief treatise on ethics attributed to Aristotle (and the only one uniformly regarded as authentic) is thus a formal inquiry into the nature of happiness

The characterization that Aristotle advances is far removed from the language of the common person. It is: "Happiness is an activity of the soul in accord with perfect virtue."[3] This is hardly what the ordinary man would *say* if he were asked what he means by "happiness," but, according to Aristotle, this is what he would *mean* when his thought process is explored at a deeper level. Aristotle's interpretation of this formula is not difficult to understand, and it is a reasonable approximation to the ordinary sense of the word "happiness."

To unpack his succinct mode of expression, we should focus on the words "soul," "activity," and "virtue," respectively.

Common sense recognizes that happiness is a psychological condition. If it simply consisted of bodily sensations or feelings, human beings would be no different from the lower animals. Beasts do not have "souls" in the sense in which human have minds or are rational. Therefore, because man is rational, happiness is more than sheer sensation; it is a condition of the soul. Aristotle is prompt to qualify what he asserts here. Some degree of bodily pleasure is needed for humans—after all, they are animals. So a life totally devoid of pleasure cannot be a happy life. But happiness is not identical with pleasure, and in saying this Aristotle thinks he is capturing the common-sense notion of happiness.

The concept of "activity" is also important. Aristotle emphasizes that happiness is neither something rigid or fixed, nor is it a kind of goal or final point. Those who hold such a view tend to think of happiness as a prize for successful living, like the trophy a tennis player would receive for winning at Wimbledon. Instead, Aristotle wishes to propose a different conceptual model for grasping the nature of happiness. He suggests that it is something that accompanies the ordinary (and extraordinary) activities of daily life. According to this model, it is something like persistence. A man who follows a course of conduct persistently does not arrive at a particular goal called "persistence." Rather, it is a way of doing something—refusing to be beaten by circumstances, practicing a skill sedulously until it is mastered, and so forth. Happiness on this conception is thus a way of engaging in the various activities of life, such as reading, working, and interacting with friends. For example, a person who is enthusiastic in interacting with friends, willingly accepts challenges, delights in solving problems, and is not depressed, tense, or insecure is a happy person. This is Aristotle's view as well as that of common sense. Happiness is thus a *concomitant* of the way we conduct ourselves in life, not a goal or end we are trying to reach.

The third key word in Aristotle's definition is "virtue." Here, his view deviates somewhat from common sense. Aristotle follows Socrates and Plato in thinking of each thing as having a specific use or role for which it is best suited. Its role will depend on the kind of thing it is. So "virtue" does not have its usual everyday meaning, such as "moral rectitude" or "chastity." Rather, as he employs the term, it is virtually synonymous with "function." Thus, the virtue of a knife is to cut things and of a hammer to drive home nails. But if each thing has its own unique function, what is that function for a human being? What is a human's peculiar virtue?

Aristotle's response hearkens back to his metaphysical thesis that a human being is a unique kind of animal in being rational—in having a soul. Accordingly, a person is fulfilling his function when that individual lives in accordance with the dictates of reason. Aristotle sees such a function being exercised in one of two ways: either through philosophical reflection or in sensibly conducting the affairs of daily living. The former function he calls "intellectual virtue"; the latter, "moral virtue." Intellectual virtue is reminiscent of Plato's account of reason. There is unquestionably a kind of happiness associated with sheer philosophical reflection. But it is moral virtue, the use of reason for dealing with practical problems, that mainly interests him. Thus, his famous formula that "happiness is an activity of the soul in accord with perfect virtue" is a way of emphasizing that the use of practical reason is an essential condition for achieving happiness. But this formula is still not specific enough for Aristotle; it does not indicate in detail how one should act in particular circumstances. The inquiry thus leads him to develop a theory to that effect. It is perhaps the most famous thesis of the *Nicomachean Ethics* and is called the "doctrine of the mean."

The doctrine of the mean

The doctrine is an attempt to answer the question, How should human beings as moral agents, act in specific circumstances? His answer is that they should live *moderately* in accordance with the dictates of practical reason. If they pursue this course of conduct, they will be happy. The doctrine of the mean is thus a more specific regimen of how persons ought to conduct their lives in order to be happy. Being happy, as Aristotle views the matter, is something like being properly nourished. If one asks, "How much or what kind of food should a person eat in order to be properly fed?" Aristotle's answer would be that no general response is satisfactory. It depends on the age of the person, how large the person is, what kind of activities he or she is engaged in, and so forth. One must thus answer the question on a case-by-case basis, taking account of various contextual circumstances. The question "How should practical reason be exercised in order for someone to be happy?" is, for Aristotle, just like the previous question. One cannot provide a wholesale answer that will make practical sense. In saying this, Aristotle breaks with Plato. He is suggesting that ethics is not an a priori discipline, with rigid principles that can be discovered by pure reason alone, as Plato's theory of forms asserts.

In contrast, Aristotle is saying that the facts matter; such facts are discovered by observation and by trial and error. If we return to the matter of a proper diet for a moment, we can see the emphasis Aristotle is putting on experience. For Plato, no information derived from the senses can lead to knowledge. Aristotle urges an opposite point of view. A large man will generally require more food than a small woman—but not always. The proper nourishment anyone needs can only be established by trial and error: If a person eats a certain amount of food and remains hungry or loses weight, then he should eat more. A professional athlete will generally require more nourishment than a clerk with a sedentary job. The moral to draw from such examples—and note that for Aristotle the example is important in a way it is not for Plato—is that the correct amount of food one should consume is thus a *mean* between the extremes of gorging oneself and of starving oneself; but there is no a priori way of determining what this amount should be for any particular individual.

In speaking of a "mean" here, Aristotle is not talking about an average or a mean in the statistical sense. Let us assume that for a particular athlete eating two ounces of meat per day is too little, and that eating forty ounces is too great. If we average these quantities we would emerge with the figure of twenty-one ounces as the correct portion. Aristotle would say that this is an absurd way of trying to solve the problem of how much one should eat. That answer might be correct for a certain person, but it is dubious that it would, in general, be correct for everyone. People differ and, accordingly, the proper amount they should eat cannot be captured in a simple arithmetical formula. All one can say is that what is right for a particular person falls somewhere between these limits—and this is what he intends with the use of the term "mean."

When the doctrine is applied to ethics, it implies that there are a number of different, but correct, ways of living for human beings. What is a right course of conduct for one person may not be right for another. Moreover, the discovery of such a pattern for living for a given individual cannot be determined by reason alone. It can only be established a posteriori, that is, by the sort of observational and experimental procedures indicated above. As opposed to Plato, Aristotle can be described as a relativist and an empiricist in ethics.

The implications for the achievement of happiness follow directly from his relativism and empiricism. The proper mode of conduct will depend on the individual's physical capacities, temperament, interests, desires, and interactions with others. The number of correct ways of living is thus multifarious—in principle, there could be as many as there are human beings who differ from one another. All Aristotle is stressing is that the attempt to lead a good life must follow the dictates of practical reason: It must be led in conformity to the doctrine of the mean. One who conducts himself in this way will achieve happiness.

Virtue is thus conduct that lies between extremes. Courage is a virtue that lies between cowardice and rashness; liberality, between prodigality and frugality; pride, between vanity and humility. In all these cases, virtuous behavior is reasonable behavior. A man who is rash is foolish because he exposes himself unnecessarily to danger; a coward is foolish because he has unrealistic fears. To act courageously is to act between the extremes of rashness and cowardness. "Courage" is thus defined as the mean between rashness and cowardice. But in saying this, Aristotle is also stressing that courageous behavior for one person may not be courageous for another. What would be courageous for a professional boxer would be rashness for an untrained fighter. Each of the virtues will thus, in practice, lead to differing forms of conduct, since what will count as the mean in such cases is context dependent.

As we indicated earlier, Aristotle's moral theory is profoundly different from Plato's. For Plato, right action is independent of the individual or the circumstances; it is simply a matter of following the form or idea. Aristotle's outlook is less austere and rigid. One can see the radical difference in their differing attitudes toward pleasure. For

Plato at his most austere, pleasure (and especially bodily pleasure) is bad and conduct that seeks to acquire it is evil. But for Aristotle pleasure is not entirely bad; it depends on the circumstances. He agrees with Plato that to identify happiness with pleasure is a mistake. Such a life would be trivial; but the good life, as he puts it, "is a serious thing." Nevertheless, a life without pleasure is barren. If there is not a reasonable amount of pleasure in a given life, it cannot be happy. As Aristotle remarks, "No man can be happy on the rack."[4]

The skeptical analysis

Aristotle argues that one cannot develop a general theory for directing specific, practical moral actions. His view is that each case should be looked at on its own and assessed in terms of a variety of factors: the interests and abilities of the agent, the contextual situation in which the agent finds himself, and so forth. The skeptic agrees, but interprets this doctrine as a form of skepticism. According to this criticism, there are no general rules that guide human agents in specific moral situations. But if this is the case, nobody can have moral knowledge of what to do. The Aristotelian outlook thus turns out to be a case of *anything goes*, provided that the action conforms to a mean between excess and insufficiency. This, in effect, means there is no objective way of distinguishing moral from immoral conduct. Accordingly, Aristotle's view, which is supposedly developed to make exactly that discrimination, fails.

The skeptic points out a second difficulty with the theory, namely, that many moral dilemmas are not cases where the doctrine of the mean can apply at all. If an unmarried girl becomes pregnant she has only two choices: either to carry the baby to term or to abort it. Which is the right action to take? Since there is no mean between these alternatives, Aristotle's doctrine cannot provide an answer. Some of the most profound moral dilemmas are like that: either one tells the truth or doesn't; either one is generous or isn't. There is no "intermediate" possibility between telling the truth and not telling the truth. Accordingly, the Aristotelian proposal simply will not do.

Bertrand Russell, who is a type of skeptic in moral matters, offers a third criticism of Aristotle. In A *History of Western Philosophy*, he writes:

There is something unduly smug and comfortable about Aristotle's speculations on human affairs; everything that makes men feel a passionate interest in each other seems to be forgotten. Even his account of friendship is tepid. He shows no sign of having had any of those experiences which make it difficult to preserve sanity; all the more profound aspects of the moral life are apparently unknown to him. He leaves out, one may say, the whole sphere of human experience with which religion is concerned. What he has to say will be useful to comfortable men of weak passions; but he has nothing to say to those who are possessed by a god or a devil, or whom outward misfortune drives to despair.[5]

Russell's objection is one that Fyodor Dostoyevsky might have made. Aristotle seems totally unaware of the profound range of human emotion. For romantic or passionate human beings a life of prudence and caution would be stultifying and cloying; it would lead to boredom and unhappiness. Russell's criticism is tantamount to saying that Aristotle, like Plato before him, overemphasizes the role of reason in human interactions. Many persons would find a life dominated by reason to be irksome, restraining, and confining. They want a different, more dynamic moral philosophy, one that reflects the strivings, yearnings, anxieties, and tensions of daily existence. For them, therefore, nothing could be less appealing than Aristotle's doctrine of a life of moderation.

RELIGIOUS ETHICS: JUDAISM, CHRISTIANITY, ISLAM

Though the moral views of Plato and Aristotle were later used by theologians for religious purposes, their original associations with Greek religion ranged from the minimal to the nonexistent. We first find a formal connection between ethics and religion in the Old Testament, whose twenty-four books constitute the canonical teachings of Judaism. This is a work whose earliest written segments, usually called the "J Document" by scholars, can be traced at least to the eighth century B.C.E. In some of these early materials, such as in chapter 20 of the Book of Exodus, there is an explicit moral code commonly called the Ten Commandments. This consists of a series of general injunctions defining the province of moral behavior for the members of the Jewish faith. These pronouncements include such commandments as: "Thou shalt not commit adultery," "Remember the Sabbath to keep it holy," "Honor thy mother and father," and so forth. In slightly later books of the Old Testament, for example, in Leviticus, there are also specific instructions connected with the moral life. These are mostly detailed rather than general rules and have a vast scope, covering all sorts of daily conduct, from dietary regulations to permissible and forbidden sexual behavior.

The Old Testament is also the basis for the other two great Western religions, Christianity and Islam. Christianity accepts the Old Testament and adds to it the New Testament; Islam accepts both the Old and New Testaments and adds to them its own Scriptural document, the Qur'an. All three of these religions thus have much in common. Each asserts that the universe was created out of nothing by a being of infinite wisdom, power, and benevolence, and though the names of this being differ (e.g., Yahweh, Allah), they are usually translated into English as "God" or "Lord." Each believes that there is a special relationship between human beings and God. God holds absolute sway over all human beings, who are sinful and who can only make adequate sense of their lives by categorically accepting God's ordinances for them. Each religion believes there is a special set of books or documents that contain God's words. All accept that God has given particular human beings a unique authority to convey his message through these books or documents, and such persons are often called "prophets." In Islam, for example, Moses, Noah, Abraham, Jesus, and Muhammad are all equally prophets spreading the word of God. All three religions posit the existence of angels. Each contain strict moral rules; in the cases of Christianity and Islam, some of these derive from the Old Testament and some are specific to each religion.

There are also differences between them. Judaism and Islam are overtly monotheistic, whereas the status of God in Christianity is less clear. It posits three divine persons united in a complex godhead— Father, Son, and Holy Spirit. On some interpretations Christianity is monotheistic and on other interpretations it is trinitarian. Islam requires that each member of the faith observe five daily public and collective prayers, that each adherent diet during the month of

Ramadan, and that each make a *Hajj*—a pilgrimage to the holy city of Mecca—at least once a year. None of these provisions are found in Judaism and Christianity. In Christianity, Jesus is a divine being, whereas in Judaism and Islam he is human, though of extraordinary moral excellence.

Skeptical challenges to religion-based ethics

Religious belief is found in virtually every known human culture. The range of doctrines, both past and present, is vast. Some are polytheistic, others have no gods, but nearly all religions have some sort of moral code. It would be impossible in this chapter to deal with a phenomenon of this diversity and scope; accordingly, we shall confine ourselves to the three great Western religions mentioned above. Again, our focus is on skeptical responses to their doctrines. Such responses fall into five categories.

(1) There are skeptical doubts as to whether there is a god.

(2) There are skeptical doubts as to whether such sacred texts as the Bible and the Qur'an contain God's message to mankind. These doubts fall into two divisions: (a) whether these books are really the creations of God or whether they are human products designed for various human purposes, and (b) whether they contain a consistent message. For example, the Pentateuch (Torah) of the Old Testament is said to have been written by Moses; yet one of these books, Deuteronomy, contains a description of the death and funeral of Moses.

(3) There are skeptical doubts about the relationship that the various prophets have to such sacred texts. The prophets in the Old Testament, for instance, often convey quite different messages. Muhammad, considered by Islam to be the last and most perfect of God's messengers to mankind, sometimes expresses doctrinal positions that differ from those of the earlier prophets, including Jesus.

(4) There are deep divisions among adherents to each faith about what the sacred texts actually say. In Christianity, for instance, Catholics believe that Scripture states that humans will be saved by good works, whereas Lutherans hold that salvation is by faith alone. In Islam, there are profound doctrinal difference between the Sunnis and Shiites.

(5) All of the sacred scriptures make claims and predictions that are frequently at odds with known scientific principles and facts. It is asserted, for instance, in the Old Testament that Joshua made the sun stand still. In all these texts, miracles—i.e., suspensions or violations of the laws of nature as a result of divine intervention in the course of nature—are described. But as Hume pointed out in his famous essay, "Of Miracles," it is more sensible to doubt that the laws of nature have been suspended or violated than to accept the testimony of persons who claim to have witnessed miracles.

Since we have discussed many of these skeptical doubts about the validity of religion in more detail in the previous chapter, we shall say no more about them here. But there is one skeptical problem that should be mentioned which refers specifically to the relationship between religion and morality.

As we have seen in the previous remarks, all of these Western religions argue that morality derives from God's commands to human beings. These moral codes are said to be an expression of "God's will." The skeptical challenge is to this particular assertion, and it can be formulated in terms of the following question: *Are moral laws good or right because God wills them, or does God will them because they are good or right?*

The skeptic points out that either alternative raises difficulties for the religious person. Consider the first option: Moral laws are good because God wills them. But the skeptic will say: This thesis assumes that God is good and wills only that which is good. But how do we know that God is good? After all, there is much evil in the world and if God is the creator of the universe and of everything in it, how can one explain the existence of evil? This raises the famous Problem of Evil—namely, if God is all wise, all powerful, and benevolent, where does evil come from? Perhaps God is not really benevolent and, if so, then his commands are not necessarily good. Indeed, given the existence of evil, it is possible that the ruler of the universe is not God but Satan. The other alternative, namely, that God wills the moral laws because they are good, entails that God is not all powerful. He is constrained to will only that which is good, so there is a limit to his power or perhaps to his wisdom. Furthermore, if moral laws are good independent of their creation by God, then perhaps they arise as human conceptions of how persons should interact with and treat one another. In such a case, the moral laws have no special need of religion. The connection with religion can thus be dispensed with and the claim that God has ordained how humans should conduct themselves is to be rejected. The outcome of this provision would be a kind of ethical code that needs no religious backing. Some "ethical humanists," have espoused exactly this position.

In a world culture that has seen the prestige of science increase, many ethicists have tried to develop moral theories that are independent of any particular religious outlook, and indeed are compatible with a scientific picture of man's place in the universe. In contemporary philosophy there are numerous such doctrines. Some of these, to be sure, have resonances of religious faith and are compatible with a general religious orientation. Others have no such connections. We shall now turn to the two most widely accepted modern moral theories, Kantianism and utilitarianism. The former has a religious tinge to it, though its fundamental ideas do not derive from any specific religious affiliation; but the latter, utilitarianism, is essentially nonreligious and secular. It proposes a moral philosophy that is compatible with science.

TWO MODERN THEORIES

The moral philosophy of Immanuel Kant (1724-1804)

Many commentators regard Kant as the greatest philosopher since Aristotle. Like Plato and Aristotle, there is almost no important area of philosophy to which he has not made fundamental contributions. For this reason his work is richly textured, having tightly woven strands that are difficult to separate for independent analysis. This is especially true of his ethical views, since they are intimately connected with metaphysical and epistemological doctrines that treat of such matters as human freedom, causality, perception, God, and immortality. Kant's moral philosophy is similar to Aristotle's in that it is designed to answer two questions: "What is the good life for human beings?" and "How can one tell whether one's actions are morally right or not?" Still, if we were to try to describe his response to these questions directly, we would find ourselves entwined in a host of metaphysical and epistemological problems that it would take several chapters to sort out. We shall, therefore, try a slightly different approach. Let us begin with a simpler question that Kant also wishes to answer: "When does a human being have moral worth?" or, in an alternative formulation, "What distinguishes a person of virtue from a person who lacks virtue?" Starting with this query we can eventually work our way into the heart of his theory.

Kant's response is that what determines the moral worth of a human being is that person's character. To explain what he means, consider the following example: Suppose a man repays a debt because he knows it will please the person who loaned him the money. Or, again, suppose he repays a debt because he feels that he will suffer reprisals if he does not. In neither case is that person morally worthy according to Kant. Kant describes the former individual as acting "in accordance with duty," but not "from duty." He describes the latter person as acting "from prudence," and not "from duty." Insofar as a person fails to act from duty, he is not virtuous. So what it is to act "from duty"? It is to act from the *recognition* that when one has incurred a debt one is obligated to repay it. That kind of recognition is a function of reason. A virtuous person recognizes that to incur an obligation entails that there be an appropriate response to it. In the particular case under discussion, this means that if one has incurred a debt one is obligated to repay it. It is the rational understanding that an obligation demands an appropriate kind of response that defines the morally worthy person. One of the terms often used to characterize Kant's view is to say it is a "deontological theory," namely, a doctrine that stresses the duties and obligations every person faces. In particular, such a theory distinguishes the rightness or wrongness of actions from the psychological motivations (fear, pleasure, inclination) to do them and from their consequences as well. One must do a moral action because duty demands it. A person having the right kind of character can "see" that obligations produce demands that *must* be met simply because they are obligations.

Kant thus distinguishes the moral worth of an agent from the consequences of his or her actions. An action is right or wrong only if there is some obligation on the part of the agent to do it—that is, if, in relevant circumstances, one could properly say to a person, "It is your duty to do such-and-such." On Kant's view, an action is right if it ought to be done in those circumstances and wrong if it ought not to be done in those circumstances. Thus, if I have promised to do something but fail to keep my promise, my conduct is wrong. It would be right only if, having promised, I carry out the promise. Even if fulfilling one's promise caused one pain or guilt or regret, it is a right action only if the action is carried out. This is why, for Kant, it is never right to lie, even from altruistic motives. We recall that at the beginning of Plato's *Republic*, Socrates argues that it would be right to tell a lie to protect a friend from harmful consequences. Kant completely disagrees with Plato. No matter what the consequences, lying is morally wrong—even if that action will benefit others. Kant's moral theory can therefore be summarized as insisting that a morally righteous person is, as he puts it, a person of "good will." To say that one is a person of good will means for Kant that the person acts "out of reverence for duty." To act in this way is always morally justifiable. As Kant expresses the point in a memorable phrase, "Nothing can possibly be conceived in the world, or even out of it, which can be called good without qualification, except a Good Will."[6]

These preliminary remarks open the door to the central domain of the theory and put us in a position to answer the first of Kant's basic questions: What is the good life for human beings? The answer he gives emphasizes two different features. The first is reminiscent of Aristotle's view, namely, that the good life is a happy life. The second component is purely Kant, namely, that the good life consists in having a virtuous character. When these are united, one can achieve the highest good or the summum bonum. Thus, the best possible life for a human is one that is both happy and conducted by a person having a virtuous character. A certain religious tinge is found here, since Kant also calls the highest good the "Kingdom of God."

Whether Kant was directly influenced by Aristotle is a matter of debate. But many of his comments about happiness sound like something Aristotle might have said. Like Aristotle, Kant maintains that all human beings aim at achieving their own happiness ("It is the essence of men to do so"); furthermore, he agrees with Aristotle that happiness is neither a goal nor an object, nor is it to be identified with pleasure. It is, as Aristotle emphasizes, connected with the way in which one's life is conducted. If there is any psychological state that all cases of happiness exhibit it is a sense of well-being or having conducted one's affairs from a sense of duty.

Kant's theory is, however, not eudaimonistic in the way that the views of Plato and Aristotle are. He points out that since all men are, in fact, inclined to seek their own happiness, such inclinations must not be confused with their duty. Therefore, he argues, it can never be anyone's duty to promote his own happiness. But since happiness, as mentioned previously, is part of the good life and should be pursued, Kant argues, surprisingly, that it is the duty of men to promote the happiness of others. This is why, as we shall indicate below, he holds that every man must be treated as an end in himself and not as a means. Kant also rejects any eudaimonistic theory in denying that the purpose of acting from duty is to attain happiness. On the contrary, he emphasizes that the moral life consists in fulfilling obligations that are binding on each of us as rational beings. In this respect, his view differs from that of Aristotle, whose doctrine of the mean is a prescription to be followed for attaining happiness. In this connection Kant writes,

> Now it follows from this that *morality* should never be treated as a *doctrine of happiness,* that is, an instruction how to become happy; for it has to do simply with the rational condition (*conditio sine qua non*) of happiness, not with the means of attaining it.

Elsewhere he says similar things:

> Hence morality is not properly the doctrine how we should make ourselves happy, but how we should become *worthy* of happiness.

These quotations make it plain that moral philosophy is not to be understood as an instruction about how to attain happiness, but rather "how we should become *worthy* of happiness." We become worthy of happiness when we act from duty, not because we are trying to achieve our own happiness.

This brings us to the second part of Kant's theory: How can we tell if our actions are morally correct or not? His answer is that an action is morally correct if one can will that it become a universal law that all should follow; otherwise it is wrong. In other words, the test of the moral rightness of conduct is whether one could rationally allow that the action set an example that everyone should follow. If one cannot "will" this, then the action is not morally correct. This is Kant's answer to Plato's original puzzle, whether lying is not sometimes just. For Kant lying, even if it is beneficial, cannot be morally correct under any circumstances, for we cannot will that lying should become a universal practice that everyone should adopt.

Kant's way of formulating this answer uses a technical concept, the "categorical imperative." Let us explain this notion briefly. As the word "imperative" indicates, the categorical imperative is a type of command. Categorical imperatives are injunctions that mandate human beings to behave in a given way without qualification. A categorical imperative thus states that one must do such-and-such, and it states this without any exceptions or reservations. Kant thus distinguishes between hypothetical imperatives and categorical imperatives. A hypothetical imperative does involve qualifications. It typically takes the form of a directive stating that *if* one wants to achieve certain goals one should act in certain ways. Hypothetical imperatives are thus concerned with prudent conduct, that is, with the most effective way or ways of achieving given ends. Their concern is with the means at arriving at a particular goal, rather than with the goal itself. For example, if one wishes to become a violin virtuoso, instructions for attaining this goal would take the form of an hypothetical imperative—if you wish to do this, then you should find an appropriate teacher, buy an excellent violin, and practice constantly. Whether being a virtuoso is a good thing or not is not in play; it is assumed rather than argued for. But the moral life is not a question of means; it is a question about the worth of certain ways of living, and this is a matter of acting from duty.

The distinction that Kant is drawing between categorical and hypothetical imperatives is thus a key element in explaining how one determines what one's duty is in a given case. Moral behavior, as we indicated above, is conduct engaged in "from duty," and *not* from prudence *or* in accordance with duty. Kant argues that one's duty in

a given situation imposes an obligation that is not subject to any qualifications or conditions. Thus, the determination or test of what one
should do as a moral agent is always arrived at through the categorical imperative. Kant formulates the categorical imperative in several
different ways. His initial rendering is:

> There is, therefore, but one categorical imperative, namely this:
> Act only on that maxim whereby thou canst at the same time will
> that it should become a universal law.

As we have stressed, Kant means by this formula that a human
being should always act as if each act were to become a universal prescription or law. Thus, no moral agent should commit murder, since
no one can will that murder become a universal practice. Similarly
with regard to stealing, one cannot will that it should always be prac-
ticed in every community. On the contrary, one should will that
keeping promises be universalized. This is why it is moral to keep
promises. The test that Kant is proposing of what one should do as a
moral agent in any given situation is to ask oneself: Can I will that the
action I am about to do should become a universal moral principle
that everyone should follow? If the answer is yes, then such an action
would qualify as one that should be done in every morally relevant
situation.

A somewhat different, and equally famous, formulation of the
categorical imperative states:

> So act as to treat humanity, whether in thine own person or in that
> of any other, in every case as an end withal, never as a means only.

This second formulation derives from Kant's idea that it is the
duty of everyone to seek the happiness of others. This entails treating
each human being as an end, not as a means or as an instrument to
achieve some particular end. The notion that one must treat each
human being as an end is virtually equivalent to the famous principle
called the Golden Rule, which says, "Do unto others as you would
have them do unto you." In political theory, the idea that each person
should be treated as an end in himself or herself appears as the
maxim that "All men are created equal." Each person counts equally

from a moral perspective and each should be respected equally. In the U.S. Constitution, this is interpreted as the notion that each person stands equally before the law, and that discrimination on grounds of race, religion, or creed is always morally reprehensible.

Skeptical challenges to Kant

The skeptic points out that Kant's theory cannot deal with cases where there is a conflict in duties. Suppose I promise to keep a secret and then, while in court as a witness, I am asked a direct question about the event. According to Kant I cannot lie, and according to Kant I must also keep my promise. But in this particular case, it is logically impossible to do both. If I keep my secret, I cannot truthfully answer the lawyer's question. If I do answer it, I have broken my promise. The skeptic infers from this kind of case that the whole theory of the categorical imperative is shot through with holes.

The skeptic also mentions that for Kant, considerations of the consequences of an action should never be taken into account, only whether the action is done from a sense of duty. Yet they point out that in Kant's own writings on ethics, he surreptitiously introduces considerations of the consequences of actions into the determination of the rightness or wrongness of those actions. They argue that Kant is tacitly presupposing that the effect or consequence of not behaving in accordance with the categorical imperative would be to make human life as we know it impossible. But to say this is to introduce the consequences of our actions in determining moral worth. Thus, suppose that everybody lied all the time; then on a Kantian view, life as we know it now would become impossible. We could not trust anyone and accordingly civil society would become chaotic and impossible. But to make these points is to talk about the effects or consequences of certain practices. Here, according to the skeptic, is a quotation from Kant where the consequences of actions are implicitly appealed to:

> Then I presently become aware that while I can will the lie, I can by no means will that lying should be a universal law. For with such a law there would be no promises at all, since it would be in vain

to allege my intention in regard to my future actions to those who would not believe this allegation, or if they overhastily did, would pay me back in my own coin.[7]

In mentioning that if everyone lied it would be "in vain" to promise and that if everyone lied the liar would be paid back in his own coin, Kant is obviously introducing the notion of consequences. The skeptic points out that a moral theory that ignores the consequences of actions is too unrealistic to be taken seriously. In everyday life, the outcome of actions is enormously important and cannot be ignored.

Utilitarianism

This doctrine in its modern forms is a product of two Englishmen, both famous figures of the nineteenth-century Enlightenment: Jeremy Bentham (1748–1832) and John Stuart Mill (1806–1873). Both were political reformers who searched for a principle that would allow them to determine with scientific objectivity whether an act (in particular, a legislative act) was morally justifiable. In attempting to find such a maxim, they rejected any appeal to authority, tradition, intuition, religious guidance, feeling, sentiment, or emotion. The principle they finally hit on seemed to them to avoid these defects and to provide a publicly verifiable standard for establishing the moral worth of any action. They called this maxim the "Principle of Utility," and it formed the basis of what they argued was the first scientific moral theory. Like many of the moral views we have discussed, utilitarianism emphasizes happiness as the goal of moral conduct; but in nearly every other respect it differs from earlier moral theories, especially from Kant's. It has scientific connotations, it takes "pleasure" to be identical with "happiness," and it stresses the importance of the consequences of actions in determining their value.

A typical formulation of the Principle of Utility states that an action is right if it tends to produce the greatest balance of happiness over pain for the greatest number of persons; otherwise, it is wrong. Bentham and Mill were both psychological and ethical hedonists, that is, philosophers who equate happiness and pleasure. *Psychological hedonism* is the thesis that each human being aims at achieving pleasure in life and in avoiding pain; *ethical hedonism* is the doctrine that the attainment of pleasure is the goal that humans *should* seek. Psychological hedonism is thus a factual thesis and ethical hedonism is a normative one.

Utilitarianism is thus a moral philosophy that embodies two assumptions: (1) that pleasure is the only thing worth having in its own right—i.e., that it is *the* ultimate goal for which humans should strive, and (2) that all moral agents should act so as to produce the greatest balance of pleasure over pain for the greatest number of persons. This second principle thus implies that utilitarianism is also a social/political philosophy. It maintains that it is an obligation of every individual (and of every public policy) to further the happiness of the greatest number of persons. In suggesting that this is what each agent should do it exhibits resonances of Kant's philosophy. Kant contended that it is never one's duty to seek one's own happiness; rather, it is one's duty to seek the happiness of others. But, of course, Kant denied that happiness consists in pleasure. But this is what Bentham and Mill believe, both for psychological and ethical reasons. When given such a hedonistic twist, their doctrine holds that it is an obligation for each human to act in such a way as to produce the greatest balance of pleasure over pain for the greatest number in society.

In speaking about "the greatest balance of pleasure over pain," they did not mean absolutely the greatest amount of pleasure per se. Rather they construed this formula to mean that it should be the greatest *proportion* of pleasure over pain that should be produced. They were fully aware that efforts to produce the greatest amount of pleasure could produce enormous amounts of pain as well. Therefore, the Principle of Utility was more circumscribed than the initial exposure to their formula might suggest, since it was only the largest excess of pleasure over pain that humans should aim to bring about.

The fundamental thrust of utilitarianism is thus to make a sharp distinction between the moral worth of an action and the moral worth of the agent who performs it. Bentham and Mill stressed that the effects of actions, not the motives from which they are done, are what make them right or wrong. Persons may act from the highest motives, yet they may do something that has undesirable consequences. Joseph Stalin may have acted from the desire to improve the Soviet economy by eliminating private farms, yet his actions led to starvation in the general population, to the displacement and even murder of the so-called Kulaks, and to disastrous results for the well-being of most citizens. A utilitarian would condemn his conduct on the ground that it produced more pain than pleasure. One can think of many examples where persons act from the purest motives and yet the effects of their conduct lead to unfortunate consequences. A doting parent may be protective with respect to how his or her child is raised, but the effect may be to spoil the child. All sorts of actions are initiated from such commendable motives as honor, love, duty, or justice while having undesirable long-range effects.

The feature of utilitarianism that Bentham and Mill stressed was that it provided a criterion or test of a perfectly objective kind to determine the moral worth of any action. Bentham even went so far as to invent what he called the "hedonic calculus," for making calculations about the consequences of actions. The calculus contained seven factors on the basis of which anyone could measure the amount of pleasure or pain an act produces (among these factors were the intensity of the pleasure, its duration, and its extent). Bentham assumed that in calculating the amount of pleasure an action will produce each person is to count equally; and he further assumed that there were no *qualitative* differences between pleasures, but only *quantitative* differences such as intensity and duration. He said famously that the "quantity of pleasure being equal, pushpin (a popular game) is as good as poetry."

Mill disagreed with Bentham on this point. He believed that the pleasures of the intellect are qualitatively differ from and are superior to those of the body. He thus distinguished between different kinds of pleasures, contending that some were more valuable than others. He also believed that since only the "wise" are capable of acquiring intellectual pleasures, the effects of actions upon the wise must be given a superior value than the effects on the nonwise. Mill thus ultimately rejected the thesis that each person is to count equally in any assessment of the rightness or wrongness of an action. In a frequently quoted remark, he states:

It is better to be a human being dissatisfied than a pig satisfied; better to be Socrates dissatisfied than a fool satisfied. And if the fool, or the pig, are of a different opinion, it is because they only know their side of the question. The other party to the comparison knows both sides.[8]

Skeptical challenges to utilitarianism

There are three important skeptical challenges to the utilitarian philosophy. First, the skeptic points out that once Mill distinguishes between kinds of pleasures, the view becomes paradoxical. According to that philosophy, the Principle of Utility is supposed to provide an objective, publicly verifiable standard for determining the moral worth of any action. A morally worthy action produces a balance of pleasure over pain. Bentham argues that it is a simple matter to calculate such effects. But once the doctrine is modified to allow for qualitatively better or worse pleasures, then one will no longer be able to use the Principle of Utility to make what should be purely quantitative assessments of the amount of pleasure or pain. One will need a wholly different standard to decide how much better some qualitative pleasures are than others—and this is to leave the camp of scientific objectivity for sheer preference and opinion. It is not an objective matter to claim that listening to classical music is better than listening to jazz. But if this is so the Principle of Utility is no longer of any "utility" in helping us decide what a morally correct act should be.

A second skeptical objection is essentially a practical objection about how to calculate the effects, results, and consequences of any action. It is assumed by Bentham and Mill that it is the total number of consequences that must be taken into account in any moral appraisal of an action. If we merely count the immediate amount of pleasure or pain we may be wildly wrong in deciding that it is right or wrong; a long-range survey of the results may give different results. Television, for instance, may produce immediate pleasures for its viewers, but its long-range effects on persons may be to dull their sensibilities and stultify their interest in reading and other pleasurable activities.

The objection is that if the total effects of an action must be considered, we immediately face a practical, technical problem. Any action may have an infinite number of effects, and therefore to wait an infinitely long time for deciding whether an action is right or wrong is simply not to decide at all. The Principle of Utility was developed as a practical test for ascertaining whether actions are right or wrong, but if we cannot apply the principle in a practicable way then its value for making decisions seems nil.

A third, still deeper objection, is the following. Utilitarianism completely discounts the importance of motives and reasons with respect to the assessment of the moral worth of actions. But this leaves out an enormous part of the moral life of human beings. Consider the question of responsibility, for instance. Clearly this is a fundamental moral concept. Agents should be held responsible for some of their actions. Someone like Adolf Hitler, who arranged to have persons tortured and murdered, should be held accountable for these deeds. But to say that a person is responsible entails that he or she intended to do a particular act. We do not morally condemn a surgeon whose patient dies on the operating table from some unpredictable cause. The surgeon did not intend for the patient to die and accordingly we do not hold him *morally* responsible in the way we would Hitler, who intended to kill people. It follows that no moral action can be fully evaluated as right or wrong unless some consideration of the agent's intentions is included in that assessment. Bentham and Mill argue that we should consider only the consequences of the action. But in making such a discrimination between the motives of an agent and the consequences of his action, they rest their case on a misleading contrast, for what is meant by "moral action" is behavior that results from someone's intention. Subtract the motive, and the action does not fall within the scope of morality at all. The skeptical conclusion is that utilitarianism is too one-sided to be acceptable as a comprehensive moral doctrine.

We therefore conclude this chapter on a skeptical note. The skeptic argues his case inductively. He puts it this way: We have looked, he will say, at the whole history of moral philosophy, a history of theorizing. From Plato to the present, philosophers have attempted to construct broad-ranging theories about morality. But each of these has been subjected to devastating criticisms. Under the pressure of counterexamples, not one such theory has been able to withstand scrutiny. The correct conclusion to draw from twenty-five hundred years of theorizing about human conduct is that no theory will do. We are thus left with the skeptical attitude that life will simply have to go on without such theorizing.

NOTES

1. Ludwig Wittgenstein, *On Certainty* (Oxford: Blackwell, 1969), entry 253.
2. Ibid., entry 156.
3. Aristotle, *Nicomachean Ethics*, book 1, chap. 13.
4. Ibid., book 7, chap. 13.
5. Bertrand Russell, *A History of Western Philosophy* (London: Allen & Unwin, 1946), p. 206.
6. Immanuel Kant, *Groundwork of the Metaphysics of Morals*, trans. H. J. Paton (New York: Harper & Row, 1964), p. 61.
7. Ibid., p. 70
8. John Stuart Mill, *Utilitarianism* (1863), chap. 2.

7 POLITICAL PHILOSOPHY

WHO SHOULD RULE?

From as far back as we have information, human beings have been living in groups. Over time, many of these groups have evolved into societies in which some people ruled and directed the activities of others. The societies became political entities, from the Greek term *polis*, for "city-state." The political structure of these societies varied from rule by a warlord, a warrior priest, a group of people, or rulers chosen by some subgroup of the society, to something like a democratic society in which the majority of the people chose the rulers.

In ancient times, thinkers like Plato and Aristotle, living in fairly highly structured societies, pondered over the questions: Who should rule? Is there a right or just or good society? They knew about the varieties of groups in and around Greece. They lived in different kinds of rulerships, from that of Athenian democracy to the rule of tyrants and of conquering kings. Aristotle sought to investigate the differing constitutions of the time. Plato tried to outline an ideal society, the Republic, in which philosopher kings would rule.

The question, "Who should rule?" has been discussed and, unfortunately, fought over up to the present time. Most societies derive from traditions and/or conquests. Their political structures are imposed by those in power without much philosophical consideration. In two major modern cases, those of the government developed by the thirteen American colonies and that developed by the French revolutionaries, debates went on exploring the possible ways governance could or should occur.

In the American case, there was the possibility for thoughtful men to examine who should rule in a relatively calm context, whereas in the French case, twelve years later, the working-out of answers to political questions had to go on in a society in turmoil, in the face of civil war and threats of invasion. In the American case, the members of the Constitutional Convention included several who had carefully studied political philosophers from ancient times, including Plato, Aristotle, Cicero, and Seneca, and modern thinkers such as John Locke, Montesquieu, and Jean-Jacques Rousseau.

Figures such as Thomas Jefferson, Alexander Hamilton, John Adams, and James Madison discussed whether the new country that was being formed out of the union of the thirteen original British colonies should be a republic or a monarchy; whether the people, or a subgroup of them, should rule; and how they should rule. Since the new country had been formed as a result of a rebellion against Great Britain, the Founding Fathers had little interest in having rule by one individual. They had experienced the ways a tyrant king could limit the freedoms and activities of the rest of the people. Even George Washington, who was the only obvious choice for king, opposed such a way of running the country. Instead, the Founding Fathers opted for the formation of a democracy, a government ruled by the people. The question then became, How was this to be accomplished?

Both the Americans and the later French revolutionaries were only too aware of the ways in which an autocratic king could force his will upon a powerless public. And, as had been observed back as far as Plato's time and biblical time, an unrestrained monarch could cause much public unhappiness and misery. An unrestrained monarch could do as he or she pleased with regard to the activities of the subjects, so people could be jailed, executed, forced into military service, deprived of their property, and so on, at the whim of the tyrant.

Although the monarch might claim he or she was doing what he or she did for the public good, it could appear obvious to the subjects that the monarch's decisions were wrong or disastrous or even worse. Kingdoms had been plunged into wars and ruined financially by unrestrained monarchs. Even though it might be argued that the ruler were the wisest and most just person in the society, he or she could nonetheless make mistakes that affected everyone.

Hence, a restrained monarch might avoid such error-prone actions. But how to restrain without taking away all of the power of the monarch? The French revolutionaries sought ways of doing this, but when they felt that the king was not accepting the limitations, they moved to the extreme of arresting and executing the king. Then it was decided that the elected members of the national assembly should rule, and then a subgroup of these ruled, leading finally to the Reign of Terror by the subgroup, the end of the revolutionary government, and its replacement by a new monarch, Emperor Napoleon.

Of course rulers can make mistakes—monumental mistakes—if not restrained. Then what are the alternatives? The English philosopher John Locke at the end of the seventeenth century had advocated that government should be based on the consent of the governed. Locke's political philosophy is one of the basic philosophies of democracy. The consent of the governed would appear to make "the people" the sovereign.

Locke's view is offered in contrast to those of Thomas Hobbes and Benedict de Spinoza, just before him. Hobbes, who had been forced into exile by the Puritan Revolution, theorized that people left to their own devices will be in constant conflict with one another. Each human desires everything. This quickly leads to a war of all against all. This human civil war only ends when somebody has enough force to make others stop fighting and submit to the will of the stronger. Human beings need peace and tranquility, but can only have it if they each cede their power to a sovereign, who can then make all decisions. The powerless public gains peace but loses all control of their lives. In the extreme, Hobbes was willing to let the sovereign decide everything, including what religion the people should accept, what science they should accept, what education they should have, and so on.

The ultimate limitations that Hobbes saw for his sovereign, the Leviathan, was that he could not order people to destroy themselves. And if he did not supply the populace with a protected environment, they would no longer be obliged to follow him. A monarch who loses a war loses his public, which will have to find another sovereign who can protect them.

Hobbes's sovereign can obviously make mistakes in terms of adopting policies that damage or destroy his country. He can also try to force bad views or false science on his subjects. Spinoza, a contemporary of Hobbes, agreed on the need to have a strong sovereign in order to keep people from fighting with each other. But for Spinoza, a chief reason for favoring rule by a complete sovereign was to allow those who can to have the opportunity to understand the world. The rational man needs peace in order to live a life of reason. Although Spinoza accepts a fair amount of Hobbes's view, and actually provides no ways of limiting the sovereign, he nonetheless insists that a sovereign who tries to prevent people from thinking freely will soon find himself without a job.

For Spinoza a strong government, not necessarily ruled by one man, is needed to keep people from disturbing each other. The ultimate value in this is having a society in which rational, creative people can function unhindered. In order to do this, the irrational people have to be forced to obey the laws of the state. For Spinoza the role of organized religions is to teach such people to obey. At the same time, the all-powerful state should not interfere with the rational, creative people, and should allow them the opportunity to think for themselves and to express themselves.

Thus, though Spinoza did not endorse what we now call a democratic state, he saw two important aspects of such a state freedom of thought and freedom of expression.

Because these freedoms were for him crucial for the development of human understanding of the world, the state could not and should not make any effort to limit or suppress them. In fact, the state—and through it, the churches—should force those who don't have the capability for understanding to obey laws that would guarantee a tranquil state in which intellectuals and scientists could carry on their activities.

The history of human tragedies due to faulty rulers, economic ruin, and so on made it imperative to examine who should rule. The Hobbesian and the Spinozian rulers could quickly become tyrants who could order policies that would destroy societies and personal lives. A skepticism developed concerning allowing rulers to have complete power. Plato had long ago made the claim that ruling is an activity based on knowledge in the same way that medicine is based on knowledge. Plato, through his spokesperson, Socrates, showed that the democratic rulers of Athens, the ones who arrested and condemned Socrates, actually knew nothing. The burden of Plato's *Republic* was to describe the proper education of true rulers, a daunting education that involved years and years of study of mathematics, among other matters. The end result would be a philosopher king who would know what should be done. Plato was only too well aware that the actual rulers of states were fallible humans, not philosopher kings; and these rulers made mistakes, often catastrophic mistakes. Plato ended by saying that the world would be safe only when philosophers were kings and kings philosophers. When would this happen? Wise Plato realized it could only occur by accident if those choosing the ruler did not realize who they were choosing.

About two thousand years later, after the Puritan Revolution in England and the restoration of the monarchy, ending with James II, there was an attempt to reestablish Catholicism in England. This was followed by the Glorious Revolution, which put the Protestant William of Orange on the throne. It was felt that a limited monarchy, plus rule by the people, was what was needed.

Locke, in contrast to Hobbes and Spinoza, did not see the basis of society resting on a forced contract between an all-powerful sovereign and a terrified populace, but between more or less coequal persons who wanted a social system that would protect their physical persons and their individual property. Whoever was in charge could only be in power by the consent of the governed. Without such consent there would be unrest and even revolution.

Locke then propounded a semiskeptical system of government

that would sufficiently limit the actual ruler and would recognize the fallibility of both ruler and subjects. If government rested on the consent of the governed, how was this consent expressed? In Lockean democracy it was expressed through elections of representatives who would then express the consent of their constituents to the ruling executive, as long as said executive stayed within limitations. The sovereign was the king, but he ruled in consort with the parliament, the representatives of the people. The people could withdraw their consent when they next voted. This did not guarantee the truest or best decisions, but did avoid some of the worst possibilities.

Later in the eighteenth century, English colonists in America, raised on Locke's political philosophy, found themselves in a most unpleasant situation in which the British government in the name of King George III imposed taxes on the colonists. They screamed against taxation without representation. When their petitions to the British government fell on deaf ears, they withdrew their consent, and began the American Revolution.

When the American colonists convened after the Revolution to construct the fabric of the new government, they eliminated the role of a king, and substituted a president as the executive ruler, limited not only by Congress and the courts, but also by the length of a four-year term. Skepticism about the merits of even the best people of the time—George Washington, John Adams, Thomas Jefferson, and James Madison—led the Founding Fathers to keep the executive in check by this time limit, which would then give the people a chance to give or not give their consent for the next term.

In both the English and American cases, representative democracy was designed first to avoid the varying judgments and attitudes of the populace as events unfolded. Aware of how large numbers of people can be swayed by events, by orators, and by passions, representative government was a skeptical check on direct government. A direct democracy might find itself open to constant changes of opinion providing no settled course of action for the society. By limiting popular democracy to election of representatives, one had government based on the consent of the governed, consent given only at fixed times and places.

The French philosopher and political theorist Jean-Jacques

Rousseau, a firm believer in government by the will of the people, remarked that the English people were only free on election day. The rest of the time they were at the mercy of their so-called representatives, who might no longer actually represent them. Since they could not express their views until the next election, they were captives of their representatives between elections. To deal with this, some procedures were introduced for the recall or removal of representatives if their behavior was too awful in terms of legal or moral activities. The chief executive also was subject to removal before the end of his or her term by the complicated process of impeachment.

One also has to mention that Locke and the framers of the U.S. Constitution were skeptical about the ability of some of the people to render serious consent. "People" includes every human being living as a citizen of the country. Some are obviously too young to know what is involved in governing and giving consent; hence, age limits have been imposed as to who can vote. In the United States it has been decided that people can vote if they are eighteen years of age, although until recently the age limit was twenty-one. The change recognizes a new view of maturity—if people are old enough to be drafted into military service, they should also be considered old enough to participate in political choices.

Besides age limits, the right to vote was originally restricted to males, and mostly to white males. Women were seen as not sufficiently aware of what was involved in the political process and, under then-existing laws, were ruled by their husbands or male relatives. Slaves were also excluded. In fact, in both England and the United States, only property owners were originally considered adequately involved in political business to have a need and right to vote. In England the restrictions went further. Catholics and Jews could not vote, since the established religion of the country was that of the Church of England. The United States was the first country to have universal suffrage regardless of religious convictions or commitments. Only after the Civil War were racial restrictions removed, and only after World War I was suffrage extended to women.

When one studies the American system of checks and balances, it can be seen as an extremely clever way of dealing with skeptical problems about human nature and about finding the right or true course of action. The actual governmental structure, which many Europeans find quaint, with its eighteenth-century trappings, was developed in part from David Hume's thoughts in his "Essay on the Idea of a Perfect Commonwealth." Hume, the great skeptic, was in grave doubts about the optimistic views of French Enlightenment political theorists who were trying to frame a way of government that would lead to the infinite perfectibility of human nature and to the solution of all human problems. Hume had fundamental doubts about how much humans could be perfected, and more doubts about how many human problems could be solved. Hume saw human nature as more or less fixed through the ages.

After listening to such French optimists as Anne-Robert-Jacques Turgot, Jean Le Rond D'Alembert, Jean-Jacques Rousseau, and others, Hume wrote his essay. He saw that political projectors, like the French Enlightenment thinkers, could do much more harm than good if they could put their projects into operation in the political sphere. So Hume offered the design of a government that could do the least harm by being difficult to change or mobilize. He offered it as a way of avoiding passionate pushes toward military action: a proposal that each county, modeled on England, would have to agree separately to declare war. And he saw that this would result in inaction because by the time each county had deliberated and voted, the cause of war would probably have gone away. This would be the case with a lot of other issues. Hume's delaying mechanism may be based on what had developed in the Netherlands in the seventeenth century after the Dutch rebellion, when the Spanish authorities were driven out. It was not clear who was in charge in the territory, so a kind of government developed of the United Provinces of the Netherlands, in which each province had to decide on crucial matters such as going to war. This often had the effect of delaying decisions until the immediate cause of the crisis had disappeared. Hume may have seen the virtue of this diffused sovereignty in which each province had to give its consent. In most cases, though not always, this could avoid precipitous errors.

Hume's hobbled government was incorporated into the American scheme in the form of the United States Senate. This body, less representative than the House of Representatives, would have two mem-

bers from each state. (Originally, these were chosen by the state legislatures, not by popular election.) The Senate was given various ways
to delay actions. The Senate had to give its advice and consent to executive appointments. It had to ratify treaties by a two-thirds majority.
And it had, as we have recently seen, to adjudge the House of Representatives' impeachment of a chief executive or any other high executive, requiring a two-thirds majority to accept an impeachment of a
high official and to remove him or her from office. So the Senate,
designed in part on Hume's delaying plan, reflects skepticism about
the decisions of the populace and of its representatives.

The chief executive, chosen independently, supposedly enacts
and enforces the will of the people by putting laws into practice. But
since there are enough doubts about the wisdom of the representatives and their choice of laws, the chief executive is given the power
to veto, to refuse to accept, the laws passed by Congress. This veto
can only be overturned by a two-thirds majority of both houses of
Congress.

Last in the structure, laws and actions of the executive can be
challenged in the courts; so another level of review takes place on
the judicial side. And many levels of court are established, since
judges can make mistakes; the highest level is the Supreme Court.
These judges have been chosen and approved by a political process.
Everyone knows they are fallible, but society accepts that they are
the court of last resort and that there is no appeal beyond the
Supreme Court. However, when we see that many important questions about how our society should function are decided by five-to-
four votes of the justices, and we know that some of the judges are
aged, ill, or politically biased, we may be skeptical of the results.
When they decide by such a vote, for example, that human life
begins at a certain point before birth, there is some doubt as to the
scientific or religious value of the decision; but we accept it nonetheless for all legal purposes and the society proceeds by accepting
Court decisions for the time being. And often the decisions get modified or changed altogether by future justices.

SOME SKEPTICAL CONSIDERATIONS

In addition to the structure of the U.S. government exhibiting strong skeptical doubts about finding a best or right solution to human problems, the Bill of Rights and the judicial system also involve a strong skeptical outlook.

The First Amendment, guaranteeing freedom of speech, the press, and religious belief, was added because of doubts about whether the various states could be trusted to grant all of their citizens such freedoms. Jefferson and Madison felt it necessary that all citizens be granted the right to say what they wished, to publish what they wished, and believe what they wished, lest some dogmatic powers attempt to impose beliefs on the people. Alexander Hamilton, who actually opposed adding the Bill of Rights to the Constitution, said at the time that if it was stated in print that Congress can pass no laws abridging freedom of speech, the press, and religion, it would take just a few years before some bright lawyer would twist words around and argue that Congress *did* have such rights or powers. So Hamilton, perhaps more skeptical than the other Founding Fathers, thought it better to say nothing and hope for the best.

The Freedom of Religion Clause, which is fought over year after year in the courts, was advocated both by deists like Jefferson and Madison, who probably thought no religious view was any better than any other, and by the religious sectarians who made up about half of the original framers of the Constitution. The deists were skeptical about religious-knowledge claims and wanted to keep religious groups from imposing their versions of the truth on others. They also wanted to make sure that Congress would not use its power to aid and abet any religious group or to interfere with any religious group. A skepticism about religious-knowledge claims, then, could be a basis for separating state and church.

On the other hand, the many sectarian groups in colonial America were very worried that there might be an established church, a religious group that would have special privileges and control over other groups. Some had suffered under the control the Church of England had exercised in New York, Virginia, South Carolina, and other states. Some were worried that the kind of Protestant theocracy that had existed in Massachusetts and Connecticut would try to control their lives. A historical awareness of the state of affairs in England, where dissenters were barely tolerated and where neither Catholics nor Jews had suffrage, made many sectarians fearful of any group gaining control. They also knew of the extreme cases of intolerance that developed during the Puritan Revolution in mid-seventeenth-century England, the wars of religion that devastated Europe in the struggle between the Catholic states and the Protestant ones.

Just as tolerance developed in seventeenth-century Holland because different religious groups feared the others and wanted to guard against their gaining power, so something like this carried the day in the United States. Catholics represented about 1 percent of the population in 1789 and needed a noninterfering government in order to persevere. The various Protestant groups felt much the same way. The Church of England, of course, wanted to be reestablished where it had had such status before the Revolution.

Thus, the different religious groups were united in wanting to make sure that no American government could foster a particular religious teaching on the populace. In the late 1780s especially there seems to have been real fear that there might be an established church in the new country. Holland, tolerant as it was, had (and still has) the Dutch Reformed Church as the official church, and the ruler must belong to it and protect it. However, in the seventeenth century, the Dutch, de facto, worked out how to have an established church but at the same time a government that did not enforce the views of that church. The United States made this easier by separating church and state, but only after looking into what might happen. The German philosopher Moses Mendelssohn, at the end of his book *Jerusalem*, added a note that he was very worried that the United States would have an established church. The decision not to, endorsed by both the nonbelieving deists and very believing sectarians, created a state in which, for the first time in Western history, there was no established religion—a state in which everyone could believe as they wished.

When the First Amendment was ratified in early 1789, the new

United States was the first Western country in which Jews could be citizens. This reversed a long tradition in the Christian world, which felt that the true faith would be threatened if the Jews were given political equality. Since the fourth century, when the Emperor Constantine declared the Roman Empire to be Christian, the Jews were set apart from the political structure. They had to have special permission from popes, bishops, and kings to reside anywhere. They were regarded as a pernicious, evil force that had to be carefully controlled and kept out of the political process, lest they undermine Christian states by questioning the central Christian religious claim that the Messiah had already come and had established a Christian governance of political societies.

In the late Middle Ages, the Jews were driven out of England and France and ghettoized in Germany and Italy. They were expelled from Spain in 1492 and from Portugal in 1497. Where they were permitted, their religious behavior was carefully controlled, lest it produce skeptical doubts in the minds and hearts of "true Christians." Toleration proposals were offered tentatively by the French political theorist Jean Bodin, by the skeptic Michel de Montaigne, and by the great Protestant skeptic Pierre Bayle.

Bodin, in an unpublished work of the late sixteenth century (only published in the nineteenth century), offered a dialogue between believers in various religions of the time. In the interchange, the Jewish participant wins, and offers a plea for universal tolerance. The problem of finding the ultimate true religion is regarded as too difficult for human beings. Therefore, we should suspend judgment and let each have his or her beliefs. Montaigne, living through the great religious wars in France in the sixteenth century and coming from a family that was part Jewish, part Catholic, and part Protestant, maintained that humans could not obtain religious knowledge through reason and had to accept belief by faith and custom. If one purged one's mind of all dogmatic beliefs and attitudes, then maybe God would inscribe truths in it. Until and unless this happened, Montaigne pointed out, one did in fact accept the religion one was born and raised in. In his case, this was Catholicism. And if there were no valid reasons for another religious view, then one stayed with the religious community by birth and custom. One should recognize that everyone is like this, from the savages in America and Africa to the non-Western civilizations of China. And each religious group should be tolerated, since we cannot tell by reason which is true or right.

A century later, Pierre Bayle, son of a persecuted Calvinist minister and a refugee in the Netherlands from French Catholic intolerance, argued that religion is a matter of faith and not knowledge, and that religious belief did not lead to any specific moral consequence. On the first score, each person had his or her own personal faith, and had no way of telling if it was objectively true. No matter how subjectively certain one might be, this provided no evidence beyond one's own convictions. So said, each person was entitled to believe according to his or her conscience. An erring conscience had as much rights as a nonerring one, if we could ever tell which was which. Bayle was one of the first to advocate tolerating Jews, Muslims, and other non-Christian groups without restriction or qualification. His second point, that religious belief and morality had no necessary connection, startled his contemporaries. In his great work *The Historical and Critical Dictionary*, Bayle provided case after case of religious people who did terrible things. From biblical times to the present, religious leaders had committed sexual crimes, financial crimes, and social crimes. On the other hand, Bayle contended that the few public atheists we know of had been exemplary citizens. In the modern world he pointed to Benedict de Spinoza who, Bayle said, made atheism into a philosophical system *and* lived a life without moral blemishes.

When Bayle was accused by his religious group, the French Reformed Church of Rotterdam, of arguing for atheism, he insisted he was just telling it as it was, and that if anyone knew of any immoral atheists he would gladly enter them into his picture of the human scene.

Bayle's separation of religion and ethics provided a basis for separating church and state. If the state had the job of protecting the welfare of its citizens, then this should only involve moral crimes, not religious ones. Murder or stealing are moral crimes, not religious ones, and can be committed by Christians and non-Christians.

Bayle went further and suggested, much to the dismay of his contemporaries, that a society of atheists could be more moral than a society of religious believers. He appealed to the historical record of how awful religious societies inside and outside of Christendom have been, and to the disconnection between religion and morality. If one could entertain his hypotheses, then there would be no need or reason for establishing any religious group as moral leader of a political society.

Bayle's skeptical divorce of religion and moral behavior was even more pressed in Spinoza's *Theological and Political Tractatus*. For Spinoza religious groups had no special knowledge. Whatever they claimed to know had to be evaluated in the same way as any knowledge claims; and it would be found that their so-called knowledge claims were expressions of human fears and superstitions. It was up to rational persons to determine what was true or false. What religious groups can and should do is teach their ignorant members to obey the laws of the state and the customs of the society. The religious groups, since they have no special knowledge, should not be allowed to determine the laws of the political society. However, they can be of great importance in controlling dangerous emotional outbursts of people by teaching them the great importance of obedience to the state.

Bayle and Spinoza have views that obviously would lead to separating church and state, and disestablishing any religious group in a political society. Their views appear so hostile to traditional religion that little thought has been given to whether and how they influenced the emerging democratic societies in America and France. Two facts should make us realize these thinkers may have played some role in what emerged first in the United States and later in France, separating church and state. Bayle's *Dictionary*, in which he argued his case while giving a panorama of the human comedy from ancient times to the present, was one of the hundred books Thomas Jefferson ordered for the Library of Congress when it was set up. Half of the money for the hundred first books was paid for the four folio volumes of Bayle. His work was known to at least some of the Founding Fathers. It had appeared many times in the original French as well as in English translations in the eighteenth century. Spinoza's *Tractatus*, which was banned in Holland, was published in a clandestine French edition with fake titles. It was also translated into English in 1689, probably by an English deist. The English edition has hardly attracted much scholarly interest. It presents the text, which was being denounced hither and yon as subversive, in a neutral fashion and suggests that the reader can decide for himself what he thinks on these matters. This English edition was republished in 1739. A copy of this printing is in the collection of Benjamin Frankin's library that was used as a reference source during the writing of the U.S. Constitution. The copy has no markings to indicate who used it; but it was available to those taking the monumental step of creating a secular state.

All the European countries of the time claimed to be Christian states, blessed either by the pope or some Protestant group or groups. The U.S. Constitution, setting up a new state, a new secular order, makes no mention of religion or specifically of Christianity. It has been claimed that because James Madison was influenced by Cicero's skepticism, he left out any specific link between the state and the religion of almost all of its citizens.

Except for a few thousand Jews and far fewer Muslims, just about everyone who lived in the new state was a Christian of some kind. Many were neither practicing nor churchgoers. The oft-repeated contention that America is and always has been a Christian country may be an accurate description of who most of its citizens have been, but it has no political relevance in terms of the state.

AMERICA AND FRANCE CONTRASTED

What is striking about this skeptical attitude of the state toward the religions of its citizens and of the religions toward the state can be brought out forcibly by contrasting the American and French situations at the end of the eighteenth century. In France at the time of the Revolution, almost all citizens were Christians, mostly Catholics, in a world where the Catholic Church was deeply entrenched. It kept track of who was born, who got married, and who died. It educated the children. It determined the rhythm of each year in terms of religious holidays and festivals. And it was completely entwined with the monarchical state. The French king was called the most Christian king, and the French monarchy claimed to be the most ancient Christian monarchy in Europe. When the revolutionaries began their attempt to create a better world, they quickly saw that they had to dismantle the ecclesiastical apparatus and the monarchical system. As some claimed, the world would not be safe until the last king was strangled with the entrails of the last priest.

The state and church structure covered almost every aspect of life. So from the very beginning of the Revolution, laws were proposed to make the Catholic Church and all others organs of the state and not religious organizations. All the churches would become state property, assigned by the state to groups that applied for them. The clergy would become civil servants of a new nonmonarchical state. The educational system would move from the church to the state, and would be run centrally from state bureaus. The impact of the church on street names would be washed away by renaming everything. The calendar would be redone to eliminate the religious bias in it and to recognize that a new era was beginning with a new year 1.

The French revolutionaries found an all-encompassing church-state apparatus that had to be eliminated before they could create a new society. In contrast, the Americans had a fragmented religious society, no central government, and little tradition to sweep away. Many French revolutionaries became negative dogmatists rather than skeptics, positively fighting to get rid of every trace of the ancien régime. This led to setting up models of what might be better and forcing them on the society, such as creating the Religion of Reason to dethrone Christianity and making Notre Dame Cathedral the central edifice of this new religion, embodied in the naked form of a Parisian actress who was placed on the altar.

Two areas of concern underline important differences in the American and French cases. In the French case, eliminating the church-controlled educational system involved creating a secular school system. In order to make sure that the old system did not creep back in, the whole system had to be run by the central political government with an army of inspectors to make sure that students all over France were learning the same secular subjects. In the American case, schools were local at the time of the Revolution, most financed by religious groups, some by citizens. A diffuse school system developed all over the country. Schools receiving public funding could not teach religion or engage in religious practices. Beyond that, each school was locally governed. A kind of skepticism seemed to encompass this—nobody was absolutely certain what was to be taught or how it was to be taught. So, many different curricula were employed. Attempts even now to have more central control, to have uniform tests and uniform requirements for teachers, are met with much hostility and seen as a threat to local political power. On the other hand, there is a recurring attempt to eliminate the U.S. Department of Education in Washington, D.C., but this fails because no one seems willing to see what would happen if there were an attempt to abolish all control and standards. In France, there are recurring rebellions by the students against the almost complete central control, the inflexibility of the curriculum, the inability of the system to adjust to new conditions, and so on.

With regard to religion in France, the negative dogmatism of the French revolutionaries has left a lingering and often raging feud between the Catholic world and the secular world. In America, the multiplicity of religious groups, many of whom crossed the Atlantic Ocean to escape religious persecution in Europe, have been able to live fairly comfortably in coexistence with a secular state. There are, of course, many strains. There is a continuous series of legal cases about whether the state can regulate religious practices that involve ingesting drugs, whether the state can force people of certain religious groups to avail themselves or their children of medical resources, whether the state can force orthodox Jews to accept secular practices in a secular school system, and so on. By and large, the state has tried to avoid describing what constitutes a religion, and is usually willing to allow for state purposes, such as tax exemption, a group's self-designation of itself as a religious group. The state has taken a skeptical attitude about whether there is a fixed essence of religion. What seems a limiting case is a group, the Universal Life Church, which has no stated beliefs or creed and no practices, but which for $10 will enroll anyone and send him or her a certificate for tax purposes designating the person as a minister of the church, and his or her home as a church. Another sort of case, which never rose to consideration by the High Court, was an alleged Egyptian mystery cult in Los Angeles whose high priestess gave religious devotees sexual favors; in return, they made donations to the church. The Los Angeles police arrested the high priestess and charged her with prostitution. Her lawyer made a brief effort to claim that the state could not interfere with religious practice and then gave up before it became a full-fledged constitutional issue.

In recent years a religious group has appeared that rejects the whole American attitude of separation of church and state and that wants to make all law simply biblical law. This group, called Christian Reconstruction, was founded by the Armenian American theologian Rousas John Rushdoony. From his first writings in the 1950s, Rushdoony insisted that there were no absolute standards for judging the world, human nature, and social groups. In his first work, *By What Standards?* (1951), Rushdoony raised the ancient Greek skeptical problem of the criterion. He contended that there were two possibilities, the criterion of the Enlightenment or the criterion of religion. Neither was justifiable. If one chose the Enlightenment criterion, one then ended up with a naturalistic picture of the world and a secular picture of society. If, on the other hand, one chose the religious criterion, then everything would be interpreted by religious standards, which, for Rushdoony, was that of biblical religion.

Viewing America in religious terms, Rushdoony portrays America, or at least the New England colonies, as having covenanted with God and operating by divine law. Then, between 1776 and 1897, this true America was pushed aside and the blasphemous secular state was set up. The American state then followed the Enlightenment vision, which included cutting off religion from the state and using the state to take over the people's economy by setting up banks and printing currency. The secular state also took over the raising of children by setting up a secular school system.

Rushdoony set forth a definite political action program for those who accepted biblical religion to pursue. This has been advocated by the Christian Reconstructionist political party, called the U.S. Taxpayer's Party, which runs a candidate, an associate of Rushdoony's, for president in U.S. elections. The party advocates in general that U.S. law should be biblical law. Specifically, the party advocates repealing the income tax, canceling the Federal Reserve Bank, allowing home schooling instead of state schooling, a return to using just gold and silver coinage, and applying biblical punishments for crimes, including blasphemy.

The Christian Reconstructionists, then, reject the entire notion of the secular state that appears in the U.S. Constitution. Although its political party does not fare well in national elections, followers have been elected to various state and national offices, and its program, whole or part, has been accepted and advocated by conservative religious groups such as the Christian Coalition. Pat Robertson and Jerry Falwell have made some of the Christian Reconstructionist proposals their own, and in Robertson's Regent's University, many of the law professors and students are adherents of Rushdoony's views. Many of the demands of the Montana Freemen are drawn from the Christian Reconstructionist program.

So, two hundred years after the adoption of the U.S Constitution, there is a viable religious group ready to repeal the essential features of the American way of dealing with political skepticism through a secular society.

SYSTEMS OF JUSTICE

Another aspect of the American democratic system that shows its skeptical approach to human problems is the Anglo-American system of justice involving trial by jury. This system, developed in England and America in the eighteenth century, involves having twelve citizens, who supposedly have no opinion about the case before them, decide matters of guilt and innocence "beyond any reasonable doubt." Before looking at this notion of "reasonable doubt," let us first consider that the jury trial system at first glance seems counterintuitive as a means of establishing truth about who is guilty and who innocent. The twelve people who are to decide this are not experts on the matters at issue and are supposed to judge only on the basis of what is presented in court. No one is allowed to be on the jury if he or she knows any of the participants in the legal case. One would never want to decide medical matters or scientific matters in this way. In medical cases, it is considered a plus that anyone making a medical decision knows the patient. And expertise is definitely a plus in making a decision. So why do we decide legal questions this way? The answer seems to come from legal history in England in the seventeenth century. Courts and trials were used as means of persecuting opponents. Star chambers were set up. Judges ordered the conviction of people without regard to the evidence. The passions generated by the religious conflicts in England obviously carried over into the legal system. So in the latter part of the seventeenth century, legal reforms were developed to limit the interference of passions and prejudices in legal proceedings. The modern American and British legal systems grew out of this.

An important and notorious case in the late seventeenth century centered around the arrest of the Quaker leader William Penn for preaching in the streets of London. The presiding judge ordered the jury to convict Penn. They retired to deliberate but then acquitted him. The judge was furious and ordered both Penn and the jury to be incarcerated without bread or water until the jury would follow his orders. This led to a higher court ruling that a jury cannot be held criminally responsible for its verdict.

The jury freed from the tyranny of the judge was supposed to consist of twelve open-minded persons who could listen to the evidence without prejudice or passion. They were supposedly like the people described by John Locke as having a blank slate for a mind on which experience could then write. Then, using common sense, the jurors independently (so that they would not be prejudiced by one another) would make up their minds. And in major cases they were supposed to decide "beyond all reasonable doubt."

This phrase, which encapsulates a key, central feature of our legal system, defies definition. When judges have tried to define it for the jurors, higher courts have ruled that this is an attempt to force jurors to decide one way or another. The California legal code tried to offer explanations of the phrase and this was ruled out of bounds.

What is a "reasonable doubt," and what is "beyond all reasonable doubt"? English case law in the late seventeenth century suggests that it grew out of discussions among philosophers, scientists, and theologians in the Royal Society who were seeking a standard for probable and reliable knowledge. They realized, following Descartes, that all knowledge claims could be called "in doubt." We might be dreaming. A demon might be infecting our minds. God might be deceiving us. So we cannot gain infallible certainty. But, they insisted, we can and do gain indubitable certainty, that is, certainty "beyond all reasonable doubt." If we accept that God is not a deceiver and that he is responsible for our faculties, then it is not reasonable for us to doubt what we "know" by the exercise of our faculties. Building on this, we can recognize why we find mathematics is certain beyond all reasonable doubt, that the sciences are pretty certain, and that factual knowledge claims, though often less certain, are probable.

In contrast, someone who wants to continue to doubt can perversely find unreasonable grounds for doubting even if everyone else is sure. Unknown or secret forces may be operating to confuse our senses and faculties. We may think we saw an event, but it might be just our imagination. In the Anglo-American legal system, supposedly using the undefined test of certainty beyond all reasonable doubt will sort out serious, legitimate doubts from frivolous ones. Then each juror can decide. If they disagree, they can then discuss each other's doubts and see if they can come to some agreement.

The inability to codify the central notion of "reasonable doubt," and the fact that we know of too many jury decisions that have been overturned or later shown to be erroneous, lead to recognizing that our legal system is less than adequate for finding *the truth*. But it is the best way we have found so far for trying to do so. At the same time, we can see that our system can be perverted by the police obtaining forced confessions, by overzealous prosecutors who distort and misrepresent the evidence, by defense lawyers who turn trials into soap operas, and by judges who commit judicial errors or mismanage the trials. So this key element of our democratic society has its failings, but no better system seems available for reaching decisions about human events in a finite time span. We say this knowing that people have been kept in jail for years for crimes they did not commit, or sometimes for crimes that never actually occurred, and that apparently guilty people are walking around free.

Because of worries about the overweening power of judges in civil and criminal cases, a movement has developed urging jury nullification. Supported by groups as disparate as the Christian Reconstructionists, the Aryan Nation, and leftists such as Alexander Cockburn, they point to the sorry history of judicial misconduct from the Penn case onward. They then urge that the jury recognize that there are free persons who can accept or reject judicial instructions. The jury, they argue, can and should take charge of cases. This, it is claimed, would lead to a true popular democracy instead of the present system in which the jury is constrained by the judge, who represents the established powers that be. It is claimed that in such true democratic discussion, better justice would be meted out.

It has been debated rhetorically from the late eighteenth century until today whether our government is a government of the people. It is actually a government representing special interests of a smaller part of the society. Every citizen is free to run for public office if he or she meets the requirements, but the cost of running today is so great that very few people can afford it unless they have the backing of wealthy persons, corporations, or labor organizations. It has also been pointed out over and over again that the way election districts are drawn gives an unfair bias to the white establishment as opposed to the various minorities in our society. The present U.S. Senate has no African American member. The previous Senate had just one. The election laws have been drawn to try to balance the interests of the two major parties, the Democrats and the Republicans. One effect of this is that minor parties have little access to radio and TV and are not included in political debates or given much opportunity to present their message to the public at large.

In fact, some critics of modern American politics, such as the late Herbert Marcuse, have argued that what we actually have is a repressive tolerance. We are all entitled to freedom of speech, but the means of communication are controlled by large economic forces and are unavailable to most of us. Television, book publishing, and radio are all big businesses that are concerned with making money, with advertising goods and services, and little concerned with public interest matters such as personal communications. I can write a brilliant book, but can I find a publisher? In the present world, most of the publishing companies are parts of large conglomerates that judge submitted material by whether it will make money rather than by whether it is has an important message.

Critics of the present state of American democracy stress that modern methods of thought control, influence, and social pressure frustrate the original aims of the skeptical American democracy. The huge amounts of money spent on the 1996 U.S. election by both parties, the ways it was raised, and the ways it was turned into influence packages to sway voters show that we no longer have a system that relies solely on public input, in which, Locke had said, the errors of some would be balanced by others. Instead, we have professional people devoted to learning how to influence people and control public opinion without relevance to any attempt to reach a genuine consensus. In a recent election for the senatorial seat in California, one candidate spent a record amount of money. He never mentioned any policy he favored in his TV ads; he just attacked the character of his opponent, making it appear that she must be a criminal on the loose. He almost won. The next election saw even larger sums spent without any serious effort to air policy questions, or involve voters in making a thoughtful decision.

In the eighteenth century construction of modern democracy, freedom of speech and freedom of the press were seen as crucial ways in which people could state their opinions, question policies, and bring about the best answers to social and political questions. The British royal government and the French monarchical one had jailed people for what they said and had books and newspapers censored. To overcome these malevolent events, the U.S. Constitution emblazoned in the First Amendment the contention that Congress could not abridge the rights of citizens to freedom of expression.

FREEDOM OF SPEECH

The classical defense of this situation was given by the English philosopher, John Stuart Mill in his essay "On Liberty." Mill, writing in the mid-nineteenth century, was concerned to defend the right of free expression from arbitrary authorities and from the tyranny of the majority, which was becoming a problem in the emerging democratic societies.

Why should people in any society be allowed to speak and write

as they wish? From ancient times to the present, various governments have limited free expression, and have often regarded it as
dangerous. The ancient Greek philosopher Anaxagoras was punished
for making remarks that indicated he did not believe in the accepted
religion of the time. Socrates was tried and condemned and one of
the chief charges was that he taught wrong (i.e., un-Athenian ideas)
to his students. People have been labeled heretics in Christendom
and Islam for speaking or writing ideas that the authorities saw as
pernicious and dangerous. In the twentieth century, especially in
Nazi Germany and Stalinist Russia, but also in many other modern
states, people have been jailed, exiled, or killed for what they said
or did. George Orwell, in his forceful satire on modern totalitarian
states in *1984*, expanded subversive expression to include "thought
crime" (even though not expressed) and "face crime" as dangerous
and subversive. Even in modern democratic societies such as the
United States there has been worry about whether to allow "hate
speech and writing."

In Mill's day it was still a crime in England to state anti-Christian
views, and there were still trials of miscreants for blasphemy. In the
face of this, Mill argued that there was nothing to be lost and much
to be gained by allowing people to write and speak freely. If what
they said or wrote was false, it could then be refuted. If it was not
obviously false, we could learn from trying to assess what had been
said or done. If what was said or written was true, then it expanded
our knowledge. Mill pointed out that there is no idea that was not
asserted for the first time by someone. We would have no new ideas
if we did not allow freedom of expression. Mill was a moderate
skeptic and realized that what was accepted as true at any time might
have to be revised or changed. Without freedom of expression, no
such intellectual progress could occur.

If there are so many merits to allowing freedom of speech and
writing, then why are societies and many members of modern democratic societies so worried about allowing it? They point out that
people might be led astray by false or misleading expression, that
they might be led to all sorts of bad things. Mill, after writing as if he
were in favor of freedom of expression without limits, started introducing some limits. He would not let somebody teach children that

2 + 2 = 5. Children's minds are not mature enough to assess the truth or falsity of such information. Further, even grown-ups who are not sufficiently educated have to be protected from demagogues, bad leaders, and the like. He thought that in the British colonies, for instance, the natives may not be allowed full freedom of expression. And in democratic societies such as England or the United States, one still has to protect people from speech or writing that can lead to horrendous consequences before people have a chance to evaluate what has been expressed. So Mill was willing to restrict freedom of expression in cases where, as Justice Oliver Wendell Holmes expressed it, there is clear and present danger. Someone shouting to any angry mob that corn dealers are robbers in front of a corn dealer's house may lead to violent action. Shouting "fire" in a crowded movie house might lead to panic, injuries, and loss of life.

Mill, in recognizing that expression can and does have consequences, tried to separate thought and action. It is not too clear exactly how to delimit these spheres. Speaking and writing are actions that express the thoughts of someone. Should people be allowed to have whatever thoughts they wish, but not be able to act on some of them? Thought control is not easy, and it is not easy for the government, the neighbors, or any social group to be sure of what somebody is thinking.

As a result, political limitations have usually been on actions, even if the actions are just expressions of thoughts. Since the beginning of the U.S. government, the courts and the Supreme Court have been wrestling with where and how to draw the line. In looking at this we can see many skeptical issues. Take, for instance, an issue that is in the courts almost every year, that of pornography and obscenity. Is publication of a picture of a nude person an action that society should prevent? Is nude dancing something society should prevent? Is sexual activity in public something society should prevent? Is publication or depiction in the cinema of sexual activity something society should prevent?

Over the last two hundred years there have been many answers given to these questions. In Victorian times the answers were usually negative. What was banned or forbidden even fifty years ago is now permitted. The arguments for each case have usually dealt with the possible harm that such activities could cause, and whether it is up to society to do something about it. For a while the publication of James Joyce's classic *Ulysses* was banned because of its supposed pornographic content, as were the novels of Henry Miller and Vladimir Nabakov's *Lolita*. Courts later decided that regardless of the alleged possible harm that might be caused, these works had what the courts called "redeeming social merit."

Who could be the arbiters of these issues? Literary critics were called as witnesses to oppose the baleful views of prelates. They, of course, were fallible human beings who could be wrong.

These cases finally were decided by the United States Supreme Court, the ultimate arbiter in our system of government.

The court has given varying opinions over the years, from supporting censorship to prohibiting it. It has offered regulatory conditions, such as saying that societies can have time, place, and manner restrictions on where pornographic and obscene materials can be sold, and regulations about the ages of people who can purchase them. The court has held usually that such restrictions have to be "reasonable." Still, year after year, a fight goes on between those of libertarian tendencies and those who feel the need to restrict and regulate behavior. The very fact that the court has changed its view over the years suggests there is no infallible standard in this matter. It also suggests that the court itself, as the ultimate arbiter in our society, is a fallible institution. It is composed of nine human beings appointed by the chief political person, the president, and approved by a majority of a political body, the U.S. Senate. Nobody thinks that the political nature of the way people become justices guarantees that they make right or best decisions. We know all sorts of gossip about the nine justices, their quirks, their leanings in political and social questions. Given this, why do we easily accept their decisions? For the same reason, basically, as we accept the umpires' and referees' decisions in sporting events, though we know they can be wrong. The game would be playable without some final arbiter, but as skeptics we know the arbiter can be wrong. In the sporting cases there are often video pictures that show the decision was wrong, and still the game goes on. In court cases, those who lose can reapply, hope for a change of judges, and press on.

Recently one of the authors was at a panel discussion about the impeachment trial of President Clinton in which four eminent legal experts from Stanford and the University of California, Berkeley, spoke. They all said without a qualm that the U.S. Supreme Court had been wrong in its unanimous ruling in the case of *Paula Corbin Jones* v. *William Jefferson Clinton*, when it decided that permitting Ms. Jones's civil action to proceed while Clinton was the sitting president would not interfere with his presidential duties. By now, perhaps the justices themselves would agree, which shows the skeptical element still in the judging part of our system.

If we turn briefly to another kind of attempt to limit expression, that of designating some speech as "hate crimes," we can see further skeptical problems. There are some people who deny that the Holocaust ever occurred and insist that the evidence offered is fraudulent. Some of these people write books, publish journals, disseminate their views on the Internet, give lectures, and so on. Should this be permitted?

If we were to say only true information should be allowed to be published, who would judge? And would anything be published? The Millean view would be that if the publication is false, it can be refuted, so no harm is done. But in view of what happened in Europe during World War II, many people can suffer from the dissemination of false information. It can even lead to advocacy of racist legislation and injury to some people. The question is so sensitive that in countries such as France and Canada there are actual laws against denying the Holocaust and legal penalties that can be imposed.

At the present time we are told of an explosion of hate materials on the Internet. What should be done? Those who think something ought to be done point to the hate crimes that occur—people being attacked, insults, discrimination. The racist material on Internet Web sites can lead unsuspecting people astray, those who do not realize what they are being exposed to. Attempts to punish people for holding racist views have usually been thwarted by the courts as violations of the First Amendment, and the very liberal American Civil Liberties Union often defends the racists on these grounds. Others insist that too much social damage has already occurred and could happen again unless certain views are outlawed or controlled. This seems to indicate the cutting edge of the thought-action question. It would be almost impossible for even the most tyrannical government to regulate what is on the Internet. It can, however, regulate the people who put it on the Internet. Thus, child pornographers can be arrested for pictures they display, but preventing the appearance of such pictures seems technologically impossible. The debate goes on about the extent to which society can or should regulate TV and radio programs. But with the Internet, we appear to be in another kind of world of expression that may not be manageable.

There are groups that try to monitor various kinds of sites, to warn people about them, and to warn society about their dangers. And when some racist outrage occurs the monitors flood us with data about the kinds of people who do this sort of thing. But in a democracy, with the First Amendment, can one have prior restraint of expression? Occasionally some governmental agency overzealously tries to censor the appearance of a book or article prior to publication, and is forced to give up by the courts or public pressure. But can speech or publication be so dangerous that something can or ought to be done? In the 1970s an underground publication put out in Madison, Wisconsin, announced that in its next issue it would have an article describing how to make an atomic bomb. There was a public outcry and a demand to prevent the publication of this article. The magazine insisted that all of the information that was in it was available in public libraries, and that no "secret" information would be released. The author said he had gotten most of his information from the public scientific library maintained by the U.S. Government at Los Alamos, New Mexico. As the debate went on, the shock value of the intended article became obvious, the possibility of actually silencing publicly available information became futile, but cooler heads prevailed. The magazine decided to withdraw the article.

In a case a few years earlier, a government social scientist, Daniel Ellsberg, took a copy of "secret" government reports on the Vietnam War from the Rand Corporation in Santa Monica—reports that he had helped to compile, which found that pursuing the military policies of the government would not lead to a successful outcome. News was leaked that the *New York Times* was about to publish the reports that Ellsberg had taken. The federal government went to court to seek an injunction against the newspaper while its presses were rolling. They got a court order, but only after a sizeable portion of the report was published. But then the *Chicago Tribune*, the *Boston Globe*, and others put out further portions. With the report published, it did not seem that anything horrendous had happened to the government's military efforts. But President Nixon insisted on pressing charges against Ellsberg. At the trial, Ellsberg and his attorneys showed that all of the documents in the report had appeared earlier in newspapers, in the Congressional Record, and in public governmental hearings. Yet the government kept insisting that something in the mass of data was a secret so dangerous that it should not have been made public.

This effort to suppress information, put forth by many government agencies since World War II, since the assassination of President John F. Kennedy, and through all sorts of investigations of purported governmental misconduct, has bred perhaps the greatest level of skepticism among the populace.

Partly as a result of the atomic bomb project, the government has declared some expression to be classified, that is, that it can only be known by people authorized by the government. President Truman set up the machinery that led to the classification of documents, classified "secret," "top secret," and on and on. People who have been granted access to such classified information have to apply for clearance before they can state orally or in writing some classified item. This system of limiting freedom of expression in a democracy is enforced by severe legal and criminal penalties for the unauthorized disclosure of classified information.

The supposed rationale for this limitation on freedom of expression is that some information, if disseminated, could aid and abet enemies of the United States. Hence, there would be a clear and present danger in allowing such classified information to be expressed in open circumstances where anyone might become aware of it. And over the last fifty years we have had a culture where we are constantly told of dangerous efforts being made by enemies of the United States to obtain such classified information. We are told that we are threatened by spies trying to obtain either our military secrets or our special industrial secrets. This post–World War II culture has led to some wonderful spy movies and novels, and also the arrest and trial of actual spies.

CLASSIFIED INFORMATION AND SKEPTICISM

However, in the course of the agitation to keep spies away and to guard our classified information, enough silliness leaks out to raise the level of skepticism very high among the public. Over and over again, examples come to light in which trivial information has been classified, where the fact that embarrassing mistakes have been made or that somebody has misbehaved have been kept secret by classifying the data.

This then raises the basic question: Who decides what is a secret? And who knows if the classification process has been carried out soundly? Over and over again the public finds that material has been classified to prevent embarrassment, to aid and abet some political end, to cover up mistakes, to avoid public scrutiny, and so on. If one looks at the sequence of declassification of documents from 1963 to the present about the assassination of President John F. Kennedy, all sorts of bureaucratic bungling becomes apparent. The general public had great interest in knowing what had actually happened to the president that fateful day in Dallas. All sorts of unusual claims surfaced from eyewitnesses, from reporters, from people involved in investigating the case, and from people who had known some of the principals such as Lee Harvey Oswald. There was tremendous public concern to know what had actually happened, how many gunmen were involved, what kinds of injuries the president had suffered, and, most of all, what were the cause or causes of his murder. Was there a failing on the part of the Secret Service in protecting him? Were there conspirators plotting to end his life? Was the investigation of his death carried out properly? Within a few days after the assassination, the new president, Lyndon B. Johnson, set up the Warren Commission, named after its head, Chief Justice Earl Warren, to investigate and to allay the fears and rumors that were affecting the populace. The Warren Commission carried on most of its work in secret, and less than a year after the murder issued its report saying that Kennedy had been killed by a lone assassin, Lee Harvey Oswald, whose motives were not known. Much skepticism was aroused by the failure of the report to explain many of the points that bothered people.

Over a year later, twenty-six volumes of evidence and testimony were released, purportedly to justify the report's findings. When this material was examined by careful investigators, they found more questions than answers, and found in many cases that the documents and the testimony did not justify the conclusions of the report. And then it was found that any further information was classified. This included medical records, investigative materials of many governmental agencies, and information about Oswald, his life in Russia, and his activities in the United States. Over the years, poll after poll has shown that over two-thirds of the public doubt the conclusions of the Warren Commission, and has demanded that more information be made available. As we have become aware of the huge amount of classified information on the subject, there has been a growing public skepticism. This has spread from the official claims about Kennedy's death to official claims about the Vietnam War and many other matters.

So far, in the vast declassification that has taken place, especially since President Clinton ordered all except the most secret materials to be released, nothing seems to have surfaced that should have been classified in the first place. People might have been less convinced of the reliability of governmental agencies and personnel, but because of the long, long fight to force the declassification of documents, the general public is by now overwhelmingly convinced that the Warren Commission was mistaken, and that some governmental agencies were involved at least in covering up what had happened. A huge credibility gap has been created that now makes it very difficult for governmental agencies and figures to satisfy the public as to what has occurred in all events. A former means of overcoming this kind of public skepticism, that of appointing special commissions of people whose integrity is beyond question, has been eroded.

The simple, original democratic belief that if the public could freely obtain information and discuss and argue about it, they could most likely reach a better conclusion regarding policies to be adopted no longer seems to hold. If the public cannot obtain or discuss critical information, and cannot examine expert opinions about policies, then can the public make an "informed" judgment?

The military situation since World War II seems to have created two blocks to previous democratic procedures. One is the classification of information, and the other is the shielding of experts, who have access to such classified information, from public scrutiny and question. So we have to consider the consequences and whether they are desirable in a democratic society. For example, the budget of the Central Intelligence Agency (CIA) is a secret. Congress is not given a monetary figure, as it is for other agencies when it has to decide how to appropriate public monies. The people who know the budgetary amounts given to the CIA are shielded, and are not examined or questioned—they are *required* to keep this information a secret. So how can we, the American public, decide if enough, too little, or too much is being appropriated?

In the investigation in 1998 and 1999 regarding whether the Chinese government obtained secret information about our nuclear weapons, much of the material at issue is classified. When Congress called various witnesses to testify, that is, to tell them and the American people what had happened, the witnesses, usually after consulting lawyers, said that they could not answer the questions in open hearing. So their answers were given in secret, and cannot be divulged except to those with proper security clearances. Even the congressmen who drew up the report about what had happened had to allow the government the right to restrict portions of their report, that is, to classify them.

An absurd picture of the situation occurred during the Senate Watergate hearings in 1973. The senators asked a witness about a secret government report, the Houston Report, a plan to arrest all subversive Americans in time of danger. The witness said he could not discuss anything about it, even its existence, because it was classified. However, classified or not, the Houston Report had been published that day in the *New York Times*. Senator Sam Erwin, the chairman, had a copy, and started reading it aloud. He was told it was classified. He then and there declared that he, as a U.S. Senator, was declassifying it, and putting the issue of the newspaper into the public record. Of course, once it was made public, it became apparent that some bureaucrats had devised this plan for rounding up subversives—a plan that never went into effect. And the open publication of the plan did not cause any hardship to society, but it ruined the reputation of a couple of bureaucrats.

When one starts applying our skeptical questions to what is involved in classifying knowledge, and in declaring some persons as authorized to have knowledge of it, some basic doubts arise. If one asks is this system designed, perhaps, for the common good, the security of our country, compatible with a democracy, we may realize what has developed.

The original classified knowledge presumably had to do with military-scientific information about building and employing various weapons systems. The information involved was discovered by human beings in the course of intellectual investigations. It was an outgrowth of previous developments of scientific ideas that had, prior to World War II, appeared in public scientific journals and publications. If those working in America and Great Britain could generate the technology to build atomic weapons from previously published information, what would prevent others from doing so? Nothing, except the difficulty of testing some of the hypotheses. What was involved in classifying the information gained by the British and American scientists was to prevent the development of the same weapons in the immediate future when they would constitute clear and present dangers to the Allies. In time, our enemies would have found out what we knew. If they found it out too soon, the results might have been disastrous for the Allied side. So, though we might not have kept the classified knowledge secret for very long, we did forestall our enemies' developing such weapons until after the war. Now, over fifty years later, at least eight countries have developed such weapons, even though we still treat the information involved as "classified."

A critical problem in a democracy deals with who makes the decision to restrict knowledge, who continues to apply the decision, and who has the power to change the decision. Prior to World War II the United States did not really have an intelligence service. The secretary of war before 1939, Henry Louis Stimson, held that "gentlemen do not read other people's mail." It was presumed that all scientific findings were public. With the outbreak of the war, it was immediately seen by the highest governmental authorities that some information had to be kept from our enemies, lest it be used against us. Once the decision to attempt to build an atomic bomb was made, a vast military-industrial undertaking was "classified." And from it grew a larger and larger system of classified knowledge, reaching to such matters as the actual budget of the CIA, the existence of some other secret agencies, the names and addresses of some of their personnel, and areas of scientific investigation undertaken by military or intelligence agencies. Each time some leak or dramatic disclosure occurs, the questions again is raised: Why and how do some cognitive matters become classified knowledge?

Some examples indicate the kinds of problems involved. In 1975, a commission headed by Vice President Nelson Rockefeller to look into some of the activities of some of our intelligence agencies mentioned in its report that a member of a research team committed suicide after taking an experimental drug years earlier. The family of the person, who could never get any information from the government, recognized the case mentioned in the report. It turned out that the government had classified all information about some CIA psychological experiments in brainwashing by using drugs such as LSD. The experiment, carried on unbeknownst to the participant, was to drug the drink of someone at a party in Washington. In this case, the person became so disoriented that he was secretly rushed to New York (to keep him out of sight) and put in a hotel room, from which he jumped or fell ten stories. One can well ask, as the family did, Why keep this matter secret, and call all information about it classified knowledge? The CIA did not want to reveal that it was carrying on such experiments, but did that give it the right to cover up what it had done and what had happened? A similar but more massive experiment financed by the CIA was subsequently revealed as carried out in Canada, where patients were given drugs to see if they could be brainwashed. Some of the patients never recovered.

In these cases, the classifying of information seemed to have no vital national defense quality, and only served to cover up incompetent, possibly illegal, and certainly unethical research.

Another example is a bit more touchy. A onetime CIA agent, Philip Agee, defected and started telling stories about what the agency did. He wrote a book about it, which the CIA tried to ban because it was full of classified information. The book, published in the United Kingdom, had some "secrets," that is, things most people did not know, some information about how our intelligence agencies operate. As a result, some changes had to be made in some activities, but no drastic damage seemed to occur to the republic. The book was subsequently published in the United States without any evident damage to the security of the country. In fact, that author claimed he was aiding in fortifying the security of the country by showing some of the illegal things the CIA had done. Some applauded his efforts, some decried them.

Another stage of this case occurred when Agee started publishing the names, addresses, and phone numbers of CIA intelligence agents in foreign countries in a magazine called *Covert Action*. A loud howl went up that he was endangering people's lives, and when one of the people he named was killed, the seriousness of the matter became clear.

Here, simple mundane information—the names, addresses, and phone numbers of certain people—was classified because of the potential damage to these people if the information were public. At the same time, there must have been all sorts of people—maids, servants, tradespeople—who knew the information without having any idea that it was classified. So classifying the information did not completely restrict the data to a special select group. The information only became dangerous if known to some of the nation's enemies. It would, then, become very tricky to design a way of classifying the information so that some would not be able to obtain it, while allowing those like the mailman and the telephone operator to know it.

The above is to suggest that the question of who should be in a position to classify knowledge, as well as the problem of how to control the classifiers, are basic problems for a modern democratic society. Looking at this in a less earthshaking way may help reveal the problems and the skeptical possibilities. As this is being written, there is great agitation in the United States about controlling the content of TV shows, movies, and Internet information. It is alleged every day that children are being damaged by the violent and sexual content of TV programs and movies. And it is evident that anyone can gain dangerous information about how to build or purchase explosive devices from certain Internet sites. Messages inciting hate against all sorts of groups appear on Interet sites. And books such as *The Turner Diaries,* describing how to carry on a violent revolution against the government of the United States, are available in most major bookstores. There are cries to restrict some of this material, to classify it for certain mature, thoughtful, adult groups, while keeping this information away from children, unbalanced people, and so on. After some socially disruptive event, like the shooting spree at Columbine High School in Colorado, there are cries to police the Web, restrict and reform TV programs and movies, and ban certain books. But given our experience with overzealous, dogmatic people, who would we trust to do the restricting, to police the Web, to limit access to libraries and movies? Would we trust a political appointee, an ideological appointee, a religious or irreligious appointee?

MODERN DEMOCRACY AND SKEPTICISM

If, as we have argued earlier in this chapter, the very structure of modern democratic government—as designed by Locke, Bayle, Hume, and Jefferson, among others—was the result of a fundamental skepticism about human beings being able to find true and unquestionable answers about how people should live, we should not be surprised to find this same kind of fundamental skepticism carried over to such applications as restricting knowledge and appointing censors.

In the threefold division of the American government, there was a basic attempt to limit what any of the branches could do. The legislative branch has the function of designing and enacting laws, as well as keeping watch on how the laws are being enforced. The executive branch has the function of appointing law enforcers. The censors and classifers are appointed by the executive branch. And the judicial branch has the power to determine if both of the other branches are operating within their constitutional authority.

The separation of powers may seem an economical way of dividing up the work of government. It is also a fundamental part of the skeptical character of the American government. The Founding Fathers and the authorities upon whom they based their views had grave doubts about whether the members of any of the branches could be trusted to do their job, and only their job. The government was formed historically in the face of autocratic governments in which the executive had too much power and could not be controlled or limited. The U.S. Constitution carefully delimited what the executive branch could and could not do.

According to the Constitution only Congress, the legislative branch, can declare war. Presumably, a powerful executive would not be able to enforce his military will unless he could convince a majority of the legislative branch to agree. Hume, in his "Essay on the Idea of a Perfect Commonwealth," had such doubts about the reasons for going to war that he wanted to require that the legislature of each English county individually declare war. (This was the case in the seventeenth-century Dutch Republic.) In the American case, the presumption was that the legislature, the two houses of Congress, would more represent the popular will than an executive leader, and possibly be more cautious. What this has led to since World War II is that wars have been fought but not declared. Presidents from Truman to Clinton have found that they have the ability to mobilize and commit military forces. Congress may insist that only they can declare war, so military actions go on without being declared wars.

This has led to other ways by which the legislative branch can delimit what the executive branch can do if it has doubts about the wisdom of the executive's policies. Its greatest deterrent is that of withholding money to finance executive activities. In the separation of powers, only the legislature can appropriate money and impose taxes. This would seem to be the strongest way that doubtful or poor policies could be stopped. And it has worked on some occasions, when Congress has set a deadline on when expenditures can be made for military actions in certain parts of the world. But in the winter of 1994–95, when the House of Representatives under Speaker Newt Gingrich refused to pass a budget, thereby forcing a shutdown of the government, the legislators found that there was a further force, public opinion, which would not tolerate the effects of the cessation of governmental action.

This indicates that our system of limited powers works as long as it is supported by the public. The public can show its support or non-support by the choices it makes at the next election, by threatening to make different choices at the next election—or by not voting.

Perhaps the most important control of the system is the role of the judiciary. The members of the various levels of courts are nominated by the executive, and must be approved or confirmed by part of the legislature. So the judges are political appointees in the nature of the case, but they serve apart from the ongoing political process. The ultimate judges, the Supreme Court justices, serve for life once nominated and confirmed. And they are the arbiters about whether the other two branches are acting constitutionally, that is, within their designated roles. For example, when Congress passed legislation making it a crime to burn the U.S. flag, the Court ruled that this is unconstitutional, thereby nullifying the law.

Congress at this point can either try to amend or change the Constitution, or to impeach the judges who have thwarted their will. For better or worse, as part of the skeptical nature of the state, it is extremely difficult to amend the Constitution, which can take many years, and it is even more difficult to remove justices.

The executive is often thwarted by courts deciding he cannot do certain things. Presidents Nixon and Clinton tried to withhold certain information from Congress and the investigatory groups. The presidents claimed they had an executive privilege that allowed them to withhold such information. The Supreme Court, in both cases, with different justices, ruled unanimously that this was not the case. At these points in history, the parties involved, the presidents, obeyed the court rulings; otherwise, a constitutional crisis would ensue from which it might not be determinable who was ruling the society. A genuine impasse would create a total political crisis. At this point, both presidents, in fact, meekly backed down, and the system of limited powers and skeptical democratic means of finding answers could continue. If either president had insisted on the rightness of his case, then the Supreme Court could have held the president in contempt and ordered the police or the the military to arrest him.

Had some such scenario taken place, the carefully crafted system would have collapsed, and a new kind of government would have had to be constructed.

In order to avoid such dramatic developments, and such threatening ones to the governmental consensus, the various branches of our government have often gone out their way to avoid reaching the collision point. When Special Prosecutor Kenneth Starr sought President Clinton's testimony before the grand jury investigating allegations against him, he first sought ways of gaining the testimony voluntarily and indirectly, that is, gaining it in conversation at the White House, rather than in a courtroom. When, for various reasons, no satisfactory arrangement could be worked out, the special prosecutor let it be known that a subpoena would be issued requiring the president to appear before the grand jury. Before such a step was taken, an intermediate arrangement was worked out whereby the president could be questioned in the White House, with the grand jurors, watching on TV, able to submit questions. This procedure avoided testing what might have happened if a court issued a subpoena requiring the president to present himself in a courtroom at a certain time, and he did not appear.

Earlier there was serious concern about what would happen if President Nixon defied the Supreme Court's unanimous ruling that he had to turn over his secretly recorded tapes of conversations with his aides. There was genuine fear that Nixon might order a military force to protect the White House and its properties. There was fear that Nixon, in his constitutional role as commander in chief, might order the military to protect him. Either case would have had one branch of the government literally at war with another, thus destroying the civil society. Fortunately, this test did not occur.

The only time the civil society has been really tested was in 1861 when a group of southern states refused to obey the orders of President Lincoln. The southern states realized the enormity of what they were doing, namely, that they were seceding from the United States and setting up another, different country, the Confederate States of America. It took four bloody years of war to restore the kind of government that had prevailed previously.

Before leaving this subject, another indication of the degree of skepticism involved in the United States Constitution is the fact that the commander in chief of the *military* forces is designated as a civilian, the president, rather than the top general or admiral. This again reflects doubts about whether the military, with the forces at their disposal, can be kept from seizing political power. Various military leaders seem to have had desires to extend their control from that of the military forces to the entire country. But each time there has been a crisis about this, the military has followed the orders of the civilian commander in chief. When they have publicly opposed these orders during a military action, they have been removed by the civilian leaders. Afterward, we have had the spectacle of military commanders contending that the civilian commander in chief made wrong or harmful decisions, but at the time these orders had to be followed.

What we are trying to show is that the American form of government has been designed to avoid acting on policies that are claimed to be *true*. Rather, a system has been designed to avoid as much error as possible.

Over and over again, political leaders such as President Clinton have announced that what they want to do is "the right thing to do." The more a political leader makes this kind of claim, the more the skepticism of the public and its elected representatives comes to the fore.

Is it better to have such a system as ours, which thwarts dogmatic proposals of solutions to problems? One can say that in thwarting them it is often the case that social and political problems do not get solved, or get mixed up by partial or limited solutions. If we take as an example the problem of eliminating drug use in the United States, we can see that various ways of solving the problem are thwarted by the Bill of Rights, by laws passed to protect people against overweening governmental authority, by judicial restraints, and so on. The solution to the drug problem adopted in some less skeptical countries, such as inflicting fierce punishments or even death sentences on drug users, may curb drug usage. But so far nothing this extreme is even considered here because of limitations on types of punishments that are allowed and limitations on instances in which the death penalty can be employed. Drug usage could probably be curtailed if the police were able to have surveillance over the life activities of citizens, through some kind of monitoring of the form portrayed in George Orwell's *1984*. But this would be unconstitutional, since the Bill of Rights limits the police ability to search people and their activities without "probable cause." Here we can see another skeptical element. Society has doubts about what the police would do if unsupervised and unrestrained. So the burden is put on the law-enforcement authorities to cite reasons that make them think there is a probable cause to investigate the lives of X, Y, or Z, and the courts can later decide that these reasons were inadequate. In order to enter peoples' homes the police are supposed to first obtain a search warrant, that is, an authorization by a judge giving them the right to search a place because they have "probable cause." Judges have often refused to issue such warrants when they have doubts about what the police assert.

In the War on Drugs, which has now gone on for almost three decades, the authorities empowered to carry on this fight have been pressing over and over again for the suspension of civil rights in order to enable them to faster and more indiscriminately pursue drug users and those who import and sell drugs. As this war drags on without any sign of victory or abatement, another order of skepticism is developing, a skepticism about the very policy that has led to the war. Some people are questioning whether there is any "good" reason for carrying on the war at all, or whether it might be carried on in a less forceful and military manner. Our drug czar speaks as if he would like to be able to send U.S. military forces into foreign countries where drugs are produced; he would like to suspend constitutional rights within the United States.

He can advocate such policies, but he can only enact them if the system authorizes it. He needs the support first of his superior, the president. Then he needs Congress to authorize the funds, which now are spoken of in billions of dollars, and he needs the support of the courts. The built-in skeptical mechanisms prevent any precipitous action or decision.

We can say that is a hell of a way to solve a dire social problem. But the proponents of our kind of limited democracy can reply that any other known way of dealing with social problems has the potential to be much worse in terms of the harm it may do to people and to the society as a whole.

In fact, it has been pointed out over and over again, representative democracy is not a good or sure way of reaching the best solution to social and political problems. It has been pointed out over and over again that the separation of powers in a government makes it less able to cope in real time with real problems. It has been pointed out over and over again that some of the key features of democratic government, such as trial by jury, are inefficient and liable to abuse and mischief. Studies of the American jury system have shown that jurors often make decisions based on their prejudices, and not on the basis of the evidence presented to them. One study showed that jurors in prominent trials make up their minds long before they hear most of the evidence. And it goes without saying that since the jurors are usually not technical experts, they are in no position to judge technical matters presented to them. Further, there is ongoing evidence that jurors have reached wrong decisions, that innocent people have been convicted and even executed.

When all of this has been taken into consideration, we can still ask, Is there any better system of government that is not liable to even worse faults? The history of political societies, especially those in the twentieth century, leads many to opt for a skeptical democracy, faults and all.

Leading alternatives during the twentieth century included various forms of fascist and communist governments, both of which replaced the basic democratic features with totalitarian ones. These governments had central authorities that *knew* what to do in order to deal with social and political problems. No hint or whiff of skepticism entered into the political process. The communist governments based their policies and actions on a claimed knowledge of the necessary forces of historical development. With this knowledge there was no place for doubt about what to do. The fascist governments—the Italian one, the German one, the Japanese one, and many Latin American and Asian ones—were led by authorities who professed absolute knowledge that was not allowed to be questioned by the citizens. Both kinds of governments saw no need to allow free expression on the part of citizens. Such expression could only interfere with the solution of pressing problems and lead to social disorder.

In the theory of communism developed by Karl Marx and

Friedrich Engels, the kind of democracy that exists in England and the United States is really just a government operating in the interest of the capitalist class. The capitalists control the means of production and the means by which governments are chosen. So the so-called democracy is just the way the capitalist class carries on its domination. All of the democratic safeguards are just ways by which the capitalists keep the oppressed, the working class, in check. In contrast, a real democracy would be a dictatorship of the proletariat, the working class, which governed in terms of advancing the interests of the people, that is, the working class.

Since the members of the working class may not recognize their own interests—since they have been misled by the capitalists for so long—it is necessary to have a central government, a dictatorship, run by the Communist Party, which claims to be the spokesperson for the working class. In this way decisions are made without all of the impediments that the capitalists and their dupes could put in the way. As this kind of government developed in the Soviet Union, more and more emphasis was put on control and elimination of dissent and dissidents. In fact, in the history of the Soviet Union from 1917 to 1991, the rulers kept discovering capitalist plots involving leading members of the Communist Party. Leaders who were thought to be selfless officials always working in the interests of the masses were said to be actually agents of anticommunist forces. This finally included the great dictator Joseph Stalin, unmasked at the twentieth Communist Party Congress in 1956. Naturally, this bred a kind of skepticism among the populace; a skepticism which could not be expressed openly until the controls of the government were stripped away.

The fascist and Nazi governments decried democratic governments as inefficient, corrupt, and unable to deal with real social problems. In Italy, then in Germany, and later in Spain and France, Fascist leaders claimed that the democratic governments of those countries were too weak, lacked vision, and were letting the countries go to rack and ruin. Only strong governments with the power to act could meet the demands of the time. The various fascist groups insisted that the state was more important than any individuals and that they, the Fascists, spoke for the state. Part of their rationale was usually drawn from the nineteenth-century German philosopher G. W. F. Hegel, who saw the state as the fulfillment of human history. In this vision, the state was seen as the organ of historical development.

The various fascist governments in countries such as Portugal, Spain, Italy, Germany, and France, pointed out the inability of the democratic governments that preceded them to solve social and political problems. The previous democratic governments never had a strong governmental majority in order to act. The fascist governments all claimed to be much more efficient. As was said, Benito Mussolini made the trains run on time. Adolf Hitler eliminated unemployment. Francisco Franco and Antonio Salazar produced social order from the somewhat anarchic worlds that came before. This efficiency might have solved problems, but these governments curtailed human freedom and the governments could only be maintained by the use of a massive police apparatus. The twentieth-century fascist governments silenced opposition through terror and intimidation. However, they were unable to keep control as the result of World War II and the spread of democratic governments all through Western Europe.

The communist governments that arose in Russia and other Eastern European countries took over the previous governments, and set up enormous apparatuses to deal with everything. This proved quite inefficient, but was protected by a fearful police state. Contrary to Marxist theory, the actual states that arose in Eastern Europe made little headway in dealing with basic economic problems. In the decades after World War II there was more and more hardship for citizens unable to cope with extreme shortages, black markets, and the like. The Communist control collapsed in the late 1980s and in various ways the states of Eastern Europe have been trying to develop democratic systems of government to deal with their problems.

To close our discussion we should mention that democracy, even though less efficient than other alternatives, is emerging as the preferred form of political power in much of the world. The skeptical democracy of the United States is among the most stable and, by now, one of the oldest continuous democratic governments. It obviously has not yet been able to deal satisfactorily with some of the pervasive problems in our society, such as racial inequalities, control of weapons in private hands, and the development of a successful educational system for all of the students in the state. A worrisome sign is that many citizens seem to be getting disillusioned with the democratic process, and with the politicians who are supposed to make it operate successfully. At each national election fewer and fewer potential voters actually take the time to cast their ballots for representatives and executive leaders. In the last two national elections, President Clinton actually received fewer than half the votes of those who chose to participate; participants numbered half the actual number of eligible voters. If this trend continues, the political process will be controlled by a smaller and smaller minority, and the government will no longer be based on the consent of the governed. The theoretical safeguards developed in the eighteenth century and the levels of skepticism introduced may no longer be a basic feature of our political system.

8 SKEPTICISM TODAY

A Debate between Avrum Stroll and Richard H. Popkin

LETTER FROM AVRUM STROLL TO RICHARD H. POPKIN

Dear Dick:

As colleagues and friends of long standing we have personally debated the merits of skepticism for many years. Now that we have finished our manuscript about the role of skepticism in the history of philosophy, and have done this by presenting major philosophical theories and the skeptical challenges to them in a neutral, objective manner, I think we should discuss skepticism as we view it today. I also suggest that we extend the discussions about skepticism we have had in the past: with my arguing against it and you arguing for it. These positions would accurately reflect views we have in fact held over the years and would provide our readers with the opportunity to hear these matters broached from a contemporary perspective. In a sense I am asking that our ongoing personal talks about the merits of skepticism now be made public.

As I mentioned in an earlier chapter of this book, the research into skepticism that you and your students have done has altered our understanding of the history of philosophy. Before your seminal work, skepticism was always treated as a trivial nuisance that was not important in its own right and could therefore be dismissed as a kind of pathology. You have shown that this reading is completely mistaken; that skepticism is one of the driving forces behind most of the major theories from the time of the ancient Greeks to the present, and that every important thinker has felt the need to respond to it. In that chapter I quoted a passage written by Benson Mates emphasizing this point and I agree with it. The preceding chapters in this book are all directed to spelling out this thesis in greater detail. But skepticism can raise probing criticisms without being correct in itself, and it is this issue that I think we should discuss. I will focus the matter by asking: Is skepticism correct? I deny that it is and the material that follows will support this position.

As you have made abundantly clear, there are many forms of skepticism, some of which professedly do not advance arguments. One of the most important of these is "Pyrrhonism."As you point out, such approaches have been extremely influential throughout Western history. But since they are not systems of beliefs or doctrines it is hard to know how to argue against them. I will therefore simply set them aside in what follows, which, of course, does not mean that you must do so as well.

Instead, my focus will be on an argumentative tradition that is at least as important, and it is *only* this set of doctrines that I shall refer to when I speak of "skepticism." This tradition is parasitic upon a kind of philosophy it calls "dogmatic" and its aim is, and has been, to show that dogmatists are mistaken in believing that knowledge and/or certainty are attainable by human beings. Interestingly enough, skepticism and its dogmatic opponents share certain deep beliefs: that epistemology is dedicated to the justification of knowledge claims; that justification consists in argumentation, i.e., in providing reasons (grounds, evidence) in support of such claims; that in the justificatory process some of these premises function as criteria; and that such criteria must be satisfied by any true assertion of knowledge. While accepting these principles, skeptics also deny that there are any criteria whose satisfaction will guarantee that p is known to be true.

As you know from our conversations and from things I have written elsewhere, I reject these principles and the skeptical challenge to them. I hold, for example, that criteria may not exist where true knowledge assertions are made, and that even where criteria do exist they are sometimes relevant to the determination of knowledge claims and sometimes not. I regard the dichotomy that one must either be a dogmatist or skeptic as spurious and, further, I deny that every defense of knowledge and certainty must follow a justificatory pattern. I am thus neither a dogmatist nor a skeptic.

It is important in beginning our discussion to stress that the forms of skepticism I will be focusing on presuppose the same conception of knowledge as is espoused by their dogmatic opponents. This conception rules out any claim to the effect that a high degree of probability could be a case of knowledge, i.e., the kind of view that W. V. Quine has made famous in the twentieth century. This shared conception has three facets: first, that if A knows that p, p is true; second, that if A knows that p, it is impossible for A to be mistaken; and third, that if A knows that p, A must have "suitable" grounds—a justification—for the claim to know.

These last two facets are the factors that the skeptic seizes on in challenging any claim to knowledge or certainty. The idea that if A knows that p it is impossible for A to be mistaken about p is obviously a key element in the skeptical challenge. This is because, as the skeptic views the matter, it is not necessary to show in any given case that A, who is asserting a knowledge claim, is *in fact* mistaken. All that needs to be pointed out is that it is *possible* for A to be mistaken; for if that is so, it follows from the conception of knowledge that the dogmatist also accepts that A cannot know that p is true.

This inference gives rise to the second key element in the skeptic's armory, namely, to the doubt that any form of justification, such as evidential backing, is ever airtight. Once this possibility is surfaced, the skeptic is in a position, via such arguments as the Dream and Demon Hypotheses, to challenge the contention that any species of evidence is conclusive. If it is always possible that statements describing the evidence are true, while the conclusion, p, derived from them is false, one can never know that p is true. One might give a true description of what one is sensing, say, a fire burning in a fireplace, while in fact one is dreaming or hallucinating that such an event is occurring. Historically the skeptics have developed a panoply of arguments emphasizing the gap between the evidential base and the conclusion upon which it rests—a gap that allows for doubt about the conclusion. The strategy also has parallels in formal logic wherein showing that an argument is invalid, one need not show that its premises are false, but only that it is possible for them to be true and the conclusion false. In the same way, it is sufficient for the skeptic to show that true premises do not guarantee the truth of a knowledge claim based on them.

I can illustrate both points with an actual historical example. In a famous paper, "Certainty," G. E. Moore claimed that he knew that he was not dreaming because (at the moment of speaking) he knew he was standing up. The skeptical response to this argument was not to make a counterclaim, i.e., to deny that at the moment he was speaking Moore was standing up; rather, it was to indicate that since Moore *might* have been dreaming at the moment in question, he could not know that he was standing up. This rebuttal thus turns on the notion that if A could possibly be mistaken, A cannot know that p.

This mode of argumentation is powerful. If no grounds for any claim to know are conclusive, then even if p is true and even if A believes correctly that p is true, it does not follow that A knows that p. No matter how much sense information one possesses, it is always possible that it is insufficient to guarantee truth. One is therefore never justified in assuming that any statement based on the evidence of the senses is known to be true.

This line of reasoning underlies the two famous skeptical arguments: the Problem of the Criterion and Descartes's Dream Hypothesis, which I will now consider. In different ways each turns on the point that there is always a logical gap between reasons given and the knowledge claim that is based on those reasons. I will examine both arguments to see if the skeptical position is really cogent. I will argue that it is not, and if I am right there is no reason to believe that human beings cannot attain knowledge and/or certainty. So let's have a look at those famous arguments now.

The Problem of the Criterion

Robert Amico's book *The Problem of the Criterion* (1993) contains an excellent discussion of the history of this problem as well as his solution to it. His solution is that what he calls "metaepistemic skepticism" is self-refuting because the conditions laid down by the skeptic are in principle impossible to meet. He asserts that settlement of the dispute is possible only if agreement on the metastandard for acceptable justification is reached by the disputants, and he outlines an approach where both disputants would agree to an acceptable metstandard that would justify their first-order knowledge claims. His solution is ingenious, and yet in my opinion it is unacceptable, for it attacks the problem in the wrong place. In effect, Amico has bought into the conceptual model upon which the skeptic's strategy rests: namely, that one must always justify knowledge claims and must invoke criteria in order to do so. Amico fails to see that such presuppositions can be rejected without the need to a develop countertheory, for that in turn will have its critics, and those theirs, and so on; and in the end nothing will have been decided. The skeptic will thus stand unrefuted.

To make these objections more specific, and eventually to show how the argument can be defeated, let us see how Amico sets up the problem. I will quote him at length to avoid any misrepresentation of his position:

> Wonder brings questions, and these questions constitute a natural beginning to philosophy. Yet beginnings can be difficult and elusive, at least if we take the philosophical skeptic seriously. The skeptic would have us believe that we cannot begin at all, and this claim is the challenge posed by "the problem of the criterion." Before we can know just how seriously to take this skeptical claim, we must come to understand clearly the problem of the criterion.
>
> Suppose you had a basket of apples and you wanted to sort out the good apples from the bad apples. It seems that you would need a criterion or standard by which you could sort them, either a criterion for recognizing good apples or a criterion for recognizing bad apples. But how could you ever tell whether your criterion for sorting apples was a good criterion, one that really selected out all and only the good ones or all and only the bad ones? It seems that

in order to tell whether or not you have a good criterion, you need to know already which apples are good and which are bad; then you could test proposed criteria by their fidelity to this knowledge. But if you do not already know which apples are good and which are bad, how can you ever hope to sort them out correctly? And if you already know which are good and which are bad, by what criterion did you learn this?

This analogy is a paraphrase of Roderick Chisholm's explanation of the problem of the criterion, which itself was inspired by Descartes's reply to the seven set of objections. Chisholm claims that if we substitute beliefs for apples, we encounter the problem of the criterion—how do we decide which beliefs are "good" (actual cases of knowledge) and which beliefs are "bad" (not knowledge at all)? In the case of apples, there is no real difficulty because we already know the criteria for their goodness—firm, juicy, no worm holes or bruises, and so on; but in the case of beliefs we do not. What is the correct criterion, method, or standard for picking out good beliefs or bad ones? It seems as if we need such a criterion or method for sorting out our beliefs. But how will we know whether or not we have the correct criterion, unless we already know some actual instances of good beliefs or bad ones so that we can check our proposed criterion against these known cases? So if we do not already know which beliefs are good ones and which are bad, how can we ever hope to sort them out correctly? How can we ever hope even to begin in epistemology?[1]

Before discussing these passages, I will quote Roderick Chisholm. He writes:

> To know whether things really are as they seem to be, we must have a procedure for distinguishing appearances that are true from appearances that are false. But to know whether our procedure is a good procedure, we have to know whether it really succeeds in distinguishing appearances that are true from appearances that are false. And we cannot know whether it does really succeed unless we already know which appearances are true and which ones are false. And so we are caught in a circle.[2]

In this citation, Chisholm does not speak about beliefs but about appearances; nonetheless it is possible to construe his remarks as referring to beliefs about appearances. In any case, as Amico correctly indicates, Chisholm in many other places explains that the problem is about belief. Let us accept that this is so. That the problem catches us "in a circle" is one reason why it has been called the "Wheel Argument" or *diallelus*. Commentators historically have interpreted the argument in at two different ways, as concluding: (1) there exist no criteria for distinguishing "good" from "bad" beliefs, or (2) that criteria exist but will never succeed in helping us make such discriminations. Chisholm's claim that "we are caught in a circle," buttresses the second interpretation, since it presupposes that there are criteria whose application will lead to vicious circularity.

Amico and Chisholm reflect the tradition in espousing both interpretations. When Amico writes, "It seems that we need such a criterion or method for sorting out our beliefs," the context indicates that he is presupposing that no such criteria exist. This would be a case of interpretation (1). When he goes on to say, "But how will we know whether or not we have the correct criterion," he seems to presuppose that criteria exist but that they will fail to help us sort out good from bad beliefs. This is interpretation (2). That Amico and Chisholm, like many of their early modern predecessors, adopt both interpretations is puzzling, since the two interpretations seem incompatible with one another. The former denies there are criteria and the latter asserts the opposite. Perhaps the argument cannot be given a consistent formulation. But I will not pursue this question since it is philosophically less interesting than the claims made in (1) and (2). It is also worth mentioning that there is a vast literature that supports interpretation (2) in a way that differs from Chisholm's notion that we are caught in a circle. According to it, the argument contends that in order to know that A is a good criterion for selecting beliefs, we require another criterion, B, that will select A as a good criterion; but then we will need another criterion, C, for deciding that B is a good criterion, and so on ad absurdum. According to some of your essays, Dick, this is Montaigne's position. It sustains interpretation (2) by holding that the attempt to apply criteria leads to an infinite regress. These two construals of the argument have something in common; they conclude, though for diverse reasons, that no knowledge claim can be justified. In arriving at this result, they both assume that every knowledge claim must be justifiable.

The Cartesian Dream Hypothesis resembles the Wheel Argument in certain ways, and differs from it in others. It also presupposes that knowledge claims require justification, and that criteria based on sense experience exist for adjudicating such claims. The thrust of the Dream Hypothesis is that the application of such criteria will never guarantee knowledge, i.e., that data based on the senses will never fill the gap between evidential premises and the conclusion derived from such premises. So in effect, Descartes concurs with proponents of interpretation (2) of the Wheel Argument in holding that criteria exist and that such criteria can be satisfied without producing knowledge. Of course, apart from these affinities, the Wheel Argument and the Dream Hypothesis are basically dissimilar, and are generally subject to differing assessments. But since my main concern here is to show that both interpretations, i.e., (1) and (2), are mistaken, it would be repetitive to discuss both arguments with respect to each consideration. Accordingly, I will defer consideration of interpretation (2) until I turn to the Dream Hypothesis below and I will confine my analysis of the Wheel Argument to interpretation (1) that there exist no criteria for discriminating good from bad beliefs. I shall show that the thesis is false, and accordingly that the Problem of the Criterion is a misnomer, for it turns out to be no problem at all. This result would constitute a partial refutation of skepticism.

Criticisms of the Wheel Argument

Let us look carefully at what Amico says, in particular how he formulates the problem. He begins with an analogy, the sorting of apples. His point is that we lack criteria for sorting apples and, by analogy, for sorting beliefs. But as he continues to describe the problem of sorting apples, he admits that "[i]n the case of apples . . . we already know the criteria for their goodness—firm, juicy, no worm holes or bruises, and so on." He then adds, "[B]ut in the case of beliefs, we do not." If we do have criteria for sorting apples how can this case be assimilated to that of sorting beliefs? Clearly it cannot, and Amico's analogy is self-defeating.

Moreover, if Amico concedes this much how can he contend that we do not have criteria for sorting beliefs? It is just as plain as in the case of apples that we do. Good beliefs are true, are buttressed by evidence, have a high degree of probability, and so forth. Truth and strong evidential support are criteria for discriminating good from bad beliefs. The correct conclusion to draw from Amico's presentation is that the analogy is well taken after all. There exist criteria for sorting both apples and beliefs. Similar remarks apply to Chisholm's version. We can surely distinguish, at least some of the time, true from false appearances. Artificial flowers may look like real flowers and, given certain circumstances (uncertain light, bad eyesight on the part of a percipient, very good imitations), it may be difficult to distinguish one from the other. But in general it is not. There are criteria for making such discriminations. Since Amico and Chisholm give accurate renderings of how the Wheel Argument has traditionally been formulated, I see no reason to accept its conclusion that we lack criteria for distinguishing good from bad beliefs.

My purpose here, however, is not merely to discredit the Wheel Argument. It is rather to stress that behind the Wheel Argument lie presuppositions that are the deepest sources of conceptual perplexity. In this particular case, we are given a factitious dilemma: we must either accept that there are no criteria or that even if there are, they are inevitably abortive in allowing us to distinguish good from bad beliefs. The fact of the matter is that where knowledge claims are advanced we *sometimes* lack criteria and *sometimes* do not. This is true in the case of beliefs, for example. It is also true that even where we have criteria they may or may not be needed for such discriminations. It depends on the situation and other contextual factors. What is false, as the Wheel Argument presupposes, is that we *always* have or need criteria in such cases, and that every knowledge claim requires justification via their satisfaction. I will describe two cases that illustrate these points. I begin with an example where one can make a knowledgeable judgment without using criteria.

A decorator has been asked to decide between two shades of blue for a couch. She looks at two swatches and says, "They are certainly different. One is much darker than the other. I think the darker one would be more suitable." The statement "One is much darker than the other" is true. She now knows something she did not know before looking at the samples. She did not arrive at this judgment by invoking criteria. She can just see that the two shades are different. Seeing is not a criterion in this situation, though it makes the judgment possible in a way in which touching, smelling, or hearing would not. We can see why it is not a criterion if we look at our second case.

I am in a foreign country, in Italy. I meet a stranger who wishes to exchange *Lire* for U.S. dollars. Are the bills he is holding counterfeit? I have been given instructions before traveling about how to identify Italian counterfeit money. Legitimate bills held against a light will reveal a figure of Dante; fake currency will not. In addition, legitimate money will have a thread pattern that cannot be reproduced by counterfeiters. So I hold these particular bills against the light and see that that they satisfy the criteria for authenticity. In this circumstance, I have, need, and use criteria. The case thus both resembles and differs from the preceding. In the previous example one looked at samples in order to arrive at a true belief about the shades of a color. I said that seeing was not a criterion in that situation, and we can see why by comparing it with the new case. In looking at the bills against a bright light one is able see a picture of Dante and a specific thread pattern. The presence of the picture and the thread pattern are the criteria for the judgment that the bills are valid. *Looking was not itself the criterion; it made the application of criteria possible.* It thus functioned in a presuppositional relationship to those criteria. It was the invocation of the criteria that made the judgment of legitimacy possible. In the previous case, seeing a difference between the shades made a judgment possible without the intervention of criteria. But seeing was not itself a criterion.

I could continue to adduce other cases, for example, where seeing is a criterion. But I assume that piling up further illustrations is not necessary to support the point in question, namely that the assumptions upon which the Wheel Argument rests are unsound. Because this is so, I conclude that the argument does not generate a a real problem. In particular, it does not require a general theoretical solution of the kind that Amico and Chisholm wish to find.

The Dream Hypothesis of Descartes

My approach to this argument rests on various assumptions you may wish to challenge; among them, that common sense is right about the attainability by humans of knowledge and certainty, and also that common sense needs no justification. Many philosophers, from Immanuel Kant to Barry Stroud, have disagreed with the latter provision, arguing that common sense, like any set of beliefs, needs a philosophical justification. The skeptic would thus agree with them. But I demur and will show why in analyzing the Cartesian Dream Argument, which Kant and Stroud have found compelling. I start by asking: How good is the argument after all? I say not very. It can be rejected on at least three grounds. The moral to be drawn, if my analysis is correct, is not that philosophers need to justify common sense against skeptical challenges, but rather that such challenges that appear prima facie implausible invariably are. The correct response is not to advance another theory, as Kant assumed, or even to provide a countervailing argument, as Moore attempted in "Proof of an External World" or as Amico feels necessary with respect to the Wheel Argument, but to explain why one is not necessary. I reject the argument, then, for these three reasons:

(1) Since it is familiar to scholars, I will not quote the whole argument as it appears in the "First Meditation." But in formulating the argument Descartes makes several statements that undermine the very point it purports to establish, namely that we cannot differentiate waking from dream experiences. In the first of these he says,

> How often has it happened to me that in the night I dreamt that I found myself in this particular place, that I was dressed and seated near the fire, whilst in reality I was lying undressed in bed.[3]

That he can say that in reality he was lying undressed in bed implies that he then knew that he was lying there undressed, and that implies, of course, that he then knew that he was awake.

His second statement contains a similar slip. He says:

> But in thinking over this I remind myself that on many occasions I have in sleep been deceived by similar illusions, and that in

dwelling carefully on this reflection I see so manifestly that there are no certain indications by which we may clearly distinguish wakefulness from sleep that I am lost in astonishment.[4]

Here the mistake is even more obvious. In using the expressions "I remind myself that on many occasions I have in sleep been deceived by similar illusions" and "I see so manifestly," Descartes is presupposing that when he reminds himself of how he has been deceived, and when he can see so manifestly, he is at that moment awake and knows that he is. Once again, the thrust of the Dream Hypothesis has been undercut in its very formulation.

The argument also presupposes that certain sorts of sense experiences are criteria. What it denies is that the satisfaction of such criteria will guarantee the possession of knowledge. When Descartes refers to "indications" in the preceding passage he is alluding to what in modern parlance would be called "criteria." He states that because such indications are not certain one cannot distinguish waking from dream experiences. But this is a non-sequitur. There may be all sorts of things to which the notion of indications or criteria is not applicable, yet one has no difficulty in distinguishing one such thing from another. I do not possess any "indications," certain or otherwise, for distinguishing the color yellow from the color purple. Yet I have no trouble making such a discrimination. Indeed, I have no idea what such indications or criteria could be, or what sort of thing one could appeal to in judging that the colors differ. In that context I neither need nor use criteria/indications. I can just see that the colors are different. There are likewise no indications for determining in general that one is awake. If such a question might arise it will arise in a particular situation—perhaps in the case of someone emerging from an anesthetic. If in that circumstance there is need for criteria to make such a determination they will apply only to that specific situation.

In the same sentence, Descartes says something that is the basis of my second criticism of the hypothesis and the supposed skepticism that results from it. He says "that in dwelling carefully on this reflection I see so manifestly that there are no certain indications by which we may clearly distinguish wakefulness from sleep. . . ." What Descartes fails to realize is that in order to dwell carefully one must be awake. For "dwelling carefully" means to linger over in thought, to deliberate, ponder, and assess a situation. This is not something that one typically does in dreaming. Dreams are not normally subject to one's control or volition. In dreaming we do not "dwell carefully." Instead, dreams force themselves upon one, as it were. The point I am making here can be generalized into a second criticism of skepticism as follows:

(2) The Dream Hypothesis can be formulated briefly in a sentence or two. Presumably the skeptic wishes to express his challenge by uttering the words "Isn't it possible that I am now dreaming? or "For all I know, I may be dreaming at this moment." Now in certain circumstances, one who employs these words may be using them to say something that is sensible and true. Someone may have just won a lottery and may be indicating his pleasure and surprise by saying "Isn't it possible that I am dreaming—dreaming that I won all this?" In such circumstances, the speaker does not intend to say that he may be asleep and dreaming. He uses those words to express his astonishment. He might have used a different idiom, such as "I am amazed." An auditor would understand that the speaker's words "Isn't it possible I am dreaming?" were not being used as they would be if a speaker said, "Isn't it possible that he is dreaming?" The speaker might use the latter sentence if he were looking at a child who was obviously sleep and was murmuring in his sleep. But if a person said, "Isn't it possible that I am now dreaming," an auditor would certainly not take the person to be saying that he, the speaker, might now be asleep. These are the typical adjustments human beings make in communicating with and understanding others.

Now, are there circumstances in which a speaker could use those words to mean at the moment of speaking he might be dreaming and therefore might not be awake?

The answer to this question is no. The reason is that if one meant those words in that way the utterance would be self-defeating. It would violate certain communal conditions that define meaningful intercourse. We all learn from experience when to give credence to the words a person utters; and such experience is the basis for the judgment that when a person utters words while asleep he is not only not intending them in the usual way but is not intending them at all. The skeptic is, of course, a member of the human linguistic community and accepts its linguistic practices. His mistake is to think his utterance is in accord with those practices when it is not. For in order even to formulate his challenge the skeptic must be awake and must know that he is. For in order sensibly to express the thought that he might now be dreaming, the skeptic must be aware of what he is saying, must intend to mean his words in a specific way, and both of these conditions entail that he must be awake at the moment he utters them.

But if the skeptic were dreaming and hence was not awake those conditions would not be satisfied. Therefore, any speaker who uttered those words while asleep would not intend anything by them. The moral: The skeptic's attempt even to express the Dream Hypothesis entails that he be awake and know he is when he utters the words "For all I know I might now be dreaming," and thus the hypothesis that he might be dreaming and hence asleep would be self-refuting. I can formulate the objection as a dilemma. If the skeptic is asleep, he cannot mean anything by the words he utters. If he does mean something by the words he utters, he cannot be asleep. On either alternative, nothing that needs refuting has been said by the skeptic. The plain man does not have to develop a countertheory. He can just go on believing what is true, namely, that he can sometimes distinguish his waking from his nonwaking experiences.

(3) We come to the third reason for rejecting the Dream Hypothesis. Though it was Descartes who formulated the difficulty, it purports to be a general conundrum. It is not simply Descartes who cannot distinguish whether he is awake or sleeping, but presumably it is every human being who is thus incapacitated. The argument would have no philosophical import if it turned out that it was only Descartes who suffered from this particular liability. But a set of insuperable problems emerges if the argument is generalized in this way. To my knowledge, no one has previously pointed out these difficulties.

The Dream Hypothesis presupposes that everyone dreams—and indeed, it presupposes that proponents of the argument know that this is so. But how could they know this? Take a particular case—that of Mr. Smith. If they do know that Smith has had dreams, they are able to determine when Smith is asleep and when he is not. But they could not do so if they themselves were asleep. Hence, in assuming that the argument holds generally, they are presupposing that they themselves are awake on some occasions and know that they are. The very generality that the argument requires thus constitutes a ground for the rejection of its conclusion.

Finally, suppose a certain person has never had a dream. Then what happens to the Dream Hypothesis? If one has never had a dream, one has never had any internal experiences that he cannot distinguish from waking experiences. But if that is so, then he has no trouble distinguishing those occasions when he is awake from those occasions when he is asleep. He doesn't have to compare experiences. He doesn't need those "indications" that Descartes mentions. He just wakes up every morning and realizes that he has been asleep. These objections show that we don't need to justify our common sense beliefs about the so-called external world. It is sufficient to show that the arguments that question these beliefs lack cogency.

How I see philosophy

In concluding this letter to you, Dick, I might say a few words about how I see philosophy. As I have mentioned I believe that common sense can give rise to knowledge and certitude, and my philosophical views start from this presupposition. I thus reject skepticism in any of its forms. But my views also have something in common with the skeptic. As our book has shown, no major philosophical theory is immune to criticism. The skeptic takes this fact to show that knowledge and certainty are not possible. I agree with the skeptic that the study of the history of philosophy does show the fallibility of all theorizing. But what I infer from this fact is that philosophy should be done without theory. I thus concur with Wittgenstein's celebrated remark in *Philosophical Investigations*, "We must do away with all *explanation* and description alone must take its place."[5] By "explanation" in this passage, Wittgenstein means "theorizing." He is thus urging that we do philosophy in a different way—a way that is descriptive. But descriptive of what? The answer is "Of the way that the world is." From the time of Thales to the present, philosophers have attempted to give accounts of the nature of reality.

They have almost unanimously assumed that any such account must result in a theory. This is what Wittgenstein and I deny. We say let us replace theory by description.

Therefore, let me indicate what such a descriptive philosophy would look like. It assumes, as against the skeptic, that we have knowledge of the world, and that much of it derives from perception. It also denies that there is any general philosophical theory that is fine-grained enough to account for the diversity of what we know about the world. Let us call such a general philosophical theory a "holistic view." We can contrast such a holistic view with what I will call an "example-oriented view." The latter is a form of descriptive philosophy. I will illustrate the difference between them with the following example.

In the early part of the twentieth century philosophers generated holistic theories of perception that were very attractive. One of these culminated in the thesis that if a perceiver is looking at an opaque object from a particular standpoint and at a given moment the most the observer can see of that object is a facing part of its surface.

The argument they adduced in support of this thesis was powerful. It began by holding that every opaque object has an exterior, and that its exterior is its surface. Because the object is opaque, one cannot see its reverse side, or its interior, and accordingly there are parts of it, including parts of its reverse surface, that are invisible at the moment of perception and from the position the observer is occupying. What one can see, then, is at most that part of its exterior that faces the observer, and that, by definition, is part of its surface. It concluded that, under the stipulated conditions, the most one can see of any opaque object is part of its surface.

All sorts of powerful conclusions were drawn from this putative perceptual fact. To some writers (including some contempories such as Benson Mates) it seemed that surfaces stood between the observer and the whole object, blocking at least part of it, and this "fact" was interpreted as having skeptical implications. Given the opacity of the object and the perceptual situation as I have described it, Mates inferred that one could not know what the back surface or the backside of the object looked like. He thus concluded that any judgment about the total set of properties of an opaque object will always transcend the available evidence and thus open the door to skeptical doubt. This is another variant of the notion that sense experience cannot guarantee the reliability of judgments about so-called external objects. But the argument, taken in this general form, is fallacious. Once again, we do not need to mount a counterargument to this position. It is sufficient to show that the argument when examined carefully does not go through.

The examples of opaque objects that philosophers advancing this theory invoked were constrained in their topological and spatial variety. Such things as billiard balls, tomatoes, dice, inkwells, tables, persons, and planets constituted a limited range of examples that were used to support this skeptical conclusion. It just seemed obviously true that under the conditions stipulated one cannot see the back surface of a spherical object like a tomato; and since it clearly has a surface, it surely follows that the most one can see of the object is the facing part of its surface.

But with a simple change of examples the theory and the skeptical conclusion it entails collapse. Tennis courts, putting greens, roads, and mirrors are opaque; yet, depending on the contextual circumstances, all of their surfaces can be seen. One watching a tennis match from a good seat can see the whole surface of the court. But if one is sitting behind a post one may be blocked from seeing all of it. The whole surface of a large body of water such as Lake Victoria, which is about two hundred miles long, cannot be seen by a person standing at ground level on its southern shore, but that is not because one cannot see its reverse surface. Not being spherical, it has no reverse surface. One cannot see all of its surface because of its length and the fact that it dips below the horizon due to the curvature of the earth. But no part of its surface blocks any other part, as one could ascertain from a high-flying airplane. From that height, all of its surface can easily be seen. Under typical weather conditions and when seen from a high altitude Lake Victoria is opaque; so under those conditions one can see all of the surface of an opaque object.

Any holistic theory must thus take account of the differences between opaque objects having various topological characteristics, between objects which are spheres, cubes, rhomboids, rectangles (such as tomatoes, dice, etc.) and between them and those entities I call "stretches," i.e., such things as putting greens, tennis courts, sheets, lakes, and roads. These are differences we find in the real world. When we add to these differences other contextual constraints, for example, that many objects we look at are moving, that they may or may not have surfaces even though they are opaque, that the observer may also be in motion, that light playing on objects takes many different forms, that particulate matter in the atmosphere produces a host of differing effects, that the observer's visual acuity, and his distance from the object condition what he sees, it is impossible to accept a theory that claims there is single thing, such as a surface or part of a surface, that is invariably seen in each of these cases. An example-oriented, context-sensitive description of the vast range of perceptual situations is able to take account of these multifarious factors in ways that no holistic theory can. It is thus the right way to do philosophy. It is, as such, a powerful alternative to the holistic theories, including the skeptical ones, that we have been considering.

I have shown in the preceding analysis of the Wheel Argument and the Dream Hypothesis that this approach does not require new forms of model building. With its deflationary strategies it simply undermines bad arguments, leaving us less perplexed than we were before; and in its constructive phases it replaces theorizing with an example-oriented account of the world. That such an account is not only feasible but indeed exists is a good reason for thinking that argumentative skepticism is, and always has been, a paper tiger.

I await your response,

With very best regards,

Avrum

RESPONSE FROM RICHARD H. POPKIN

Dear Avrum,

Since you think the analysis of the Dream Hypothesis is one of the most important elements in dispensing with the skeptical challenge, let us consider the matter further. The problem posed in Descartes's discussion is that many people, most people in fact, have had experiences which, when they occurred, could not be distinguished from a dream world or a waking world. Some people have found that they often cannot be sure that the experiences they have had occurred when they were awake or asleep. The problem gets more complicated when one adds to this what Descartes started with, namely the inability to be sure whether there is a "real" experience or an "illusory" one. Many people, in fact most people, have had what they later realized were hallucinations or "unreal" experiences. Anyone who has smoked marijuana is aware of illusory or distorted experiences compared to normal ones. In the present age of psychotropic drugs, many who have tried them are aware that changes in their experiences occur. Similarly, people who use alcohol are aware of changes in their experiences.

The research in brainwashing techniques, such as the effects of sleep deprivation or of sensory deprivation, show that one can alter people's experiences medically or psychologically. When we reflect on this, we may no longer be so sure that we can tell a real or true experience from an induced one. When we read the psycho-chemical explanation of how some of these techniques and drugs work, we further realize that what we call ordinary or normal experience is a function of how certain brain connectors are working, how certain secretions are taking place, and so on. Then, can we ever be sure if what we take to be our real experiences correspond to events in the world? Some people go crazy pondering this. People who are kept in isolation seem to have no way of finding out if their experiences are part of their situation or are like other people's.

In our current world, where we know so much about the ways in which we can all be influenced by propaganda—for example, TV commercials, subliminal factors, environmental chemicals, sun rays, electro-magnetic forces—we should develop a much stronger personal version of Descartes's Dream Hypothesis. Is all life a dream or are parts of what we experience what the advertisers want us to experience, or what the political authorities make us experience, or what is forced upon us by biochemical factors in the world?

As you recall, no doubt, we have discussed in previous joint writings the story called *Donovan's Brain*, wherein a brain is kept functioning detached from a human body while it receives stimuli. If the brain could have the experiences of a whole human being while resting comfortably in a laboratory jar, can we be sure that we are not all in such a situation?

When you appeal to the person who has never had a dream, does this really make any difference? (In fact, clinical research indicates that certain physiological changes occur in a person when they are dreaming and if they are prevented from dreaming by clinical intervention, they will become disoriented or crazy. Physiologically, the process of dreaming seems to be essential for physical well being.) We would not consider a blind person part of a discussion about colors or a deaf person part of a discussion about sounds. If there are people who never dream, then they won't be interested in this problem. But we can offer them other skeptical possibilities. Presumably illusions are part of their life experience, from daydreaming to alcoholic effects to the effects of drugs and medications. In that context they could be asked if they can really tell what constitutes a normal veridical experience.

I think this shows that the criterion problem rears its ugly head as soon as one ponders the varieties of human experiences. We are asked by friends, by loved ones, by doctors, by lawyers: Did such-and-such really happen? Did you really feel such-and-such? Did you really receive a message from so-and-so? Are their illusory events the effect of too much alcohol, too much marijuana, too many psychotropic drugs, too much sunshine, too much vitamin C, and so on? In order to begin to answer this, one needs some criterion for selecting veridical experiences from others and here, as Montaigne said, "We are off to roll again on the wheel."

Hypnosis

Some further skeptical problems develop when one considers what we know about hypnosis. People in a hypnotic state can be made to have immediate experience of past events and experience them as if they were happening right now. When watching a hypnotic demonstration we can see the difference between present experience and what the hypnotized person seems to be experiencing. However, we can also ponder whether we ourselves are living in some sort of hypnotic state, controlled by forces outside of us. Science-fiction writers have portrayed this and have been able to scare generations.

The movie *The Manchurian Candidate* is about an American soldier in the Korean War who is hypnotized and programmed so that when he emerges from his hypnotic state, he can be made to perform terrible acts upon seeing a certain signal. Researchers in brainwashing techniques have shown that various kinds of controls of this sort are possible. Can we be sure that they're not only possible, but actual—that some bureau somewhere has programmed what we will experience at certain times? No matter how certain we may be of an immediate experience, the experience itself may be the effect of programming. So Cartesian doubts seem to be raised again.

An example from the testimony of the Warren Commission investigation into the assassination of President John F. Kennedy indicates how a reasonable, commonsense person could be driven to Cartesian doubts. An official from Scripps-Howard Newspapers named Seth Kantor reported that he had been talking with Jack Ruby outside Parkland Hospital in Dallas at the very moment that the president was dying inside. Kantor said that Ruby, whom he knew well, wanted his advice about whether he should keep his nightclub open that evening in view of what had happened to the president. The Warren Commission investigators had already decided to their satisfaction that Jack Ruby had not been interested in the events of Dallas until much later and that he was nowhere near Parkland Hospital at the time. Kantor's testimony upset their picture, so they vigorously cross-examined him. He was asked whether he was sure that he had been with Ruby. He replied, *yes, yes, yes*. Could he have possibly been mistaken? Could it have been somebody else? He insisted that he was certain; he knew Ruby well. Then he was asked the Cartesian question. Is it possible that you could be absolutely certain and yet be wrong? He pondered for a while and decided that the answer was yes, since all sorts of conditions that he knew nothing about might have been going on. The Warren Commission investigators pounced on this and said that he had admitted that he could be wrong. A skeptic might suggest that the same sort of answer could be elicited from you, Avrum, if pressed far enough since, unbeknownst to you, you might be controlled by some mad scientists testing a new drug or form of hypnosis.

Another phenomenon that raises questions about the reliability of some kinds of experiences is called "near-death experience," where people very, very close to being medically declared dead report seeing a long tunnel that they are entering with extremely bright lights at the end of it. There are many versions of what people have reported when they have been in this state. Of course, they report it after they have regained some degree of life activity. A compelling case for this is illustrated by what happened to the English philosopher A. J. Ayer, who was operated on for terminal lung cancer. When he awoke from the operation, he immediately asked a nurse to take down a report of what he had experienced and gave a very vivid description of the tunnel and lights and indications of another world at the end of the tunnel. Ayer, as you know, was devoted to antireligious philosophizing all his life. When he recovered enough, he spent a fair amount of time trying to explain that the experience he had reported did not prove anything about an afterworld or the immortality of the soul or any religious view. But he never changed the report of what he had experienced. The philosopher Paul Edwards has devoted a lot of energy to trying to show that these near-death experiences have no significance as religious data and has suggested that they may be due to internal conditions in the brain. I once had such an experience when I had a severe case of pneumonia and I saw the tunnel and the lights and all that, so I think I know what the discussion is about. It was a very happy experience and I still remember it as such but I have no idea what it signifies. I was apparently falling off a chair when this was occurring and when I hit the floor, the experience stopped. I suspect it had something to do with my medical condition at the time. If it did, then one could generalize that any experience we have is involved with our medical condition. The tunnel/light experience may occur when the oxygen going to the brain decreases radically. Other experiences could be correlated with other oxygen levels, so how does one tell which experiences are genuine, real, illusory, and the like? Presumably something like this is involved in the high that people get from using cocaine or heroin. By now, scientists can explain what is happening in the brain and nervous system at that time, but again, how does one tell what's the genuine experience? Normality may be a malignant condition and normal experience may be the effect of biochemical agents that we are used to. As Tolstoy said in his novel *Resurrection,* "Am I crazy that the world looks this way to me, or is the world crazy that it looks this way to me?"

Universal Studios

Of course you will say that all this news about illusions and such makes no real difference because almost all the time we can tell whether we are awake or asleep, whether we are having distorted vision as a result of drugs or alcohol, and so on. We usually can adjust and not feel any real uncertainties, but in extreme cases, problems arise that then reflect on all the rest of our sensory judgments. If we are forced to testify about what happened when we saw two cars collide and the lawyers question us about how sure we can be, whether we could have made mistakes because of our visual limitations, whether we were daydreaming or fully awake, whether we were seeing through a "glass darkly," we might find that we are unable to continue being sure. Some people dissolve into complete doubt on the witness stand when a modern-day Perry Mason raises these sorts of problems. When we watch this, we may realize that we, too, could be the witnesses turned into doubters.

In fact, those of us who live in this part of California know it as the land of make-believe. The main industry of the Los Angeles area is creating illusory worlds. Universal Studios takes people on tours to show how they do it, as well as allowing them to experience the illusion of being in an earthquake, an air crash, and all sorts of other horrendous events. There is now great rivalry amongst the movie studios in making special effects that create greater and greater illusions to convince the viewers, even if only for a short time. When one lives in a world where many people make their living creating fictitious experience and finding ways to make us think strange things are happening, can we really be as secure as your man of common sense?

Those of us who live in the area find that every now and then the neighborhood streets are suddenly transformed into parts of a movie scenario. Dramatic police chases take place on quiet neighborhood streets as part of the make-believe. The nice, simple Will Rogers Beach suddenly becomes part of the *Baywatch* series. So the make-believe encroaches on everybody's lives as they go through their ordinary affairs.

Psychological experiments have shown over and over again that people looking at the same situation see many different colors or figures; hear different sounds; have different olfactory experiences. This has led lawyers and police agents to say that eyewitness testimony is the most unreliable form of evidence compared to scientific evidence like photographs, fingerprints, DNA, and so on. Anyone who watches football games on Sundays sees and hears the variety of experiences as to whether a player has stepped out of bounds or performed an illegal tackle. The TV broadcasters, within a minute or so, show the audience three or more versions of what happened. Often these are conflicting or inadequate to decide. The officials make a judgment but often this disagrees with thousands and thousands of viewers—there and in their homes. And, just to add another element to this, the viewers at home don't really know if the game is going on now, last year, or ever. Universal Studios could be producing the game.

The question is not whether one feels secure and certain about one's sensory judgments, but whether one can lose this security and certainty when conflicting possibilities are raised. If the latter is the case, can this affect all of our sensory judgments?

In a very humorous 1997 movie called *Wag the Dog*, some of the president's advisors decide to avert attention from his sexual scandals by holding a war between the United States and, of all countries, Albania. (The movie appeared about a month before Monica

Lewinsky became known to the American public.) In the movie, the whole war goes on in a Hollywood studio and the public believes a real war is occurring because their access to information is controlled by the media. Some of us, on seeing this, might imagine that the Gulf War was a TV production. This is made more graphic by what is called "virtual reality"—getting the viewer to experience being a participant though still at home. We've all experienced this in the special effects that are part and parcel of current movies, where we experience the feeling of being in a crashing airplane, being in an earthquake, in a car chase, having an angry mob rushing at us. Almost all of us, even though we are in our movie theater seats, get carried away and usually feel quite relieved when the tension is broken by allowing us to revert to our audience situation instead of being part of the virtual reality of the special effects. So some of us wonder, with good reason, whether some or all of our life experience is being generated by the special effects division of some movie company. The movie producer George Lucas, one of the great geniuses of special-effects creation, has explained that all that is involved is a celluloid strip with twenty-four images per second flashing on the screen. If that is all it takes to make people believe they are present at an earthquake, a volcanic eruption, an invasion by aliens or prehistoric animals, perhaps twenty-four images per second are coursing through our brains due to the effects of genetically modified food, fluoridation of the water, or some other biochemical cause. Finding a criterion that works twenty-four hours a day to distinguish reality from special effects seems beyond us a good deal of the time.

You might say all one needs is a criterion for distinguishing possibly dubious sensory judgments from others. The example you give of looking for good apples in a store and employing a criterion about the condition of the apple's skin, texture, color may work most times, but I suspect that even you have found that after the most careful choices that you made in the store, you have nonetheless brought home a rotten apple because you could not see or find other defects. There could be chemicals within the apple that do not show on the outside. These might only be detected if one has special scientific equipment. It might take hours, days, or months to do all the checking and even this might turn out to be insufficient if some new biochemical agent has gotten into the genetic material of the apple. So the ordinary criteria that you and I and everybody else use to make judgments may work most of the time but we must also realize that they are not adequate for judging all of the time.

Let's take an example from Cicero's *De Academica*: If one had two objects that looked like apples and one had come off a tree and the other was manufactured at some biochemical laboratory, and if they looked identical to all our visual tests and yet the artificial apple contained undetectable poison, would you be willing to use your criterion? If the FBI issued a warning that there were terrorists creating poisoned artificial apples that were undetectable by visual criteria, would you be willing to apply your standard? Or, would you do what was done during the Tylenol crisis—when someone put poison into a few Tylenol bottles—that is, remove all the bottles rather than try to find possible dangerous ones. If this is the case, can you be sure that your criterion is adequate or right? And then we get into the problem of judging criteria.

The problem gets worse when one does not have reflective time to examine the features of the experience. We find ourselves engulfed by images, emotions, fears, and hopes and have no opportunity to step aside for even a moment to tell whether what we are experiencing is part of a dream, part of a movie, part of an experiment, or as some might say, part of "real life." We are forced to make decisions in a finite time that often does not allow for much testing. When we drive, we encounter this state of affairs at every intersection. We have to act, either driving forward, stopping, or pulling off the roadway. Sometimes we have a second to make the decision, sometimes we have much less time. Applying a well-thought-out criterion in these circumstances might lead to a lot of automobile accidents as we ponder which option to pursue. In fact, most of life is like that. Experience and action are closely tied together. Choices have to be made and we have to judge what type of criteria we need to apply in different life situations. When difficulties arise, we often find ourselves falling into the skeptical trap of having to judge whether our criteria are reliable or adequate for the situations we encounter and this can quickly lead to the problem Hume discussed about skepticism with regard to reason: namely, do we have to judge our judgments and do we have to judge our ability to judge our judgments and onward and onward?

The Criterion Problem

The Criterion Problem is for me the heart of the skeptical crisis that everyone has to live with. You're of course right that most of the time, we have criteria that we apply in order to judge the various aspects of our life and we do not question these. We judge what time it is by looking at a watch or a clock. This is sufficient until we find that we've arrived two hours late for an appointment, or when somebody tells us that we have not heard a certain program because we did not realize what time it was. Then we realize that we need a more elaborate criterion. In the example you offered of selecting apples to purchase, if you applied your criterion and then found that the apples you bought were sour or tasteless, you would probably realize you had to find a more elaborate criterion for selecting. If you went back to the store and complained and the grocer asked you why you selected such bad apples and you told him which criterion you used, if he replied that's the wrong way of choosing apples, at this point the skeptical problem begins.

As my hero from ancient times, Sextus Empiricus, pointed out, skeptical questioning begins when there is a controversy about facts, judgments, or opinions. The controversy can be just between what one judges by using one sense versus judging by other senses. It also occurs all the time when we find our judgment differs from other people's. At that point, the issue of what criterion to use to settle our differences becomes preeminent. In many cases the issue is settled pro tem by authority or by argument or by force, but are these settlements, to use a word you don't like, justified? If we take the example of the case of the umpires and referees at sporting events who settle differences of opinion about whether a batter is safe or out, whether a basketball player has committed a foul, whether a football player has legally caught a pass—in all these cases, there has to be a temporary judge in order for the game to be playable. Otherwise the game would break down because of the differences in opinion. But the disputants at the game, and the fans and the watchers on TV, do not placidly accept the judgment of the authority. In some cases, they carry grudges for years and years and insist that their team was robbed! They would insist that there is a better criterion if one had the time to examine photographs, make measurements, and so on. But the situation, like many things in life, requires a judgment within a finite time, so temporary criteria are used over and over again even though we know they are faulty. In 1966, in the final match of the World Cup, there was a dispute as to whether West Germany had scored a legal goal against the British team. This dispute, in fact, went on for years as more photographs and eyewitness testimonies were gathered. Now, I think most people would agree that the German goal was legal, but I have met many die-hards who insisted that if one had a photographer directly above the goal or sensors at the goal line, one might be able to reach a truer assessment of what had happened. Of course, then one would need still other criteria for judging the reliability of the photographs, the sensors, and the satellite photos and judging the reliability of the people who gathered the data.

In my discussion of the jury system in Anglo-American law in the chapter on political philosophy, I made the same point. By and large we accept trial by jury and the decisions the jury makes as the best way of deciding in questions of law in the finite time. But as happened with the decision in the O. J. Simpson case, many, many people can say the jury was wrong and had more scientific criteria been applied and if better detective work had been done another decision would have occurred. One can also imagine what would have happened in the Simpson case if the scientist who invented DNA testing had been called to the witness stand. The prosecution thought that it would overwhelm the jury with all the DNA evidence. The scientist who invented the DNA measuring system says he was prepared to testify that his system doesn't work or is unreliable. Apparently, though he is an eminent Nobel Prize winner, he is personally regarded as unreliable. If he had been called as a witness and forced to reveal his substance abuses, this might have led to people judging that he could not be taken seriously. On the other hand, his scientific standing is such that his view would appear to be authoritative. So what criterion does one use?

It is often the case that long after a trial has been held new scientific tests become available which lead to changing the judgment that was made by a jury. Recently a number of people were released from death row because of DNA tests or because of indications that the police had misbehaved. Two major criminal cases indicate that research can go on for a long time in reassessing the decision made by a jury. One is that of Dr. Samuel Sheppard who was convicted of murdering his wife. Dr. Sheppard has now passed away, but his son has been producing evidence based on DNA and other recent chemical tests that would indicate that someone else must have been the actual criminal. Bodies have been exhumed and all sorts of reassessments have been made, and the case is still pending. Another that seems destined to go on indefinitely is that of James Earl Ray, convicted by his own confession of murdering Dr. Martin Luther King Jr. Ray, shortly after being imprisoned, insisted that he didn't do it, and all sorts of evidence indicates that other people must have been involved. Recently, a businessman in Memphis said that he paid someone other than Ray a large sum to kill King. In this case, because of political implications, there are forces pressing to reopen the case and forces pressing to keep it to the original judgment. At what point are we likely to have a satisfactory judgment? The same could be said about John F. Kennedy's assassination, but nobody was ever convicted. Should cases be held in abeyance until all present and all possible future tests have been applied? This would lead to ending the system of trial by jury. However, our system of jurisprudence tries to stop retrying cases or delaying decisions indefinitely because some judgment has to be made in a finite time.

Having said this, I think all of us, including yourself, have qualms at times about the criteria we use. When we get into arguments about our judgments, we would like to be sure we have the right standards, that is, standards that are certain and cannot be challenged. So the problem of justification is not just one that was cooked up by skeptics to badger dogmatists but is a life problem for most people at some time. I don't think that you or Wittgenstein or Popper can really avoid the justification issue. Since we all get into decision problems and we all can get into controversial ones, we often find that we have to justify our means of deciding to satisfy ourselves or others. We are unwilling to accept just arbitrary authority but want some justification for what we are doing—some justification for what we believe. And so the justification problem, it seems to me, grows out of ordinary life situations. When one raises the question asked by Socrates, "Is the unexamined life worth living?" we seem to be forced to make a judgment and if pressed, to justify our judgment. Otherwise it's like the cartoon about the Generation X character who is presented with the Socratic question and replies, "Whatever."

Finale

I am not convinced or impressed by the way that you or G. E. Moore or Wittgenstein dispense with skeptical problems when all is said and done. Taking a long view of the subject, it seems to me that there have only been two or three ways of getting around the skeptical challenges. One is Aristotle's, the other is the Stoic's, and the third is the answer of Mersenne and Gassendi. Aristotle in his great wisdom insisted he would not discuss physics with people who had doubts about whether or not the external world existed. He took it for granted that in order to discuss anything, some principles had to be accepted and he would not deal with skeptical doubts about these principles. The collapse of medieval Aristotelianism is in good part due to a refusal to accept the principles and the doubts cast by skeptics like Francisco Sanches and his cousin Michel de Montaigne and other renaissance skeptics. Gassendi's withering attack on Aristotle's philosophy on skeptical grounds showed for scholars of the time that Aristotelianism was like the Emperor's New Clothes—that there was nothing that one could accept with any degree of certainty.

The Stoics played on the inability of anyone to live in complete doubt. They also heaped scorn and derision on skeptics and skepticism. But what does this show? As the skeptic Bishop Pierre Daniel Huet replied, "It is one thing to philosophize and another thing to live."[6] Living goes on undogmatically and philosophizing poses skeptical challenges to any dogmatic theory, whether it be Stoic, Aristotelian, Platonic, or anything else. I have caricatured the skeptical response here as like an anonymous letter. The recipient gets the letter and finds it is full of questions and problems about the philosophy of the recipient. The fact that the sender may also have problems is beside the point—especially if the sender is anonymous and cannot be found.

The Common Sense view of Thomas Reid and then G. E. Moore is a version of the Stoic response and I think fails to meet the challenge. All of us may be forced to believe various things that we cannot explain or justify. So believing is hardly an answer to skepticism and what we believe may in fact be dubious or even false. As Descartes said, "What is true to us may be false to an angel." We may be forced to believe the principles of mathematics and even believe them to be certain but they could still be "pipe dreams."

In light of this, Mersenne and Gassendi, in the first quarter of the seventeenth century, presented a way of dealing with the skeptical crisis. In Mersenne's thousand-page answer to the skeptics, *La Verite des Sciences Contre les Skeptiques ou Pyrrhoniens*, he puts forth the skeptical arguments from Sextus Empiricus on one subject to another. He then says, "So what?" The skeptical problems do not prevent us from having adequate knowledge to deal with the world around us, even though we are well aware that there are basic doubts and that the principles that we use cannot be justified. The variations in sense experience may prevent us from knowing what is actually happening in the real world but we can have a science of our sensory variations. We can apply the laws of optics, refractions, and so on as ways of connecting our varying experiences. These laws can be stated in mathematical terms even though we cannot justify or prove beyond any doubt that these laws are true. So Mersenne set forth 750 pages of the book, listing what we do in fact know in mathematics and physics, not withstanding the unanswered skeptical problems. His good friend Father Pierre Gassendi said that he was presenting a *Via Media* between skepticism and dogmatism. The skeptical problems raised in antiquity sufficed to undermine the dogmatism of Plato and Aristotle, Descartes, and many other such arrogant philosophers. But the skeptical problems did not prevent the development of a constructive or mitigated skepticism in which one could offer resolutions to the skeptical problems in terms of empirical science. The view of Mersenne and Gassendi has been very influential in modern philosophy of science. It shows a way in which we can carry on our intellectual pursuits while setting aside the skeptical problems but as I have argued for the last forty years, this does not answer the skeptical problems and it leaves our intellectual world without an unshakable foundation. So this way of dealing with skepticism has allowed the modern scientific quest to go on without having to stop at each point and answer the skeptic. I think that I would have to study the matter in much detail. I think that what you and Wittgenstein are proposing is a combination of all of these ways of dealing with skepticism.

Something that I wish we had time to discuss is what I dimly perceive as a radical new version of skepticism, namely, the postmodernist view that is sweeping through various academic circles. Unlike the constructive or mitigated skepticism of Mersenne or Gassendi which accepted mathematics and science as provisionally true for dealing with our experiences, postmodernism seems to offer a form of intellectual anarchy. As far as I understand, it gives up the privileged status of mathematics and science, that any view is as good as any other and one can construct intellectual worlds according to one's tastes. Greek skepticism developed parasitically in terms of the rational frame of reference of Greek dogmatism and so kept within the parameters accepted by all the philosophers. What seems to be emerging now is a forceful skepticism with regard to reason that accepts no privileged framework. What this will lead to I don't know, but it may be that you and I will have to join forces in opposing this skepticism beyond skepticism. I have been told that I am the grandfather of postmodernism, which I hope is not true. But if it is, I may have to consider my actual relations to it.

After a lifetime of skeptical questioning and brooding, I realize that I could not offer a *justification* for why my and other people's questioning ought to go on in terms of accepted science, mathematics, and history rather than in terms of some other framework that satisfies some other people's predilections. Nonetheless, at the present stage of my life I feel that I have to consider things in terms of a "rational scientific framework" even though others can point out that this is just the result of a bad education and too many scientific colleagues. But I see a kind of intellectual disaster blooming if one follows out the implications of the previous sentence. So, *que faire?*

As you probably know, there are now people studying the philosophical classics in terms of the racist and sexist implications of texts rather than in terms of the arguments. There are people studying the texts in terms of the political, social, and religious standings of the authors. A good deal of this throws some new light on the material but if it becomes a sole way of considering the material then we would find ourselves in a radically different milieu in which our arguments would only represent our own sexist, middle-class American values. I don't see that your Wittgensteinian approach will bring us back to a sane and rational world. Instead, as you know, there is much being written about Wittgenstein's sexual life, about his politics, and his problems in adjusting to the position of Jews in the twentieth century in different countries. These kinds of studies may replace reading the texts, and then where are we?

With very best wishes in hopes that you will see the light,

Richard H. Popkin

NOTES

1. Robert P. Amico, *The Problem of the Criterion* (Lanham, Md.: Rowman & Littlefield, 1993), pp. 1–2.
2. Ibid., p. 73.
3. René Descartes, *Descartes Selections*, ed. Ralph M. Eaton (New York: Scribner's, 1927), p. 90.
4. Ibid., p. 91.
5. Ludwig Wittgenstein, *Philosophical Investigations* (Oxford: Blackwell, 1958), entry 109.
6. Pierre Daniel Huet, *Treatise on the Feebleness of the Human Mind* (1723), conclusion.

INDEX